Praise for the book when it was first published:

'William T. Martin Riches has written a book for undergraduates and general audiences that provides an excellent introduction to and review of the U.S. civil rights movement' — **Michael D. Cary**, *History: Review of New Books*

The Civil Rights Movement in the United States struggled to create a nation. The Civil War ended de jure slavery but it needed the movement to dismantle laws designed to keep African Americans subordinated to white power. In this compelling introduction, William T. Martin Riches analyses the way African Americans developed a mass movement after the Second World War and overthrew state-enforced racial segregation despite fierce resistance from whites. Riches emphasises how the movement influenced others seeking justice in America, and evaluates the coalitions formed to preserve gains threatened by the rise of the New Right.

Thoroughly revised and updated in the light of the latest scholarship, the third edition of *The Civil Rights Movement:*

- sets the movement in its broader context
- stresses the changing role of black women, and their problems with the women's movement and black nationalism
- demonstrates the positive influence on some white southerners
- explores the key role played by the state and federal judiciaries
- assesses the administrations of George W. Bush
- examines the rise of Neo-Conservatism
- covers the presidential election campaign of 2008 and analyses Barack Obama's first months in office.

William T. Martin Riches was formerly Senior Lecturer and Convenor of American Studies at the University of Ulster, Jordanstown.

STUDIES IN CONTEMPORARY HISTORY

PUBLISHED

SPAIN SINCE 1939 *Stanley Black*

THE ARAB-ISRAELI CONFLICT, THIRD EDITION
T. G. Fraser

AMERICA AND THE WORLD SINCE 1945 *T. G. Fraser and Donette Murray*

THE ULSTER QUESTION SINCE 1945, SECOND EDITION
James Loughlin

GERMANY SINCE 1945 *Pól O'Dochartaigh*

THE RISE AND FALL OF THE SOVIET EMPIRE,
SECOND EDITION
Raymond Pearson

THE CIVIL RIGHTS MOVEMENT: Struggle and Resistance,
THIRD EDITION
William T. Martin Riches

THE UNITED NATIONS AND INTERNATIONAL POLITICS
Stephen Ryan

JAPAN SINCE 1945
Dennis B. Smith

DECOLONIZATION SINCE 1945
John Springhall

Studies in Contemporary History
Series Standing Order
ISBN 978–0–333–71706–6 hardback
ISBN 978–0–333–69331–3 paperback
(*outside North America only*)

You can receive future titles in this series as they are published by placing a standing order. Please contact your bookseller or, in case of difficulty, write to us at the address below with your name and address, the title of the series and the ISBN quoted above.

Customer Services Department, Macmillan Distribution Ltd, Houndmills, Basingstoke, Hampshire RG21 6XS, England

---

THE CIVIL RIGHTS MOVEMENT

STRUGGLE AND RESISTANCE

Third Edition

WILLIAM T. MARTIN RICHES

First edition published 1997
Second edition published 2004
Third edition published 2010 by
PALGRAVE MACMILLAN

Palgrave Macmillan in the UK is an imprint of Macmillan Publishers Limited, registered in England, company number 785998, of Houndmills, Basingstoke, Hampshire RG21 6XS.

Palgrave Macmillan in the US is a division of St Martin's Press LLC, 175 Fifth Avenue, New York, NY 10010.

Palgrave Macmillan is the global academic imprint of the above companies and has companies and representatives throughout the world.

Palgrave® and Macmillan® are registered trademarks in the United States, the United Kingdom, Europe and other countries.

ISBN-13: 978-0-230-23705-6 hardback
ISBN-13: 978-0-230-23706-3 paperback

This book is printed on paper suitable for recycling and made from fully managed and sustained forest sources. Logging, pulping and manufacturing processes are expected to conform to the environmental regulations of the country of origin.

A catalogue record for this book is available from the British Library.

A catalog record for this book is available from the Library of Congress.

10   9   8   7   6   5   4   3   2   1
19 18 17 16 15 14 13 12 11 10

Printed and bound in China

For Judith, Julia. Lilla and Theo
And in memory of David and Richard

CONTENTS

PREFACE TO THIRD EDITION

A friend at Harvard University in 1964 enquired about the places my wife and I would visit during our travels in the United States from our home in Canada. When we informed him that we were going to visit the southern states, including Alabama and Mississippi, he was very concerned about our safety and pressed us to buy a Canadian flag and put it in the front of the car. He warned us that we would be mistaken for civil rights 'outside agitators' and the locals would not know our Ontario licence plate proved we were from Canada but would assume it was just another northern state. We did as he suggested.

As foreigners we were naïve about the dangers we faced or more important equally unaware of the 'etiquette of segregation.' This became apparent as we approached the town of Biloxi, Mississippi. We were thirsty and just after crossing the city limits we stopped at a restaurant for a drink. It was crowded and we sat at the counter and I ordered two coffees. The woman did not respond. I asked for a second time and still no acknowledgement. I assumed it must be my accent and raised my voice, spoke slowly and distinctly. I repeated my order. The woman fled. Before we could leave a man appeared and asked politely what we wanted and I told him. Throughout this almost surreal exchange we noticed that the conversations of other customers had stopped and there was an oppressive silence. Looking around, we realised why. We were the only white couple in the place. With my long hair and beard it must have seemed that I was one of those 'civil rights' troublemakers and by integrating that café we had endangered the man, his wife and even his customers. Inadvertently, we had defied segregation etiquette. In later years as graduate students at the University of Tennessee, Knoxville, our defiance of the South and its customs was never accidental.

What we did not appreciate at the time was how we were met with politeness by the owner and that fact we were served. If they had made the mistake we had done, the white folks' reaction would have been very different. And this desire to exclude or disappear by many white Americans has shaped much of the history of the nation. It was highlighted by those, black and white, who fought against slavery and fought against all forms of poverty and discrimination in the cities. Some wanted to escape and return to Africa and a few still do; but for the overwhelming majority this was and still is not desirable. The struggle by to become Americans was, and remains, as complex as those whites who resist that aspiration. Many Americans, in Ralph Ellison's wonderful title, *The Invisible Man*, still prefer not to see their black fellow citizens. For many white folks, black folks are 'the other,' aliens and not true citizens. These barriers have eroded gradually over the years but it would be a mistake, even after the election of 2008, to be swept away by the obvious joy of almost two million people standing in the bitter cold on inauguration day. In many parts of the South in 2009 many feel the same physical weight of poverty and oppression that they felt in 1964. Some see Spanish moss as part of the romantic antebellum South but for some it is a curtain that conceals the past and current violence and deprivation.

The third edition of this book covers events that I never thought would be possible as we travelled through the United States in 1964 – or our lifetime – and this makes the writing of contemporary history perhaps more daunting than when I worked on the first two editions. I lived through these events and some would argue that this makes considered judgement impossible. In my case it is even more difficult in that I was also a participant in a small way. However, this is not a participant's history, but rather seeks objectively to analyse the civil rights movement after the Second World War. I believe that the intervening years and my views as an outsider, who has lived in Ireland and England, as well as the United States, have helped me in the quest for objectivity. I can only agree with Alan Dawley that 'the destiny of modern America was in the hands of the meek as well as the mighty.' As he points out the struggles for racial justice and sexual equality were not simply a matter of good versus bad guys but 'there is no doubt that good and evil hung in the balance. In comprehending what happened, I have aspired to objectivity. But objectivity does not mean indifference. It matters very much how things turned out' (Dawley, 1991).

As in the previous editions, I have approached the struggle for civil rights as an interaction of grassroots groups and individuals, often working through the black institutions created by segregation. Congregants, preachers, students and teachers, workers and their unions interacted with those who held political power at federal, state and local level; the men and women who joined the struggle and organised despite massive resistance. I stressed the role of the 'meek' who did so much to help the movement.

For some historians the movement was from the bottom up (Hahn, 2003), and I revised the second edition to take into account their research. Others stress the role of leaders – the top down model – and I acknowledge the formidable leadership qualities of Martin Luther King, A. Philip Randolph, Fanny Lou Hamer, Ella Baker and E. D. Nixon to name a few. In the 2008 primary campaign Hilary Clinton was criticised for stressing the importance of President Lyndon Johnson in winning civil rights for the oppressed in the United States. She was accused of belittling the work of Dr King. The important thing is that King knew he had to work with Johnson and did so until the Vietnam War endangered the Great Society programmes. Johnson predicted that if other administrations did not join the struggle later presidents could, starve his beloved child – the Great Society – and undermine many of his civil rights achievements.

In this third edition I have kept the chapter on white southerners who assisted in the struggle when it would have been easier to follow the majority and become part of the resistance. As a graduate student in the South in the 1960s and early 1970s, I witnessed extraordinary changes in southern attitudes, especially among the students and it still disappoints me that so few people are willing to acknowledge the sacrifices these people made when they refused to follow their parents, preachers and teachers down the road of racism and intolerance. I am proud that many of my friends were people who willingly made the stand. The courage of an oppressed people was not ignored by these young southerners – freeing black southerners meant freeing themselves too. The grassroots groups they established and those who worked within them have done much to preserve the gains made.

I have revised all the chapters in light of recent scholarship and included a long section to demonstrate how power gained through the Voting Rights Act and redistricting has been organised through federal and state organisations such as the Black Caucuses and the coalitions with the Free South Africa Movement, the environmental movement and LGBT rights organisations. And, importantly, I discuss those African Americans who share the ideology of neo-conservatives. In addition, I assess the two terms George W. Bush and the abuses of that administration and how its arrogance of power meant reversals of civil rights and human rights. Chapter 10 covers the election of 2008 and the first months of the 44th president.

Every historian selects a time-frame for their work and readers of this book should realise that the civil rights movement did not have its origins in post-war America as I have briefly discussed in the Introduction. The work of labour historians such as Mark Fannin have proven direct links between unions of the 1890s, 1930s and the civil rights movement after the Second World War (Fannin, 2003). Glenda Gilmore in her major study demonstrates that African Americans from 1919 to 1950 never gave up the struggle for equality and, 'African Americans always used geopolitics to fight domestic racism' (Gilmore, 2008).

In the preface to the first edition I wrote about the worries felt about Richard Nixon's election in 1968 and the gathering at Dr Vivian Gibbs' home in East Tennessee. Dr Gibbs, the son of a poor white sharecropper, made us listen to Dr King's speech and told us when we were separated to remember the words and live by them: 'I still have a dream. It is a dream deeply rooted in the American dream that one day this nation will rise up and live out the true meaning of its creed – we hold these truths to be self-evident, that all men are created equal.' It was this faith that made Mrs Annie Rankin struggle and suffer proudly for her civil rights. As she headed for Resurrection City she had a sign on her wagon, 'you Killed the Dreamer but you haven't killed the Dream we are the dream.'

No one there on a very late hot summer's night in East Tennessee imagined that the resisters would control government policy for almost forty years. But even more, if anyone had foretold the result of the election campaign of 2008 he would have been dismissed as a harmless lunatic. In 2004, I warned that young Americans 'are forgetting the history of racial segregation and discrimination' and feared that 'recent events have shown that all might be lost in their forgetting.' I was proved wrong and in 2008 a mountain was scaled – but Americans are still far from their promised land.

ACKNOWLEDGEMENTS

I would like to thank the (now former) editors of this series, Tom Fraser and John Springhall, for their advice and criticism and the University of Ulster at Jordanstown for supporting research of the first edition. In addition I appreciate especially the invaluable assistance and advice given by my daughter Dr Julia Riches and my son Dr Theo Riches who have read and commented on this and the two previous editions. When I was lecturing, my students always reminded me of the wider influence of the African American struggle and I hope I have done justice to these other fighters. In addition I would like to say how much I appreciate the assistance of Dr Simon Topping and David McAree who shared valuable sources. My graduate students, Dr Mark Fannin, Dr Stephen Milligen and Dr Matthew McKee contributed more than they realised and this brief acknowledgement does not do justice to their honest criticism and friendship.

And there are those who showed me that there is a more complex, more generous South not remotely like Hollywood's stereotypical Gothic horror. My friends, Oscar and Mary Allen, and fellow graduate students at the University of Tennessee, Knoxville, John Thomas, Tom Wilson, Dan Pomeroy and the late O. C. Richardson were native southerners and introduced me to the complexity of the region they are, and were, so proud of. In 2008 my dearest friend, Professor David Bowen, was killed in a car accident. It is impossible to say how much I owe David, a poet, historian and fellow lover of Dylan Thomas, but his courage in his fight against bigotry in his native and beloved South inspired his friends and students.

Not wishing to offend anyone I will just say that many scholars in Britain and Ireland, and the United States have helped in this work but I would like to thank the international scholars of the Milan-Montpellier Group for the Study of American History which has been meeting for every two years since 1979 when ideas and research findings are always combined with good food and excellent wine. My editors, Sonya Barker and Jenni Burnell at Palgrave have shown me great loyalty and support and I am very grateful. Of course, the responsibility for any errors is entirely mine. I must thank my friends in Stacciola and Nicola and Alessandra a special thank you because they made sure I could keep in touch with the wider world! On a lighter note, it is impossible to adequately convey my gratitude to Mark and his magnificent deli for keeping me going.

I want to acknowledge two very dear friends and teachers, the late Professors Tony Hepburn and Richard Marius. Richard best described our relationship in an inscription in one of his books: 'To a colleague in courses, comrade in causes and to Judy who endures all this.' Tony helped me immensely in my career from the time he taught me in graduate school and when we worked together at the University of Ulster. Above all, I owe everything to my wife, Judy, who is my sternest critic and who sacrificed so much to make my academic career possible. She has always been my most loyal supporter.

GLOSSARY

Baby Boom

This is an expression commonly used to describe the generation born in the late 1940s and 1950s, a period which saw a dramatic increase in childbirth in the United States.

Bossism

The corruption of democratic government primarily in the urban centres of the United States enabled parties to control local government with the corrupt use of patronage. The most notorious city Boss in the nineteenth century was Boss Tweed of New York City and in the twentieth Mayor Richard Daley of Chicago.

Bussing

After the Second World War southern states used bussing to consolidate schools, thereby eliminating many inferior rural institutions, in an effort to raise the academic quality of the school system. However, the bus was also used to guarantee the segregation of white and black school children. In *Swann v Charlotte-Mecklenburg* (1974) the Supreme Court ordered the use of bussing to achieve racial integration.

Carpetbagger

An allegedly corrupt, white or black, Republican politician from the North who had moved to the South after the Civil War and who was active in southern politics. They had come to live off and to rob the South because the only belongings they had with them were capable of being carried in a carpetbag.

Filibustering   A method of delaying or preventing legislation in Congress or in the state legislatures by prolonging the debate or using parliamentary procedures to prevent passage of legislation.

Governor   The title of the leading executive officer of a state.

Great Society   The 1964–68 liberal, social and economic reform programme of President Lyndon Baines Johnson who hoped to resolve the problem of poverty in the United States and thereby complete the New Deal begun by Johnson's hero, Franklin Delano Roosevelt.

Interposition   The argument of southerners before the Civil War and during the civil rights movement that a state was sovereign and should interpose its authority between the people of the state and the Federal Government and protect the citizens of the state from the enforcement of a federal law which the people of the state deemed unconstitutional.

Impeachment   According to Article II Section 4 of the Constitution, 'The President, Vice President, and all civil Officers of the United States, shall be removed from Office on Impeachment for, on Conviction of, Treason, Bribery, other Crimes and Misdemeanors'. The charges are heard in the House of Representatives and if a case is agreed the process moves to the Senate. A two-thirds vote of all senators is required for a conviction. Those impeached cannot hold office again and are liable for trial in the criminal courts. The only two presidents who have been impeached are Andrew Johnson (1868) and William Jefferson Clinton (1998). Both were acquitted. Nixon was impeached by the House in 1974 but resigned before being tried by the Senate. Spiro Agnew, charged with bribery, resigned before the impeachment process was begun.

Jim Crow Laws   The system of segregation of the races imposed after the Civil War in southern and some border states. The origin of the term Jim Crow is not known.

Ku Klux Klan

A paramilitary terrorist organisation founded in Pulaski, Tennessee, after the Civil War. Despite the protestations of some southerners, the Invisible Empire of the Ku Klux Klan was the paramilitary wing of the Democratic Party and was instrumental in the overthrow of the Reconstruction governments in the South. The modern KKK was launched in Georgia and claimed five million members by 1925. It not only emphasised issues of race but also gained popularity throughout the United States with its anti-Semitism and anti-Catholicism. It still exists and it is not confined to the South.

Nullification

The southern argument that every state was sovereign and had the right to declare null and void federal legislation that the people of the state deemed unconstitutional.

New Deal

The title given by President Franklin Delano Roosevelt to the wide-ranging social and economic legislation which he introduced after his election in 1932, which was designed to regulate the capitalist economy and introduce a limited welfare state.

'Ole Miss'

The popular title of the University of Mississippi.

Peculiar Institution

This was a euphemism that was used by southerners before the Civil War to describe the institution of slavery. In the North it was used to indicate that slavery was an institution peculiar (i.e. belonged exclusively) to the South.

Sharecropper

A tenant farmer in the South who paid for his rent and supplies by giving a share of his crop to the landowner.

Solid South

Following the defeat of the South in the Civil War, the South was governed by Republican state governments which were defeated with the end of Reconstruction. Following 1876, the South voted for only one party rule— the Democratic Party.

Territories   Land acquired by the United States was held by the federal government and organised into territories governed by a judge and three judges appointed by Congress until the population reached 5000 eligible voters. After that they could elect a territorial legislature and send a non-voting delegate to Congress. When the population reached 60,000 then the land was subdivided into congressional districts, a republican constitution was adopted and when Congress had approved these measures allowed to enter the Union as a state with its own members of the House of Representatives, based on the population of the state, and with two senators.

Acronyms

ACHR	Alabama Council on Human Relations
ACLU	American Civil Liberties Union
ACMHR	Alabama Christian Movement for Human Rights
ADA	Americans for Democratic Action
AFL-CIO	American Federation of Labor and the Congress of Industrial Organizations
AFOR	American Fellowship of Reconciliation
AME	African Methodist Episcopal
AFSC	American Friends Service Committee
CEEO	Commission for Equal Employment Opportunity
CIA	Central Intelligence Agency
COFO	Council of Federated Organizations
CRRA	Civil Rights Restoration Act
EPA	Environmental Protection Agency
ERA	Equal Rights Amendment
FBI	Federal Bureau of Investigation
FDR	Franklin Delano Roosevelt
FEPC	Fair Employment Practices Commission
FSAM	Free South Africa Movement

HEW	Health, Education and Welfare
HUAC	House Un-American Activities Committee
IRS	Internal Revenue Service
JFK	John Fitzgerald Kennedy
KKK	Ku Klux Klan
LBJ	Lyndon Baines Johnson
LGBT	Lesbians, Gays, Bisexuals and Transsexuals
MFDP	Mississippi Freedom Democratic Party
MIA	Montgomery Improvement Association
NAACP	National Association for the Advancement of Colored People
NOW	National Organization for Women
PUSH	People United to Save Humanity
ROAR	Restore Our Alienated Rights
SCEF	Southern Conference Education Fund
SCLC	Southern Christian Leadership Conference
SDS	Students for a Democratic Society
SNCC	Student Nonviolent (changed in 1965 to National) Coordinating Committee
SSOC	Southern Student Organizing Committee
SPLC	Southern Poverty Law Center
UCMI	United Christian Movement Incorporated
UT	University of Tennessee, Knoxville
WPC	Women's Political Council

BASIC CHRONOLOGY

1945 Harry S. Truman becomes President on the death of FDR

1947 Truman is the first president to address the NAACP annual conference

1948 Both parties support civil rights. Democrats split over the issue and Strom Thurmond, South Carolina, leads the resistance forming the Dixiecrat Party

Truman uses Executive Orders to set up Fair Employment Board and to begin the integration of the armed forces

1954 *Brown v Board of Education, Topeka Kansas* First [White] Citizens Council, Mississippi

1955 *Brown II*

Segregation on interstate transport banned

Montgomery Bus Boycott begins

1956 Martin Luther King Jr's home is bombed

Southern Manifesto published

Eisenhower re-elected President

Supreme Court orders bus desegregation

Bus boycott ends

1957 SCLC established

Little Rock Central High School integration stopped by riots

First Civil Rights Bill since 1875

Ghana wins its independence

1959 Massive Resistance to school integration ends in Virginia

1960 Sit-in movement starts in Greensboro, North Carolina

SNCC set up

Civil Rights Act becomes law

Eleven colonies in Africa gain independence

John F. Kennedy elected President

1961 CORE organises Freedom Rides
Kennedy appoints his brother Robert Attorney General and voter registration drive is started
Albany protest starts

1962 Kennedy signs Executive Order on integration of federal housing
Riots as students resist integration of the University of Mississippi

1963 Albany protest ends
Birmingham, Alabama demonstrations
George Wallace tries to stop integration of University of Alabama
March on Washington
John F. Kennedy and Medgar Evers killed

1964 LBJ elected President
Martin Luther King Jr wins Nobel Peace Prize
Civil Rights Bill Passed
Mississippi Freedom Democratic Party established
Rioting in New York, Chicago and Philadelphia

1965 Selma demonstrations
Voting Rights Act becomes law
Malcolm X is murdered
Rioting in Watts, Los Angeles
King's first anti-Vietnam War speech
SNCC advocates Black Power

1966 SCLC campaign meets fierce resistance in Chicago

1967 Civil rights demonstrations extended to Cleveland
King attacks Vietnam War
National Organization for Women set up

1968 Poor People's Campaign plans march on Washington
Martin Luther King Jr assassinated in Memphis
Civil Rights Bill enacted
Robert Kennedy assassinated in California
American Indian Movement (Red Power) established
LBJ does not seek re-election
Riots at Democrat and Republican party conventions
Richard Nixon is elected president

1969 Nixon greatly extends the use of affirmative action

1970 Nominations of Haynesworth and Carswell defeated
Students killed at Kent State, Ohio and Jackson State, Mississippi

1971 Supreme Court orders desegregation by bussing

1972   Richard Nixon re-elected
           Watergate scandal begins to emerge
           George Wallace shot and severely wounded
1973   Vice President Spiro Agnew forced to resign because of bribe
           scandal
1974   Richard Nixon is the first President to be forced to resign
1976   Jimmy Carter of Georgia elected President, appoints two black
           women to his Cabinet and extends affirmative action
           Andrew Young appointed United Nations Ambassador for US
1977   Fanny Lou Hamer, Mississippi civil rights leader, dies in poverty
           Mississippi House of Representatives unanimously passes a resolu-
           tion honouring her for her work for the state
1980   Ronald Reagan elected President
           Reagan's opposition to Voting Rights Act defeated
1988   Reagan's veto of the Civil Rights Restoration Act fails
           George H. W. Bush elected President
1990   Bush Sr first president to successfully veto civil rights law
           Civil rights law extended to include the disabled
1991   Bush nominates black conservative, Clarence Thomas to Supreme
           Court. Approved by Senate by one vote margin
1992   William Clinton elected President
1992   First African American woman elected to the Senate
1991   Clinton appoints more African Americans, woman and ethnic
           minorities to his administration that any other president in US
           history but fails to support Lani Guinier
1993   Clinton extends Voting Rights Act with 'Motor Voter' Act
           Clinton fails to keep his promise to gays in the military
           Appoints Ruth Bader Ginsburg to the Supreme Court
1994   Supports Republican welfare reform
1996   Wins re-election
1998   Impeached and is found not guilty
2000   George W. Bush declared President over Al Gore Jr after the federal
           Supreme Court narrowly rules to stop the count of contested votes
           in Florida ensuring Bush Electoral College votes. His highly dubious
           victory margin was 537 votes.
           Refuses to appoint people to the Civil Rights Commission set up by
           Clinton
2001   Attacks on New York, Washington and Philadelphia. Passage of the
           Patriot Act.

2001   Appoints Colin Powell the first African American Secretary of State and Condoleezza Rice as his Security Advisor

2002   Trent Lott resigns as Republican leader in the Senate

2004   Nominates a judge for the Fifth Circuit Court who had written the Mississippi legislation that had prohibited inter-racial marriage.

2004   Bush re-elected in another controversial election

2004   Replaces Colin Powell with Condoleezza Rice as Secretary of State

2005   Hurricane Katrina devastates New Orleans and large areas of the Gulf Coast

2006   Appointment of John Roberts as Chief Justice and Antonin Alito, Associate Justice guarantees conservative majority on Court

2006   Bush's first meeting with NAACP since his election in 2000. African American governor of Massachusetts elected

2007   *Ledbetter v Goodyear Tire Co.*

2007   Bank crash and world recession

2008   Election of Barrack Hussein Obama as first African American President

2008   Revokes Executive Orders issued by Bush, pushes through a massive stimulus programme and a several trillion dollar budget. Appoints John Holder as Attorney General.

First African American appointed head of the Environmental Protection Agency

First openly gay people appointed by any Administration

Five states legalise gay marriage

Supreme Court in *Bartlett v Strickland* seriously weakens the 1965 Voting Rights Act

Obama signs the Lilly Ledbetter Pair Pay Act

Releases documents on CIA use of torture

Sonia Sotomayor the first Latino nominated for the Supreme Court

Supreme Court avoids issue of constitutionality of the Voting Rights Act

INTRODUCTION

John Rolfe described the arrival of the first Africans in colonial Virginia. They came by accident. A Dutch ship exchanged '19 and odd Negroes' for food and supplies. Historians have argued ever since about the status of these first Africans in North America but most agree that *de facto* slavery did not emerge until 1640 and was not codified into law to become *de jure* slavery until 1660. After that most Africans in the colonies were classified as property, and despite an increase in manumissions after American independence, nine out of ten were held as slaves by 1860 (Riches, 1999). But well into the nineteenth century the lines between black and white were often breached (Hodes, 1997; Sandweiss, 2009).

White colonists fought against George III's 'slavery' and 'tyranny' but the vast majority of African Americans remained slaves, something which the British were quick to point out and sought to exploit. Although virtually all Northern states eventually granted African Americans their freedom (Davis, 2006), the situation for most black Americans declined rapidly in the South, with emancipation made virtually impossible (Davis, 1975).

The Constitution drawn up by leading intellectuals avoided the word 'slave.' According to Article 1, Section 2, representatives and direct taxes in each state were 'determined by adding to the whole number of free persons, including those bound to service for a term of years and excluding Indians not taxed, three fifths of all other persons.' These 'other persons' were black slaves. Many historians see this compromise between the North and the South as personifying the Founding Fathers' wisdom to ensure stable government. But it was achieved at the expense of African Americans and only delayed the confrontation which led to four years of the Civil War and the destruction of *de jure* slavery (Smith, 1997).

Slavery and the Civil War

The dispute over slavery was about the institution rather than about the freedom of the slaves – free labour, northerners argued, was superior to slave labour (Foner, 1970). Most northerners only wanted to limit the expansion of slavery and were indifferent about the plight of slaves. Some abolitionists, led by William Lloyd Garrison, argued that the North should secede from the Union to prevent the corruption of its democratic institutions by slave-holders. The former slave and abolitionist, Frederick Douglass, pointed out that that might save northern institutions but it did nothing for the slaves (Douglass, 1962).

Southerners considered themselves a beleaguered minority in a Union in which their 'peculiar institution' of slavery was endangered by majority tyranny. John C. Calhoun, former Vice President and Senator from South Carolina, claimed that the Union was a compact of sovereign states, not of people, and it was the duty of state governments to protect the citizens from overbearing federal authority. If a state convention declared a federal law unconstitutional, the state had the right to nullify it and the state could raise troops to interpose their authority between the state and the federal government. The first attempt to practice nullification and interposition was by South Carolina in 1832. State sovereignty, interposition and nullification were defeated when the Southern Confederacy lost but this did not stop southerners from trying to breathe life into them when they resisted the civil rights movement.

Lincoln and the Republicans argued that they only favoured barring slavery from the territories, not abolition. But if the majority of northern whites opposed emancipation, African Americans, North and South, knew that the war was about abolition. Southerners lulled themselves into believing their slaves were loyal, and were stunned as their 'happy darkies' fled the plantations and joined the Union army. Freedom was inevitable and Lincoln knew it. The Emancipation Proclamation, freeing slaves in Confederate-held territory, was drawn up in 1862. Responding to pressures from black abolitionists, he agreed that African Americans could fight. They continued the tradition of fighting in America's wars and this time they had greater incentive because it meant freedom for all Americans. As Peter Parish writes: 'Millions of white Americans, who in 1861 regarded emancipation or the use of black troops as a fantasy or a nightmare, had four years later learned to live with both. Millions of black Americans gained pride and self-respect from the knowledge that their own men-folk had shared in the fight for freedom' (Parish, 1975).The South went to war to defend slavery and ensured its abolition with the Thirteenth Amendment of 1865.

The assassination of Lincoln horrified the North. The anger and dismay at the murder was expressed not only by Lincoln's friends and members of the Republican Party, but even by those who had opposed him and his policies. The new President, Andrew Johnson of Tennessee, believed that state and federal governments were for white men 'and the negro must assume that status which the laws of an enlightened, moral and high-toned civilization shall assign him' (Nashville *Daily Union*, 1 June 1864).

Reconstruction

Many northern Unionists were conservative, even racist, but Johnson's refusal to compromise united moderates and radicals in the Union Party. Johnson did nothing when southern states passed 'Black Codes' that virtually returned the freed slaves to servitude. He fuelled the outrage of the party he was supposed to represent when he vetoed the Freedmen's Bureau Bill and the Civil Rights Bill. Johnson used an argument that was revived in the 1990s, when Republicans attacked affirmative action. Andrew Johnson argued that the Civil Rights Bill established safeguards for blacks 'which go infinitely beyond any ... provided for the white race. In fact, the distinction of race and color is by the bill made to operate in favor of the colored and against the white race.' His contention would be revived one hundred years later and ignored that African Americans had been subjected to laws for over two hundred years which provided safeguards for whites.

Johnson's obduracy benefited the freedmen in the long term. By accusing Republicans of treason he ensured the passage of the Fourteenth Amendment which made former slaves citizens. In addition it gave the country its first national law of due process stipulating that a state could not deprive people of life, liberty or property, and all had equal protection. In 1870, with the aid of southern Radical Republican governments, the Fifteenth Amendment gave male citizens the right to vote which could not be denied by any state on account of race, colour or 'any previous condition of servitude.' The civil rights movement and the vital legislative victories in the 1960s would not have been possible without these amendments.

Reconstruction was not the disaster southerners have claimed and the first black representatives at national level proved able and magnanimous (Dray, 2008). The democratic state constitutions and the first public education system in the South were introduced by the Radical Republicans (Foner, 1988). But these governments unified the white South to oppose what they believed was corrupt Carpetbagger rule only possible because the freedmen had the vote and whites were expected to acquiesce in 'Negro domination.'

African Americans did not dominate the white South; the highest state office held by a black man was lieutenant governor of Louisiana. All governors were white, as were most southern politicians at state and federal level. Whites of all classes turned to violent paramilitary organisations such as the Ku Klux Klan (KKK), the armed wing of the Democratic Party. Radical Republicans were driven out and, despite the Fifteenth Amendment, African Americans were virtually stripped of their right to vote by violence and a series of devices such as literacy tests and poll taxes. Many illiterate poor whites kept their vote. For white southerners the South was redeemed (Foner, 1988). Ironically it was this very Christian language of redemption that would be used by African Americans in their struggle 80 years later.

Freedmen Abandoned

Increasingly Republicans were unwilling to oblige the South to obey the Constitution. To gain one party control of the South, the Democrats virtually conceded the federal executive power to the Republicans who turned a blind eye to the virtual re-enslavement of African Americans through the peonage sharecrop system and forced, unpaid industrial labour (Daniel, 1972; Blackmon, 2008) With Democrats controlling the South, most African Americans sought accommodation and followed the advice of Booker T. Washington who assured a large white audience in Atlanta in 1895, 'In all things that are purely social we can be as separate as the fingers yet one as the hand in all things essential to mutual progress.' He promised to advise fellow blacks to 'cast down your bucket where you are.... Cast it down in agriculture, mechanics, in commerce, in domestic service, and in the professions' (Blight, 2001). One year later the Supreme Court accepted Washington's view of race relations. In 1896 the Supreme Court, by 8 to 1 in *Plessy v Ferguson*, upheld southern segregation of its facilities, transport and education so long as they were separate but equal. As Justice Harlan, a man from Kentucky, pointed out, the very act of segregation was a denial of equality. But Jim Crow became the touchstone of the southern way of life and it would not be seriously challenged until the 1950s (Litwack, 1998).

It was lynching that forced Washington in his Atlanta speech to seek reassurance from the business leaders of the South. From 1885 to 1917 inclusively there were 3740 lynchings – 2734 were black people. But as the National Association for the Advancement of Colored People (NAACP) reported, in 1918 white victims declined sharply between 1900 and (186 or 13.3 per cent) and the black victims of the lynch mobs increased to 1241 (or 86.7 per cent). While African Americans fought for their country in 1918, there were a further 63 lynched. The horror is vividly portrayed in *Without Sanctuary: Lynching Photographs in America* (Allen, ed., 2000). And violence remained a characteristic of the southern way of life throughout the . 1950s and 1960s and even later. In August 1955 Emmett Till's mutilated body was dragged out of a Mississippi river. He was accused of whistling at a white woman. The defence counsel told the all-white, male jurors that he was 'sure that every last Anglo-Saxon one of you has the courage to free these men' (Whitfield, 1988). They did. Nearly forty years later violent attacks on a women's commune, Camp Sister Spirit, were defended by citing the Till case. Till failed to obey southern customs, and the lesbians at the camp had brought the attacks on themselves with their assault on the southern way of life. Those involved in the civil rights movement were well aware of this violence and that they could be the next victims. In 2008 Congress passed the Emmitt Till Unresolved Civil Rights Crimes Act to re-open cold cases involving the murder of civil rights workers up to 1970 (Senatus.com). Two sponsors of the Bill were Senators Barack Obama and Joe Biden.

Millions of African Americans, from 1890 onwards, sought a better life in the North. Although not free from racial prejudice and only free to compete for the most menial jobs, at least there was no segregation, and earnings in the Chicago stockyards far exceeded anything they earned as sharecroppers. And with the United States caught up in the First World War in 1917, white workers drafted into the services were often replaced by black workers from the South. The competition for jobs and housing led to racial violence in cities such as East St Louis in 1917 (Rudwick, 1964). There were many white race riots in 1919 – the worst in Chicago saw Irish and Polish workers murder men in the black ghetto. The police and military attacked black communities and carried out appalling atrocities (Tuttle, 1980).

This white rage was also political. Simply by moving north, African Americans were enfranchised and during the war their votes decided two mayoralty elections and three African Americans were elected as aldermen. 'Black people paid a high price for their victories, however, for in several significant ways politics was instrumental in precipitating and sustaining the Chicago race riot' (Tuttle, 1980). President Woodrow Wilson's campaign slogan was 'The World Must be Made Safe for Democracy,' but for African Americans the United States lacked democracy. Wilson segregated the federal government, praised the Klan for redeeming the South and did nothing about its revival. Exploiting race hatred, the revived Klan also attacked Roman Catholics and Jews and won support in many states and cities. At its height in 1923 the KKK boasted that it had five million members and effectively controlled states like Indiana (Jackson, 1992).

The Depression and New Deal

During the Depression years of the 1930s many Americans experienced poverty that millions of African Americans had known for so long. White southerners, faced with the Dust Bowl, followed black southerners into northern cities or trekked to the West. Mississippi by 1932 was bankrupt, with barely $1000 in its treasury and with debts of $14 million. Mississippi was not untypical: 'the shrinking tax base throughout the South resulted in cutbacks in state services, and schools closed, road construction ended, and government offices closed, more workers were laid off. Low commodity prices and farm failures made a shambles of the South's economy' (Daniel, 1986).

As black Americans won back the vote by migrating North, the Republican President Herbert Hoover found that his southern policy to neglect black Americans had collapsed. It was not the Democratic Party but Roosevelt who won over black voters and eventually the party retained their loyalty. Some Republicans made belated efforts to win their votes in 1940 but they failed (Topping, 2008).

Despite Franklin D Roosevelt's New Deal, such as the social security scheme, many African Americans faced discrimination in hiring and pay on the employment schemes or were made landless by the Agricultural Adjustment Administration. Commodity prices were raised by restricting the supply and farmers were paid to plough cotton under. The result was dismissal of sharecroppers and tenants who were encouraged to go North. As Daniel has shown, the structure of the Agricultural Adjustment Administration 'made it well-nigh impossible for a sharecropper to appeal eviction' (Daniel, 1986). But some white and black tenants and sharecroppers did fight back with the Southern Tenant Farmers Union to protect their rights and land, and even conducted a successful strike (Fannin, 2003).

The New Deal reforms persuaded African American voters to remain loyal Democrats, and by 1940 America was booming and African Americans benefited because of their loyalty. A. Philip Randolph, head of the Brotherhood of Sleeping Car Porters, threatened a march on Washington in 1941 unless job discrimination was abolished. FDR issued Executive Order 8802 which established the Committee on Fair Employment Practices to ensure all workers in defence industries would not suffer discrimination because of race, creed, colour or national origin. This was the first time the federal government introduced affirmative action, requiring companies to insert a clause in their defence contracts that they would not discriminate and the same applied to federal employment agencies. In response to criticisms, FDR issued Executive Order 9346 which gave the committee independent status, field offices and staff and $500,000 budget (Topping, 2008). Despite the shortcomings there were significant improvements, such as the integration of the San Francisco shipyard, and the Orders provided the basis for post-war legislation.

World War II

Pearl Harbor ensured national mobilisation regardless of race, religion or gender. The need for labour in northern factories required massive recruitment of black workers and, despite some resistance, the first large-scale organisation of black workers in predominantly white unions. African Americans' willingness to join unions won them an ally in the future struggle for civil rights. Although the rhetoric of war was similar to the First World War – a world safe for democracy – the war added a new element. Nazism was built on racism and justified the extermination of 'inferior races' including Jews. Every assault on German racism was an attack on racism in the United States as far as African Americans were concerned. But, fearing southern Democrats, FDR did not integrate the forces and the United States battled a racist regime with a segregated military. Five hundred thousand African Americans fought in Europe and the Pacific and they used their patriotism to demand a 'Double Victory' – victory over the enemies of democracy overseas and in the United States (Weisbrot, 1990).

Protests against segregation and racial violence did not start in the Second World War and African Americans were never passive victims. Many North and South protested against Jim Crow. Much earlier, a group of black intellectuals attacked Booker T. Washington's accommodation and later they established the NAACP. Edwin Redkey points out: 'Different as these tactics were, bitter as were the struggles between the advocates of accommodation and protest, they shared the same basic strategy. Each ideology expected a black elite to win the dignity sought by all Afro-Americans' (Redkey, 1969).

Black Nationalism and Changing Attitudes

But there were African Americans who favoured black nationalism or supported going back to Africa (Bracey *et al.*, 1972). Edwin P. McCabe urged African Americans to move into the Oklahoma territory to create an all-black state. He failed but several black towns were established. Others turned to Bishop Henry McNeal Turner and his plans to establish a nation in Africa. This black nationalism, as Redkey points out, 'shares many attributes of other nationalisms. . . . Afro-Americans had a political past of slavery, oppression, and isolation. . . . As a result, blacks had overflowing recollections of collective humiliation and regret.' But nationalism was not solely based on the negative experiences in the United States but also 'stressed the glories of their African ancestors and the American rhetoric which claimed that all men are equal' (Redkey, 1969). Black nationalism was popular in the 1920s when its main exponent was Marcus Garvey and gained supporters in the 1960s, especially the Nation of Islam (Essien-Udom, 1964).

However, the vast majority of African Americans in the nineteenth and twentieth centuries wanted full American citizenship. The early leaders in this struggle were members of the NAACP and one of their first successes came in 1915 against the state of Oklahoma. This new state, like several other southern states, sought to disenfranchise black Americans when its constitution stipulated that residents whose grandfathers had not been eligible to vote would not be allowed to either. The Supreme Court declared the 'Grandfather Clause' a violation of the Fourteenth Amendment (Meier and Rudwick, 1970). The NAACP exploited New Deal support for equal opportunity. The NAACP in the 1930s attacked university segregation and gradually sought to dismantle Jim Crow laws. They aimed to prove that the South was separate but unequal. The Supreme Court upheld their view and ordered graduate and law schools in states such as Maryland and Missouri to integrate or provide equal facilities. It was cheaper for them to integrate.

The War encouraged more Americans to speak out against racism. Gunnar Myrdal, in collaboration with black and white American scholars, produced a massive (1483 pages) report called *The American Dilemma*. It stressed the gulf between the American Creed – all men are created equal with the inalienable rights of life, liberty and the pursuit of happiness – and the American 'Deed,' which was segregation, racism and inequality (Myrdal *et al.*, 1964).

It was not only the changing attitudes of many Americans which gave grounds for hope that African Americans would be included in the American Creed. It was the denial of this creed by segregation that encouraged the development of black institutions such as churches, colleges and fraternal organisations, some of whose leaders would eventually cast their lot with the civil rights movement. Preachers had always played a crucial role in the African American community, as had the college leaders such as Booker T. Washington. The religion of African Americans often led to conservatism, to stress forgiveness rather than struggle (Branch, 1989; Asch, 2008), but after the War, pressure from their congregations and black students on the college campuses transformed these bastions of a segregated society into battering rams which did much to destroy the southern way of life.

But in 1945 most southerners were sure that segregation was safe, and most northerners had no idea of the disturbances that were to come.

1

TRANSFORMATION OF POLITICS: CIVIL RIGHTS 1945–58

After the War there were an increasing number of Americans willing to accept the views of sociologists and academics which openly challenged the assumptions of racism. The continued Great Migration of African Americans from the South into the industrial cities of the North also forced politicians to question their own assumptions. Of the African Americans living outside the South in 1940, 17 per cent were residents of New York City, and the cities of Detroit, Cleveland, Chicago, Philadelphia and Pittsburgh were home to 30 per cent of African Americans living in the North and the West (Issel, 1985). It was now necessary for the Democratic Party, the party which had its strength among the working-class in the North, to face up to the challenge of the 'New Negro,' as the black sociologist E. Franklin Frazier had described them. They resided in the growing urban ghettos, increasingly they were members of trade unions and had since 1936 transferred their allegiance to the Democratic Party. Ironically, in 1944 Franklin Delano Roosevelt (FDR) had won his unprecedented fourth term as President largely owing to the combined votes of African Americans and the segregated, Jim Crow, Democratic South. In the same year the black vote ensured the election of Adam Clayton Powell of New York, who became the second black congressman to be elected in the North, and twenty years later there would be six, all from the major industrial cities (two from Detroit and the others from New York, Philadelphia, Chicago and Los Angeles) The black population in the North had grown by 40 per cent during the war and 80 per cent voted for Truman and assured his election (Topping, 2008). The political manoeuvring that would radically change the Democratic Party after the Second World War would be in response to these demographic changes.

According to Truman's biographer, the Vice President and former shop-keeper from Missouri, who took over the presidency after the death of Roosevelt, 'moved to establish himself as a friend of the Negro' (Hamby, 1973). But although he favoured some legislative help for blacks, Truman's support for African Americans never matched his support for Jewish Americans and his unwillingness to act decisively was characteristic of white liberals, both Republicans and Democrats, after the war (Fraser, 1994). Growing up in Missouri, he never escaped the prejudices of his region. 'Privately, he could still speak of "niggers," as if that were the way one naturally referred to blacks' (McCullough, 1992). In the 1920s he had paid the $10 membership to the KKK, in what has been described as an act of 'amazing naiveté.' Principle was sacrificed for ambition. And his sister Mary was confident, mistakenly, in her belief that 'Harry is no more for nigger equality than any of us' (McCullough, 1992). Truman, like the vast majority of white Americans, never understood the humiliation and fear that segregation imposed on African Americans. As Pauli Murray, a black lesbian, feminist, lawyer and poet, wrote in her autobiography: 'We knew that the race problem was like a deadly snake coiled and ready to strike, and that one avoided its dangers only by never-ending watchfulness' (Murray, 1989).

Fair Employment

The victory in Europe and over Japan in 1945 was a mixed blessing for African Americans. Since 1944 there had been discussions in the administration about conversion of military to civilian working. Members of the Fair Employment Practices Commission (FEPC) were only too aware that this would adversely affect many African Americans and they even feared the outbreak of race riots in the cities. Although the rioting did not materialise, as it had after the First World War, the disproportionate dismissal of black workers started as early as the spring of 1945. One company in Buffalo, for example, laid off 9000 female workers. 'Black women were affected in a five-to-one ratio because discrimination forced them to be the last hired and trained' (Reed, 1991). These workers, who had been earning from 80c to $1.42 an hour, were pressurised to interview for jobs that paid less and many were denied unemployment benefits. A similar pattern of discrimination existed across the country. 'By November, 1945, the exodus of minority workers from wartime jobs had turned into a virtual rout, and discrimination was "rapidly approaching pre-war levels," columnist Ted Poston reported in the New York *Post*' (Reed, 1991; Topping, 2008).

The first test of Truman's liberalism came in 1945 when the FEPC sought to end the discriminatory hiring policies of the Capitol Transit Company of Washington, D.C. The Committee had been successful in changing the policies of transport companies in 16 cities in the North and West but had been defied in the District of Columbia for three years. Senior members of the Committee sought the support of the President. Three months passed. Finally, the Presidential Assistant, John Steelman, told the Committee they could not act; a request to meet the President was refused and the chairman resigned. According to Truman, ordering the company to desist in its discriminatory practices was a violation of congressional law. Truman's support for a permanent FEPC has been described as 'routine' (Hamby, 1973). On the other hand, it has been suggested that many 'failed to understand... that as President he could no longer sit idly by and do nothing in the face of glaring injustice' (McCullough, 1992). Although he issued an Executive Order, he knew it only gave the Committee the ability to collect data and he also knew that Congress had stripped the FEPC of its funding. Despite these limitations, the Committee had some effect. 'In the new agencies created by federal legislation in the 1960s, some of these FEPC veterans would help revive the struggle for fair employment practice' (McCullough, 1992). For example, John Hope Franklin II, a distinguished black historian, worked in the 1960s and 1970s in the Office of Civil Rights and on the presidential Commission for Equal Employment Opportunity (CEEO), and Marjorie Lawson served as a federal judge and on the Task Force on Urban Renewal. Former FEPC workers were active at the state and city level, such as Theodore Jones, the former budget officer, who set up an accounting business in Illinois where he was regional director of the Office of Economic Opportunity, a trustee of the state university, and also worked for the Chicago Commission on Human Rights (Reed, 1991).

A cynic might argue that Truman's civil rights policy was more smoke and mirrors. In a message to Congress he briefly advocated the setting up of a permanent FEPC. He did nothing to stop southern conservatives from filibustering the proposal. But he did speak to a NAACP rally on 30 June 1946 and he did appoint a special committee on civil rights, chaired by the president of General Electric, Charles Wilson, which submitted a report on 29 October 1947 entitled *To Secure These Rights*, with recommendations for an anti-lynching law, abolition of poll taxes, protection of people during voter registration, integration of the armed services, denial of federal funds to recipients that discriminated, and to end segregation in interstate transport (McCullough, 1992). These recommendations, combined with action by the Justice Department, meant that it 'was not certain by the end of 1947 just how far the administration was willing to go, but no one could doubt that it was moving in a more liberal direction on Negro rights' (Hamby, 1973).

The reception given to returning African American servicemen shocked Truman. The vicious assault and blinding of a black soldier in South Carolina was one of 56 attacks on African Americans between June 1945 and September 1946 and the bloody white police riot in Columbia, Tennessee, led to demands for a federal anti-lynching bill. Truman reassured a southern friend that he was opposed to social equality but he was in favour of equality of opportunity (McCullough, 1992). Truman, like FDR, did not support such a measure but he was persuaded of the need for action; in addition there was the pressure coming from the African American community (Duberman, 1989). Concerned about the revival of KKK terrorism, Truman told the Committee on Civil Rights in January 1947 that he wanted the Bill of Rights 'implemented in fact. We have been trying to do this for 150 years.' On 29 June 1947 he told the annual meeting of the NAACP that, 'If... freedom is to be more than a dream, each man must be guaranteed equality of opportunity. The only limit to an American's achievement should be his ability, his industry and his character' (Truman, 1956). This was the first speech by a president to the NAACP and 'it was the strongest statement on civil rights heard in Washington since the time of Lincoln' (McCullough, 1992). One of the groups putting pressure on the White House was the Congress of Racial Equality (CORE), set up in 1942 by James Farmer of Louisiana, and a group of Quakers who were members of the Fellowship of Reconciliation (FOR). The aim of CORE was 'to eliminate racial discrimination' and it was prepared to use 'inter-racial, nonviolent direct action' to achieve this end. Members of the organisation were involved in sit-ins in Chicago restaurants, and demanded the end of segregation on interstate transport as early as the 1940s (White, 1985).

Even in the most dangerous and racist states, African Americans were not prepared to wait for presidents to act. With the all-white primaries declared illegal by the Supreme Court in 1946, black Mississippians tried to vote, despite dire threats from newspapers such as the Jackson *Daily News* and Theodore Bilbo who was seeking re-election to the US Senate. The Reverend William Bender, the 60-year-old chaplain of Tugaloo College, defied a mob and was only stopped from voting by an armed deputy sheriff. Medgar Evers, a Second World War veteran, later murdered by the Klan, was denied the right to vote in Decatur. Bilbo was re-elected but the Democratic Party only allowed whites to vote in the primary and his victory was challenged by the NAACP and the Progressive Voters League. As John Dittmer maintains 'the 1946 primary election and the subsequent challenge to Bilbo is a significant event in the history of the black struggle for freedom.' And although victory over white bigotry was not in sight, the courage to openly challenge Bilbo in front of a Senate Committee hearing meant that 'in that crowded federal courtroom in Jackson the shock troops of the modern civil rights movement had fired their opening salvo' (Dittmer, 1995).

Democrats Transformed

Despite the limited actions of the President in support of African Americans, black voters overwhelmingly supported the Democratic candidate in 1948 and ensured Truman's election. As Don McCoy argues, the limited action of the Democrats had had one effect: 'If Truman was not yet considered a significant champion of America's minorities, the ostensible interest of congressional Republicans in civil rights had been discredited' (McCoy, 1984). The transformation of the Democratic Party into a predominantly northern liberal party was speeded up at the 1948 convention. Exhorted by the young Hubert Humphrey and the liberals of the Americans for Democratic Action (ADA), the Democrats adopted 'the most sweeping civil rights plank ever written into a Democratic platform' (Hamby, 1973).

Angry southerners led by Strom Thurmond, governor of South Carolina, walked out of the convention and set up their own Dixiecrat Party, with Thurmond as its presidential candidate. According to one scholar, 'The Democratic party, then, no longer represented the South's interests. It had become dominated by intellectuals, self-seeking labor leaders, and most poignant of all for white southerners, insensitive Negroes' (Garson, 1974). Mississippi Senator James Eastland was convinced that Walter White, of the NAACP, was 'a negro, who, I am afraid to say, has more power in your government than all of the southern states combined' (Garson, 1974). Another enthusiastic supporter of the Dixiecrat Party who played a prominent role in later civil rights disturbances in his city was the Police Commissioner of Birmingham, Alabama, Eugene 'Bull' Connor.

Truman complained bitterly that his stand on civil rights was 'deliberately misconstrued to include or imply racial miscegenation and intermarriage. My only goal was equal opportunity and security under the law for all classes of Americans' (Truman, 1956). Truman's position was made even more precarious by Democrats who disagreed with his anti-Soviet stance, giving their support to former Vice President Henry Wallace, who was running as a Progressive. With the Democrats putting up three candidates, it was considered certain that the Republican, Thomas Dewey of New York, would be the next president. Truman's stand on civil rights was crucial in the presidential election (Topping, 2008).

The 1948 Election

Historians are agreed that the 1948 election established civil rights as the major issue, endorsed by three out of the four parties. During the election Henry Wallace, the Progressive candidate, went into the South and campaigned for civil rights. All the meetings were integrated and in Virginia they were orderly but in North Carolina there was serious violence. It was not only the willingness of Wallace to defy segregation that was significant but also the determination of African Americans and some whites to support the Progressive campaign. Boss Crump in Memphis tried to stop Paul Robeson, the great singer and actor who was awarded the Spingarn Medal by the NAACP in 1945, from addressing a Progressive rally. The black community was not intimidated and the meeting was held at an alternative meeting space offered by a black minister. Several thousand white and black people attended. In Columbus, Georgia, the KKK surrounded but failed to attack a Progressive rally because, as the politicians later discovered, there were 100 armed blacks protecting them. Robeson's biographer comments: 'It gave him hope for the future, regardless of how the '48 election itself came out – even as the outright murder of other blacks (including several who merely tried to vote) continued to feed his anger.' In Alabama white mobs attacked the Progressive presidential candidate but Wallace 'managed to hold a dozen unsegregated meetings, and he set an example of courage and moral determination which even his bitterest liberal opponents found hard to denounce' (Duberman, 1989). Academics teaching in the South, who supported Wallace, were often dismissed.

Some Republicans were so alarmed at the loss of the African American vote, which was crucial in many northern and western states, that they formed a National Council of Negro Republicans. There were Republican strategists who noted that advocating civil rights for African Americans would not benefit the party and the seed of the later Republican southern strategy was planted (Topping, 2008). Cynical observers noted that even the

limited civil rights programme proposed by Truman did not have popular
white support.

It is easy to criticise Truman for not acting on the recommendations in
his civil rights committee report, *To Secure These Rights*; he did take executive action. He desegregated Washington National Airport, his inauguration
guests in 1949 were integrated and he did appoint a black judge, William
H. Hastie, to the federal courts (McCoy, 1984). The Justice Department
supported cases against restrictive covenants and was prepared by 1950 to
challenge the doctrine of 'separate but equal' as laid down in many rulings, such as *Plessy* (Smith, 1997). The man from Missouri 'helped – often
in spite of himself – to educate a nation to its obligations and its failures.
In another sense, he unleashed expectations he could not foresee, desires he
could not understand, and forces which future governments would not be
able to restrain' (Bernstein, 1991).

Integrating the Military

Perhaps Truman's most important action was to issue Executive Orders.
In Order 9980 he established the Fair Employment Board to ensure equal
treatment of minorities in federal hiring. However, lack of funding, civil
service rules and the conservative nature of those who ran the Board all
limited its achievements. Executive Order 9981 stipulated that there should
be 'equality of opportunity for all persons in the armed forces, without
regard to race, color, or national origin' (White, 1985). Truman's action was
partly a result of pressure from A. Philip Randolph, who threatened to lead
a boycott of compulsory conscription into the armed services (the draft).
Most historians regard Truman's integration of the armed services, despite
the opposition from some of the leading generals, especially Dwight D.
Eisenhower, as having long-term benefits for African Americans. There are
those who dissent strongly from this majority view (Pinkney, 1976). By 1952
the army, navy and air force were largely integrated. There were still too
few minority officers and the Executive Order had not been enforced in the
National Guard or reserve forces. 'The greatest battles had been won, however, thanks to the persistence of Truman and civil-rights groups' (McCoy,
1984). (And one consequence was the integration of the 1950s *Sergeant Bilko*
television comedy about army camp life, in which the one black actor is
never a figure of fun.)

Presidents and congressmen were reluctant to act; the same cannot be
said of African Americans. The NAACP Legal Defense Fund continued

to challenge the accepted notion of 'separate but equal' in the courts and members of CORE resorted to sit-ins and freedom rides, tactics of non-violent direct action which were to become common in the 1960s. As early as 1947, CORE members took a 'Journey of Reconciliation' through the border states in which they sought to ensure the enforcement of a Supreme Court ruling which had challenged segregation on buses in inter-state travel (White, 1985). These tactics were adopted because many avenues of agitation were virtually closed to black Americans.

African Americans and Labour

This is particularly true of the labour movement which, during the anti-Communist witch-hunt following the War, purged communists and radicals from organised unions. The American Federation of Labor and the Congress of Industrial Organizations (AFL-CIO) were reunited in 1955 under the leadership of the conservative George Meany. Only two black labour leaders were on the executive council of the AFL-CIO, James Carney, who had been secretary-treasurer of the CIO, and A. Philip Randolph of the Brotherhood of Sleeping Car Porters. Participating unions were 'encouraged' to recruit without regard to race but the AFL did not exclude racist unions even though they had the power to expel communists. Liberals failed to change this (Marable, 1997). Even a 1970s study which stresses the benefits of union organising in the southern black community admits that the moral force of the civil rights movement came from the black church and not the unions. 'By abandoning the effort to organize the unorganized the CIO ceased being a labor movement; and this, in turn, deprived civil rights activists of political and social space in which to operate' (Stokes and Halpern, 1994). One African American, an activist from the trade union movement, was E. D. Nixon, one of the leaders in the Montgomery Improvement Association (MIA) and the bus boycott, who was a member of both the Brotherhood of Sleeping Car Porters and the NAACP (Branch, 1989).

With limited access to the labour movement and virtually no power in politics, African Americans turned to the legal system and direct action. The limits of political action can be seen when the NAACP sought to amend federal aid to education. The Association argued that such aid should not be given to segregated schools. But the man who had championed the civil rights platform at the 1948 convention, Hubert Humphrey, now a senator, opposed the suggested amendment. 'As much as I detest segregation, I love education more' (McCoy, 1984). Rejected by such politicians, the

Legal Defense Fund of the NAACP had with increasing success turned to the Supreme Court. For example, southern states had passed legislation between 1890 and 1915 allowing the Democratic Party to limit voting in the primary elections to whites only. In 1944 the Supreme Court ruled white primaries unconstitutional but as late as 1958 it upheld the literacy tests required in North Carolina (Miller, 1967).

Eisenhower

It was Truman's successor, the Republican Dwight David Eisenhower, who inadvertently strengthened the Supreme Court which would become a major factor as Americans struggled to resolve the conflict between the American Creed and the American Deed. Certainly the new President was not prepared to act vigorously to defend the rights of African Americans. Even a sympathetic biographer admits: 'Essentially, Eisenhower passed on to his successors the problem of guaranteeing constitutional rights to Negro citizens' (Ambrose, 1984). After all, Eisenhower and the Republicans were aware that many southern Democrats had bolted the party because of the race issue. General Eisenhower, as candidate of the hated Republican Party, a party which had been feared and loathed by most southerners since the Civil War, won four southern States – Virginia, Tennessee, Florida and Texas. He did well in other states such as Arkansas and North Carolina. Having won the election of 1952, the former general had to satisfy all the powerful elements in the Republican Party, and one of these was the gover-nor of California, Earl Warren, and his supporters, who had delivered the California delegation at the 1952 convention in favour of Eisenhower (Blum, 1991). By-passed for the post of Attorney General, Warren was promised the first vacancy on the Supreme Court. It was an appointment that Eisenhower deeply regretted (Ambrose, 1984). Chief Justice Warren, unlike President Eisenhower, was willing to meet the challenge of civil rights.

The *Brown* Decision

One of the most famous cases in US history was decided by the Warren Court. The NAACP had successfully chipped away at the 'separate but equal' doctrine of *Plessy* and now it was decided to challenge segregation in schools in four states – Kansas, South Carolina, Virginia, and Delaware – as well as the District of Columbia. Twice, in 1951 and 1952, the Court referred the South Carolina case to a three-man panel who simply enjoined the authorities to ensure that the schools, if separate, were equal. In Prince Edward County, Virginia, the struggle to win equal education started at Moton High School and was led by Barbara Jones whose uncle Vernon Jones was the radical pastor in Montgomery, Alabama.

Oliver Brown decided to challenge segregation in the schools of Topeka, Kansas. Under state law any city with a population of over 15,000 could impose segregation in its grade schools. Under this legislation Oliver Brown was prevented from sending his daughter to the nearest school, a mere five blocks away, because it was white and instead she had to travel 20 blocks to attend an all-black school. Brown lost his case in 1951 when three federal judges ruled that Topeka schools complied with *Plessy*. He was given leave to appeal to the Supreme Court. The choice of this case, *Brown v The Board of Education, Topeka, Kansas*, to represent the findings of the Court was not accidental because it was ruling on a northern state with a flexible segregation law. The attack on *Plessy* was led by Thurgood Marshall, the leading black lawyer for the NAACP and director of the Legal Defense Fund. He relied not only on expert lawyers but also called on leading sociologists and psychologists to argue that segregation by race was inherently unequal and a denial of equal protection under the law as guaranteed by the Fourteenth Amendment. (Marshall would be the first African American to be appointed a Supreme Court justice.)

Earl Warren was insistent that the Court should be unanimous and on 17 May 1954 the Court's decision, written by Warren, posed the question: 'Does segregation of children in public schools solely on the basis of race, even though the facilities are equal, deprive children of the minority of equal educational opportunity?' And answered that it did. Warren and the Court also ruled that segregation in the District of Columbia was unconstitutional and a violation of due process (Miller, 1967). These rulings were made despite opposition from Eisenhower, and the Executive can have considerable influence on the Court. The President had invited the Chief Justice to the White House and insisted Warren sat next to John W. Davis, the lawyer representing the segregationists before the Supreme Court. Eisenhower told Warren that the southerners 'are not bad people. All they are concerned about is to see that their sweet little girls are not required to sit in school alongside some big overgrown Negroes' (Ambrose, 1984). Eisenhower was not the first white man, nor the last, to exploit sexual fears in combination with racial prejudice. Eisenhower's efforts failed. The ruling in *Brown* was a major achievement for the NAACP and a vindication of its policy to seek redress through the courts and it has been called 'the single most important moment in the decade, the moment that separated the old order from the new and helped to create the tumultuous era just arriving' (Halberstam, 1993). But it was not a complete victory by any means. The Court had overturned *Plessy* but there was no attempt to set acceptable standards for schools and especially there was no indication of when desegregation was to be achieved. On this latter point Marshall and the NAACP lawyers were invited to return to the Court and argue their case. In *Brown II* the Court was unanimous in ruling that integration should be done 'with all deliberate speed.' There was no date for compliance (Miller, 1967; Blum, 1991). In this decision the Court made a serious error but it was based on Warren's belief that schools were being desegregated and that school administrators needed time to adjust to the new ruling (Ely, 1976). Previously the Courts had always ruled that a constitutional right was always personal and present and, as Loren Miller points out, 'in the 1955 case [*Brown II*], the Court held that a personal and present constitutional right could be deferred and extended gradually to those who were entitled to exercise it by virtue of a constitutional amendment. There was no constitutional warrant for such a ruling' (Miller, 1967).

And it was not only white folks who were critical of the Court. In 1955 Harlem Renaissance author and conservative Republican, Zora Neale Hurston, said the ruling insulted black children and their teachers. Desegregation did not mean integration. She asked, 'How much satisfaction can I get from a court order for somebody to associate with me who does not wish to be near me' (Patterson, 1996). It was an argument that would appeal to later black conservatives.

Warren hoped for gradual compliance with the Court. In this he and his fellow justices underestimated the resistance of white southerners to change. After the first *Brown* case, white Citizens Councils were formed, starting in Indianola, Mississippi, to ensure segregation would remain. Within a year they had spread throughout the South and have been called 'the bourgeois Klan.' In Virginia there was a 'massive resistance' campaign against integration and some public schools were even closed. The Harry Byrd state political machine concerned itself with registering and caring only for the white voters of the state and frequently exploited the race issue. At first the Senator called for passive resistance but a few days later, seeking to keep his support, he changed this to massive resistance (Lewis, 2006). One former governor recalled that during his term in office; 'Negro influence was nil.' There was little support for integration from academics at the University of Virginia and the weak AFL-CIO unions were actively opposed. For example, in Warren County from 1958 until 1960 the local textile workers' union paid to keep open a segregated school when the county schools were closed. In 1958 union members overwhelmingly voted for the Byrd machine despite its anti-union measures. James Kilpatrick, editor of the *Richmond News Leader*, recalled: 'There was talk then of blood flowing ankle deep in the gutters. Men were saying "never" then; and then they meant it' (Ely, 1976). It was the Virginians and the Citizens Councils which used the Old South arguments that it was the duty of the leaders of the "sovereign" states to interpose their authority between the federal government and the people of the state and nullify unconstitutional rulings of the Supreme Court or acts of the federal government. The Southern Manifesto was also designed to win support from northerners (Lewis, 2006). In virtually every southern state, integration plans submitted by school boards were challenged in the courts, even by the NAACP, on the grounds that the plans were inadequate. Most of the congressmen and senators from the South signed the Manifesto, in which they committed themselves to fight the *Brown* decision. There were three notable exceptions – Albert Gore Sr. and Estes Kefauver of Tennessee and Lyndon Johnson of Texas (Ambrose, 1984; Dallek, 1991). Unlike Gore, Johnson refused to do so with the approval of southerner senators who wanted him to run for the presidency.

As for President Eisenhower, he insisted that the problem of integration of schools was a local matter. Despite rioting at Clinton, Tennessee, and Mansfield, Texas, he maintained that the federal government had no power to intervene. He angered members of the NAACP when he compared them to the white segregationists. At a press conference he said that the South was 'full of people of good will' but he condemned 'the people ... so filled with prejudice that they can even resort to violence; and the same way on the other side of the thing, the people who want to have the whole matter settled today.' His biographer admits that 'he had gone to great lengths to divorce himself from the problem of race relations, and especially integration of schools' (Ambrose, 1984). He set the example for other presidents who hoped that desegregation would be achieved by the courts. Eisenhower was later attacked by Truman, who argued that the General as President had failed to give leadership. 'He didn't use the powers of the office of the President to uphold a ruling of the Supreme Court of the United States, and I never did understand that' (Miller, 1974). Partly because of the Association's role in this case, it has been suggested that the NAACP was conservative and reluctant to support direct action. Their persistent challenges to segregated education so angered southern segregationists that state by state the Association was virtually destroyed by repressive legislation (Morris, 1984). Despite this repression, it was members of the Association who supported

families involved in the integration of schools, and frequently organised and
led direct action campaigns. It was the Legal Defense Fund that represented
people caught up in the mass arrests that were to come.

Little Rock

Politicians of both parties soon realised that attacks on the *Brown* decision and the Supreme Court were an easy way to gain votes. The chief
executive officer of Arkansas, Democrat Governor Orval Faubus, was just
one of many southern Democrats who used this tactic. Faubus was running for re-election and he faced stiff competition. His opponents had also
discovered that Faubus' father had been a dedicated socialist and that his
schoolteacher's son had been a student at the radical Commonwealth College before the War and had helped his father set up a socialist local [group]
(Green, 1978). Seeking to divert the electorate from his radical past, Faubus
played the race card and challenged the ruling of the Supreme Court. The
city of Little Rock had drawn up plans for very gradual compliance with the
Brown decision which would not see the integration of the schools until 1963
(Miller, 1967). Nine African American students reported to Central High
School in September 1957 but found it surrounded by units of the Arkansas
National Guard. Faubus issued orders that no black students were to enter.
   Faubus claimed that he was seeking to protect the lives and property of
citizens of the state. But already one of the students, Melba Pattillo, who
had volunteered and had been selected to go to Central High, had been
the victim of violent assault and an attempted rape by a white man who
yelled at her: 'I'll show you niggers the Supreme Court can't run my life'
(Beals, 1994). Although the children had the support of the NAACP and
most church leaders, the battle to integrate Little Rock Central also brought
about divisions. Pattillo's father opposed her, arguing that it only endangered her life and his job. Writing under her married name, Melba Pattillo
Beals, she graphically depicts the appalling treatment of the students who
integrated the school. While the governor sought to keep the students out
by surrounding the school with troops, the administration in Washington
was forced to act. After obtaining an injunction against Faubus preventing him from interfering with integration, Eisenhower had no choice but
to send in the 101st Airborne because the Governor had withdrawn the
National Guard and the children were attacked by hysterical racist mobs
(Miller, 1967; Beals, 1994). Pattillo drew strength from meeting Thurgood
Marshall:

I looked at this man who seemed to have none of the fears and hesitation of my parents or the other adults around us. Instead he had a self-assured air about him as though he had seen the promised land and knew for certain we could get there. We had only heard rumors of freedom, but he had lived it, and it showed in his every word, his every movement, in the way he sat tall in his seat. (Beals, 1994)

She survived the ordeal at Central High because she had strong support from her mother, grandmother and many members of the black community as well as encouragement from a small group of whites. In her own account she admits, 'I wonder what possessed my parents and the adults of the NAACP to allow us to go to school in the face of such violence.' And Arkansas put the Association under increasing pressure with the state Attorney General, Bruce Bennett, demanding all its records, including names of members, their addresses, telephone numbers as well as contributors to the organisation. As the young Melba Pattillo wrote in her diary: 'What will become of us if the NAACP is not strong? It feels as though segregationists are attacking from all sides' (Beals, 1994).

Despite the sacrifices she and the other eight made in 1957, it was not until 1960 that Central was integrated and by 1964 only 2.3 per cent of all African American children were attending desegregated schools (Blum, 1991). But Beals observes: 'Once President Eisenhower made that kind of commitment to uphold the law, there was no turning back. And even though later on he would waver and not whole-heartedly back up his powerful decision, he had stepped over a line that no other President had ever dared cross' (Beals, 1994).

In other schools it took even longer. The Moton High School Prince Edward County, Virginia, was closed. But massive resistance in the county collapsed and by 2003 a new high school was fully integrated with 47 per cent black students and 43 per cent white. The Virginia Assembly passed a resolution which was a formal apology for the campaign to keep segregated schools. Unfortunately recent statistics demonstrate the rapid re-segregation of schools in the United States (Leadership Conference on Civil Rights Report, 2006).

Ironically, the deeply conservative President, as a result of pressure from the African American community (to be discussed in detail in the next chapter) and the claim that the United States was a leader of the free world in a global struggle against atheistic communism, was forced to act on behalf of the African American community. However reluctant he might have been to enforce the *Brown* ruling, the Supreme Court was not so reluctant to act.

In 1958 in *Cooper v Aaron* it made a sweeping ruling which made unconstitutional any law, 'ingenious or ingenuous,' which sought to keep public
schools segregated. Three new justices appointed by Eisenhower after 1954
reaffirmed the *Brown* ruling which had been made before their appointment
(Ely, 1976).

Republicans felt that their work on civil rights had not been appreciated
by African Americans. They pointed out that despite desegregation of military bases and the city of Washington, and the appointment of Frederick
Morrow, a former NAACP field secretary to the White House in 1956,
blacks continued to vote for the Democrats. Republicans did not admit the
failure of the President to condemn the killing of Emmett Till in Mississippi
or his silence on the expulsion of the first black student from the University of Alabama, Autherine Lucy. (Miss Lucy successfully sued for admission
to the university. However, it was a Pyrrhic victory because the university
authorities expelled her, accusing her of lying because she had claimed that
she had not been admitted initially because of her race.) Eisenhower refused
to give any federal support for the Montgomery, Alabama, bus boycott.
He believed that the South was law-abiding and that it was impossible for
decisions of the Court to be completely enforced (Ambrose, 1984).

The FBI and Black America

Eisenhower's biographer says his reluctance was partly based on the reports
from J. Edgar Hoover, director of the Federal Bureau of Investigation (FBI),
that communists had infiltrated the civil rights movement. If this was the
case, it was a very different assessment from the one given to the House
Committee on UnAmerican Activities two years earlier. The committee,
better known as HUAC, had published a report on 22 December 1954 entitled *The American Negro in the Communist Party* which cited Hoover's assessment
of the previous year. Of the 5395 communists who were considered leading
members of the party by the FBI 'only 411 were Negroes. . . . The fact that
only 411 Negroes were found in this select group is strong evidence that the
American Negro is not hoodwinked by these false messiahs.'

Hoover's opinion underwent a dramatic change. In 1956, Hoover warned
Eisenhower that the NAACP, along with members of the Communist Party,
were exploiting the murder of Emmett Till and a 1957 report, based on
information obtained through illegal burglaries and telephone taps, was
given to 'various opinion molders within the government, with portions
leaked to "reliable and cooperative" newspaper reporters.' Publicly Hoover

denied that communists were influential in the NAACP. In subsequent years he and his Bureau members would not just search for communists but would seek to destroy the civil rights movement and its leadership (O'Reilly, 1994).

The 1957 Civil Rights Act

It is undeniable that Hoover held great power in Washington, but the best assessment of Eisenhower's attitudes towards civil rights is that made by a survivor of Little Rock. Beal's suspicions that the President was not 'whole-hearted' in his support for civil rights can be seen in his reaction to a proposed Civil Rights Bill which proposed a bipartisan civil rights commission, a new division in the Justice Department to investigate civil rights abuses and one which especially sought to ensure all citizens the right to vote. But the Republicans faced opposition from the powerful leader of the Senate, Lyndon Baines Johnson (LBJ). His biographer has summed up Johnson's political shrewdness well: 'Johnson saw a Senate fight over civil rights legislation in 1956 as a losing proposition for the country, the Democrats, and himself.' As a result he sent the Bill to the judiciary committee headed by Mississippi Senator James Eastland where it was buried (Dallek, 1991; Caro, 2002). The revival of civil rights legislation was due to black pressure and an acute awareness on behalf of the presidential aspirants that something had to be done.

> It was clear to Lyndon that pressure from southern blacks made change in the region inevitable.... If he could lead a major civil rights bill through the Senate, it would be the first Federal legislative advance in this field in eighty-two years. Such an achievement ... would be a boon to his presidential ambitions. A civil rights bill credited to Johnson would help to transform him from a southern or regional leader into a national spokesman. (Dallek, 1991)

Moreover his supporters, even Senator Richard Russell, understood the need for such legislation if the Texan was to go to the White House. For the Republicans, Vice President Richard Nixon, who had never championed civil rights legislation before, was also a convert and eager to make a gesture to satisfy the demands of the African American community.

The Bill went before the House of Representatives in the winter of 1955, and Eisenhower gave public and private support. But things changed when the Bill ran into opposition when it was sent to the Senate in 1956. Georgia

Senator, Richard Russell, denounced the Bill as not only seeking to ensure the right to vote but rather to give power to the Justice Department and 'the whole might of the federal government, including the armed forces if necessary, to force a commingling of white and Negro children.' Hubert Humphrey, who had so strongly advocated the civil rights platform in the 1948 Democratic convention, said that Russell's 'tremendous ability was weakened and corroded by his unalterable opposition to the passage of any legislation that would alleviate the plight of the black man throughout the nation. He was the victim of his region, the victim of a heritage of the past, unable to break out of the bonds of his own slavery' (Dallek, 1991). Russell was not completely opposed to the Bill but rather sought to weaken the powers of the Justice Department and he was particularly keen to retain jury trials for breaches of civil rights because he knew that only white voters were eligible to sit on juries. Like Russell, Eisenhower was prepared to allow a weakened Civil Rights Bill to pass and even claimed that he did not understand what was in it, even though he had supported it for two years (Ambrose, 1984). Faced with southern opposition to it, the President refused to fight for the Bill. Although most historians agree that the Bill 'was more symbol than substance,' they also agree that it was a radical break with tradition and that more effective legislation would be inevitable.

Strom Thurmond, who had led the walk-out from the Democratic convention in 1948, bitterly opposed any legislation and filibustered for over 24 hours in an attempt to kill the Bill. Eventually a much weakened Civil Rights Bill was passed, the first since Reconstruction. For many African Americans struggling to survive and tear down the walls of segregation, the Bill was seen as a sham. Ralph Bunche, a Howard University professor, critic of the NAACP and active in the National Negro Congress, and labour leader A. Philip Randolph believed that it would have been better to have had no bill. Bayard Rustin, the black pacifist and CORE member, not only acknowledged that the legislation was inadequate, but also he believed that it was 'very important because it was evidence that Congress was prepared to act' (Dallek, 1991).

Truman, the Cold War and Civil Rights

Apart from the pressure from the African American community for change, it was America's role in world affairs after the Second World War that had a significant impact on the struggle for civil rights in the United States. The Democratic Party and the Republicans and their presidential leaders

Truman and Eisenhower were engaged in a Cold War with the Soviet Union. The stark contrast between America's claim that it was the leader of the 'free world' and its treatment of the black minority was all too obvious. Truman's urgency to support democracy in Western Europe with billions of dollars in the Marshall Plan contrasted with his approach to democracy in the United States. No American president would ever show the same concern about the freedom or economic progress of African Americans in Mississippi or Alabama as they expressed concern for the peoples of Europe and Southeast Asia (Gilmore, 2008).

Immediately after the War, Truman had capitulated to pressure from his European allies by supporting French attacks on nationalists in Indochina. The Truman Doctrine, according to the President, was essential to stop totalitarianism. 'The free people of the world look to us for support in maintaining their freedoms. If we falter in our leadership, we may endanger the peace of the world – and we shall surely endanger the welfare of the nation' (Hamby, 1973). And it was this lack of national welfare that concerned many in the South. One white southern historian argues that the South as a whole was a colony and its political leaders evaded the issue, preferring to preach racism and segregation. However, he notes:

Like other colonial people, Southerners were restless, impatient with the oppression of the past, and uneasy about the direction of the future. National political leaders realized that the racial system of the South presented a diplomatic problem, for to attract countries emerging from colonialism, the U.S. could not afford the embarrassment of segregation and disenfranchisement. (Daniel, 1986)

Critics in the African American community were concerned about Truman's policies. Paul Robeson warned that the United States was supporting Britain in denying freedom to the colonial peoples of Asia and India. In addition, he argued that black Americans would have to fight to achieve democracy in the United States. Leaders of the NAACP, such as Walter White and Roy Wilkins, were concerned not to alienate potential allies and refused to support Robeson's crusade against lynching. But three thousand black and white delegates met in Washington DC, to demand a federal anti-lynching law and Truman agreed to meet a delegation led by Robeson. Truman told them the time was not right for such legislation and when reminded of the Nuremberg trials then in progress, he retorted that Britain and the United States represented 'the last refuge of freedom in the world.' Robeson rebutted this accusing the British of being 'one of the greatest enslavers of human beings.' He also warned Truman that the mood in the African American community was changing and if the federal government did not act to protect its black citizens then they would protect themselves (Duberman, 1989).

In an address to the World Freedom Rally at Madison Square Garden, New York, on 14 November 1945, Robeson warned that the American government was 'helping British, French and Chiang Kai-Shek governments to crush the people's struggles toward democracy, freedom and independence.' He pointed out that while the American administration relied on vast arsenals of weapons, world peace could not be secure so long as millions of Africans suffered from starvation, or the Jews were denied a homeland. Duberman has pointed out: 'In Robeson's mind, the domestic civil-liberties issue was inescapably linked to the international question of peace' (Duberman, 1989).

It was not only Robeson who linked America's support for European colonialism with its failure to defend the democratic rights of African Americans. W. E. B. Du Bois, the eminent black historian and for many years editor of the NAACP magazine *Crisis*, published in 1945 a volume entitled *Color and Democracy*. In this study Du Bois linked civil rights, African nationalism and socialism. In 1947 he authored an appeal to the United Nations and, like Robeson, attacked American intervention in the Korean War (White, 1985). Paul Robeson told delegates of the National Labor Conference on Negro Rights in 1951 that they were not to be diverted by warnings of the threat of communism, but rather blacks, Jews and aliens should unite with the working class to attack 'White Supremacy and all its vile works.' The enemies of African Americans 'are the lynchers, the profiteers, the men who give FEPC the run-around in the Senate, the atom-bomb maniacs and the warmakers. . . .' Despite Robeson's defence of the Vietnamese in their struggle against the French, the invasion of South Korea by North Korea saw the passage of a new and infamous Internal Security Act, the McCarran Act, which equated dissent with treason and set up detention centres for so-called subversives in times of emergency. The act was passed over Truman's veto (Duberman, 1989).

Both Robeson and Du Bois were persecuted in the United States. Efforts were made by HUAC to have Robeson cited for contempt of Congress and the State Department refused to give him a passport (Duberman, 1989). Du Bois became increasingly disillusioned by the failure of white liberals to support civil rights in the United States. Liberal intellectuals such as Arthur Schlesinger Jr, David Reisman, Daniel Bell, and Reinhold Neibuhr preferred to join the anti-communist Congress for Cultural Freedom. Although the Congress attacked the excesses of HUAC and of Joseph McCarthy, they also policed 'the intellectual community for signs of weakening will in the anti-communist struggle. Most of the Americans affiliated with the Congress presumably did not know that its activities were partly subsidized by CIA funds laundered through dummy foundations' (Matusow, 1986).

Eisenhower and the Cold War

While white liberals and conservatives promoted democracy in the 'captive nations' and opposed subversive activities in the United States, they did not share the urgency that African Americans felt about their mistreatment in the United States. The Secretary of State, John Foster Dulles, made continual promises to free Eastern Europe from the oppression of Soviet domination. Although the United States had no intention of undertaking such a task, Hungarian students and workers were not aware of this. In 1956 they sought to overthrow the communist government and were crushed by an invasion of Soviet and Warsaw Pact countries. Many fled into Austria and Vice President Richard Nixon was sent on a fact-finding mission and wrote a report for the United States government. In his report on the refugee crisis, Nixon wrote without any apparent sense of its irony that 'it is essential that in our necessary and understandable concern over the immediate problem of providing for the needs of refugees we not lose sight of the historical significance of this mass migration of people from an area of slavery to an area of freedom' (Lasky, 1957).

Nixon's professed concern for the Hungarians was not shared by many black leaders. Paul Robeson attended the Soviet Embassy reception in Washington DC to celebrate the 39th anniversary of the Soviet revolution and later, despite the efforts of an angry crowd, attended an American-Soviet Friendship peace rally. And the singer's contempt for the majority Cold War views was shared by the wider black community. Black newspapers from Pennsylvania to California shared his doubts about the attention given to Hungarian freedom fighters. The San Francisco *Sun Reporter* asked rhetorically: 'How can America in good faith blow such loud horns about the freedom of Hungarians, when such a large proportion of her own population is deprived of freedom guaranteed by the Constitution of the United States?' (Duberman, 1989).

African Americans were concerned about Eisenhower's policy in regard to European colonial ambitions. It is true that the administration opposed the attempt by the British, the French and the Israeli invasion of Egypt in 1956 to overthrow Nasser on the pretext of defending the Suez Canal. According to Stephen Ambrose, 'American policy, in general, was to support colonial peoples attempting to win national independence' (Ambrose, 1984). Certainly the United States imposed a financial and oil embargo on Britain, and Eisenhower was able to follow his policy of trying to keep the support of the newer nations – many of which were attracted by the Soviet model or preferred to remain non-aligned. But whatever success Eisenhower can claim for his willingness to defy his three leading allies, it seems that African American doubts about Eisenhower's anti-colonialism were justified because of the administration's willingness to support French colonial rule in Indochina. And they contrasted his eagerness to make a stand over Egypt with his unwillingness to challenge southern governors who openly defied the rulings of the Supreme Court. This defiance and the denial of democratic rights in the South hurt the United States in its efforts to speak for the 'free world.' Southerners, especially Senator James Eastland, used anti-communism to discredit civil rights and labour organisations. Ironically, the more he denounced the lack of democracy in the 'captive nations,' the more he undermined his efforts to maintain an undemocratic South (Asch, 2008).

Indochina

But both Truman and Eisenhower were reluctant to confront the issue of civil rights in America while at the same time they supported the French efforts to regain control over its former colony of Indochina. Both gave lavish monetary support to the doomed French effort and Eisenhower even contemplated intervention. Some have suggested that the French were offered the atomic bomb, but all are agreed that Eisenhower was determined to keep Vietnam divided and he was confident that he could achieve another Korean solution. In his efforts to persuade the American people that action in Asia, unlike action in Alabama, was vital, he outlined why it was essential for the United States to act. He stressed the advantages in raw materials essential to the economies of the industrialised nations; but more important was 'the possibility that many human beings pass under a dictatorship that is inimical to the free world.' And Vietnam would not be the last to fall. Eisenhower warned, 'You have the broader considerations that might follow what you would call the "falling domino" principle. You have got a row of dominoes set up, you knock over the first one and what will happen to the last one is the certainty that it will go over very quickly' (Ambrose, 1984). This domino theory dragged the United States into the

Vietnam War resulting in the killing of millions of Vietnamese, over 50,000 Americans, a disproportionate number of whom were African American. Eisenhower's commitment to freedom in a foreign land would also destroy LBJ's dream of liberty for black Americans in a Great Society, and lead to the radicalisation of American politics.

Perhaps it was merely coincidence that in the same year as the Russians invaded Hungary and the British invaded Egypt, a civil rights bill was introduced in Congress and became law a year later after the British gave independence to Ghana, a former British colony in Africa known as the Gold Coast (Weidner, 1962). There is no doubt that the rapid decolonisation of Africa by Britain and France had a marked impact on African Americans. Ironically these new African presidents would not suffer the humiliations of Jim Crow legislation when they travelled in the southern United States.

African Nationalism

To black nationalists the link between their status and colonialism is explicit because 'Afro-Americans have always been responded to as a colonized people, not unlike the overseas victims of European colonialism, and relegated to a system of birth-ascribed stratification, similar to that of India's untouchable caste' (Pinkney, 1976). And it was not only black nationalists who were influenced by the growing and successful independence movements in black Africa. Even groups such as the NAACP, which had traditionally avoided involvement in African politics, saw the need for co-operation. 'The contradiction of a "free" Africa and their "unfree" descendants in the US was an immediate and important parallel which was reiterated by many civil rights advocates (Marable, 1997).' It was not a black nationalist who acted as legal adviser to Kenyan nationalists in their talks with the British government in 1960, but rather Thurgood Marshall of the NAACP who had argued before the Supreme Court in the *Brown* case (Weidner, 1962). Later civil rights workers black and white, in the Free South Africa Movement (FSAM), would take up the cause against apartheid.

African American leaders were not only inspired by the demise of the British Empire in Africa. Gandhi, who greatly influenced African independence movements, was also a hero to those who formed the frontline in the battle against the southern way of life. At the height of the harassment from white students at Central High, Melba Pattillo Beals' grandmother told her to read and understand what Gandhi had accomplished without resorting to violence. As she recalls, 'I knew about Gandhi, about his courage even in the face of people beating up on him and calling him ugly names. I didn't think I was that strong and pure' (Beals, 1994). But the young girl had heroes closer to home than the nationalist leaders in India or Africa. On 1 December 1955 she read in the local newspaper about the arrest of Rosa Parks in Montgomery, Alabama, who had refused to give up her seat on a bus to a white man. 'Our people were stretching out to knock down the fences of segregation.... I felt such a surge of pride when I thought about how my people had banded together to force a change. It gave me hope that maybe things in Little Rock could change' (Beals, 1994). It was that sense of hope that motivated hundreds of thousands of African Americans to take up the challenge and tear down the walls of segregation.

2
GRASS-ROOTS STRUGGLE IN THE SOUTH

It was Thursday, 1 December 1955. Mrs Rosa Parks, who did so much to inspire the young Melba Pattillo, was 42 years old when she was arrested. Returning home after her day's work as a tailor's assistant in a department store in Montgomery, Alabama, she took her seat on the bus and soon it was full and a white man was left standing. The bus driver ordered her and three other African American passengers to move because under the city ordinance no black was allowed to sit parallel with a white passenger. The others reluctantly moved but Mrs Parks did not. Three times the bus driver, J. F. Blake, told her to move and then she simply said, 'No.' Warned that she would be arrested, Mrs Parks told him to go right ahead. Blake left the bus, called the police, and Mrs Parks was arrested. The events that sparked off the Montgomery bus boycott were completed with her being charged with violation of the city bus segregation ordinance (Garrow, 1988).

Mrs Parks has often been portrayed as an old woman whose failure to obey the driver was due to her tiredness, or because her feet hurt. As Angela Davis has observed, 'Now of course, this particular way in which history is remembered represents the central woman as a passive participant – as someone without agency' (Davis, 1994). In her autobiography, Rosa Parks has pointed out that at 42 she did not think of herself as old and although she was tired after a day at work her refusal to give up her seat was because she was tired of giving in.

African Americans throughout the South were tired of giving in. It was this emergence of a mass movement of African American women and men, young and old, middle class and poor that would destroy Jim Crow. The

33

national parties were forced to act because of pressure from people, most of whom were denied the vote and all of whom were denied political office. By segregating their fellow black citizens, white southerners forced black southerners to teach in their own schools and to study in their separate colleges, to worship in their own churches. Out of these institutions African Americans forged an army and weapons to war against their daily humiliations. And although Marxists regard religion as an opiate of the masses, it was this Christian faith taught in the black churches which inspired the civil rights movement. The Bible, with its stories of Egyptians enslaving the Jews and the flight of the chosen people to the promised land, had inspired African Americans when they were slaves. It was this deep and passionate Christian longing for justice and belief in redemption that inspired the struggle for freedom.

Many of these black church leaders and their congregations, as well as educators and their students would find themselves in the front line in the assault on segregation because southern racists resisted any change in their way of life following *Brown*, and they attacked the major campaigning organisation, the NAACP. Many states either banned it or restricted its activities and often forced state employees to resign from the Association. African Americans responded by turning to their community leaders, especially in the churches and educational institutions, and they formed groups which operated at city, state and regional level such as the MIA, the Alabama Christian Movement for Human Rights (ACMHR), the United Christian Movement Inc (UCMI) of Louisiana, the Southern Christian Leadership Conference (SCLC) and the Student Nonviolent Coordinating Committee (SNCC). These were just a few of the many groups throughout the South. Many of the leaders had been members of the NAACP. Ella Baker, for example, served as national field secretary for the NAACP in 1941 and 1942 and in 1943 was the director of branches. During these years she toured the South extensively, covering nearly 27,000 miles and attending 519 meetings. She was president of the New York branch of the NAACP after the War before becoming the first associate director of the SCLC (Morris, 1984). But her efforts working with the NAACP and SCLC did not always ensure good relations with the Association's national leadership under Roy Wilkins.

Most white southerners in 1954, when *Brown* was decided, were surprised that African Americans wanted to go to integrated schools, and were blissfully unaware of the growing dissatisfaction of black southerners with their status as second-class citizens. White southerners in the 1950s did not remember the streetcar boycotts by blacks that had occurred across the region between 1900 and 1906 (Meier and Rudwick, 1970) or of the 'wave of rebellion that engulfed most of the leading black colleges of the 1920s [which] was one of the most significant aspects of the New Negro movement' (Wolters, 1975). Ignorance was not only a southern problem. Most northern politicians, when not ignorant, were indifferent about the treatment of the African American community. Truman and Eisenhower, no different from presidents after Radical Reconstruction, were not prepared to challenge Jim Crow.

Louisiana Protest

Ignoring the views of politicians North and South, blacks in the South were prepared to act and the first major protest did not happen in Alabama but in Louisiana. In March 1953, more than a year before the Supreme Court's ruling in *Brown*, African Americans in Baton Rouge had successfully petitioned the city council to allow seating on local buses on a first-come, first-served basis. Although the passengers on the city bus service were mostly black, all the drivers were white and they refused to obey the ordinance. After a four-day strike, the attorney general supported the drivers and declared the ordinance violated the segregation laws.

In June the black community began a mass boycott of the transport system. The leader of the boycott was the Reverend T. J. Jemison of the Mount Zion Baptist Church, who was a relative newcomer to the city, moving there in 1949. As pastor and past president of the local branch of the NAACP, he was held in high regard in the community and his radio appeal on behalf of the boycott resulted in virtually total support. The church was used as a centre for meetings and when the audience of enthusiastic supporters proved too numerous for the church hall they moved to the segregated school. During the boycott the community leaders closed down the bars in the evening, organised a community police force, and provided thousands of cars which ensured a free ride to all the participants. (The movement leaders knew that if they charged for the rides they would be prosecuted for operating an unlicensed taxi service.)

Jemison was not the only black preacher to challenge the Jim Crow system. All the black preachers took an active part in the Baton Rouge community action group, the United Defense League, and urged their congregations to stay off the buses. Sunday morning sermons were not only used to exhort the faithful but were also a time when money was raised to keep the boycott going. Although the Baton Rouge action ended with Jemison accepting a compromise solution, it was the first mass, direct action campaign led by church leaders. Other preachers were soon informed of the success of the Baton Rouge community. The Reverend C. K. Steele of Tallahassee, Florida, and the Reverend A. L. Davis of New Orleans both knew Jemison and about the action in Baton Rouge. They were leaders of similar action in their cities. Martin Luther King Jr and Ralph Abernathy in Montgomery, Alabama, continued the battle started by Jemison (Morris, 1984).

Mrs Rosa Parks

Although the first boycott took place in Baton Rouge, the action in Montgomery included all the elements that were characteristic of the civil rights movement. Activists in the NAACP joined forces with college lecturers and students who in turn combined with the leading black preachers and their congregations. Mrs Parks was not just a tired seamstress on her way home from work but rather an active member of the NAACP since 1943 who had served as secretary of the Montgomery branch of the Association for most of the previous decade. She had worked closely with the young members of the Association's Youth Council, which included Claudette Colvin, who had been arrested in March 1955 because she had refused to give her seat to a white passenger. Mrs Parks had taken part in the discussions with E. D. Nixon, a fellow member of the NAACP and Alabama branch president of Randolph's Brotherhood of Sleeping Car Porters, about the possibility of using Colvin's arrest as a way of challenging the Montgomery segregation law. No action was taken because Colvin was charged with assault as well as breaking the segregation ordinance. In addition, it was felt that Colvin would not win the support needed for a successful boycott because she was a pregnant, unmarried teenager.

Mrs Parks not only knew Nixon, who had been an activist in the black community since the 1920s, but she had worked with him on voter registration drives undertaken by the NAACP. And it was Nixon who had introduced her to Clifford and Virginia Durr both of whom were white southern liberals. A friend of Lyndon Johnson and Hugo Black, the Supreme Court justice from Alabama, Clifford Durr had resigned from the Federal Communications Commission in protest over Harry Truman's loyalty programme. It was Clifford and Virginia Durr and E. D. Nixon who went to the jail on hearing of Mrs Parks's arrest. Nixon, who posted the bail bond, had agreed with the Durrs that Rosa Parks would be the ideal test case and it was his certainty that a boycott would succeed that persuaded her, despite the reservations of her husband, to be the test case (Garrow, 1988; Branch, 1989).

Not that she needed much persuasion. Mrs Parks was well aware of the implications of her action. She had attended the Highlander Folk School in Tennessee run by Myles Horton, a friend of Clifford and Virginia Durr – both of whom acted as sponsors to the school. In a letter to Highlander nearly six months before her arrest, Mrs Parks wrote that she was 'hoping to make a contribution to the fulfilment of complete freedom for all people' (Garrow, 1988). 'Highlander has been described as a 'modern American movement halfway house.' According to Aldon Morris these houses are distinctive because of 'their relative isolation from the larger society and the absence of a mass base.' Although not equipped to lead a mass move-ment the organisers at Highlander, such as Myles Horton and Ella Baker, trained activists, held workshops, developed media contacts and imbued those who attended their meetings with a knowledge of past struggles and a vision of a multi-racial democracy (Morris, 1984). Certainly, Mrs Parks' faith in such a democracy was reinforced by her stay in Tennessee. When she refused to obey the bus driver's order, she was acting – not merely reacting.

In this respect, Mrs Parks was no different from other women active in the civil rights movement. Once African Americans, women and men, refused to accept their segregated inferior status, the impact was widespread and felt by all sectors of American society. However, in the civil rights movement, the women were often treated as second-class citizens. It was black men who saw themselves as the leaders and it was white male politicians and press that focused on the role of these men, such as Martin Luther King Jr, Ralph Abernathy, John Lewis or Robert Moses.

When they first became involved in the civil rights movement, African American women were not gender conscious but rather they were con-cerned with the struggle for justice and liberty for all – male and female. In these early years, women and men put their bodies (literally) on the line when they challenged the white supremacy of the South. When civil rights activists called for 'jail no bail' they did not suggest that this applied to men only. Cynthia Fleming argues black women grew impatient with white women in the movement who, in 1964, complained they were only doing menial tasks. Black SNCC staffer, Cynthia Washington, told Flem-ing that the grumbling of Casey Hayden did not make sense to her because she had her own project. ' "What Casey and other white women seemed to want was an opportunity to prove that they could do something other than office work. I assumed that if they could do something else they'd probably be doing that" ' (Fleming, 1994).

Although black women accepted black male leadership it would become a source of difficulty. However, at first they were accused by white women co-workers of deferring to the black ministers who led the movement and, even if they criticised male activists, still they accepted male leadership. Anne Standley's explanation for this behaviour is that black women 'did not consider themselves oppressed by black men either in or out of the movement, and in some respects believed that black men were worse off than black women' (Crawford, Rouse and Woods, 1993). In these early years, women of colour were concerned about race not gender. It was their experience in the movement and the growing rivalries with white women that made them much more conscious of gender issues.

Mrs Parks was concerned about freedom – not simply her rights as a woman. Following her arrest, Mrs Parks not only gained help from fellow activist, E. D. Nixon, but also from faculty at Alabama State College, an institution for black students only. Mrs Jo Ann Robinson had joined the English faculty in 1949 and was a keen community activist in the city. At the time of Rosa Parks' arrest she was president of the Women's Political Council (WPC). As soon as she was informed of the incident, Mrs Robinson called E. D. Nixon with whom she and the WPC had worked throughout the early 1950s in attacking the poor treatment of African Americans on the Montgomery buses. Robinson, Nixon, and Rufus Lewis, former football coach at the college, businessman and head of the Citizens Steering Committee, had applied pressure on city commissioners to modify the segregation ordinance. As early as 21 May 1954, Jo Ann Robinson had written to the Mayor, W. A. Gayle, warning him that the WPC were considering a bus boycott. With the arrest of Mrs Parks, Robinson and Nixon agreed that the WPC should write a leaflet which call on the black community to stay off the buses the day of the trial. With the aid of student volunteers thousands of copies of the leaflet were run off the college's mimeograph machine and distributed throughout the community. In the leaflet she appealed to all, including children, to stay off the buses. About Mrs Parks' arrest she wrote:

> This has to be stopped. Negroes have rights, too, for if Negroes did not ride the buses, they could not operate. Three-fourths of the riders are Negroes, yet we are arrested, or have to stand over empty seats. If we do not do something to stop these arrests, they will continue. The next time it may be you, or your daughter, or mother. (Garrow, 1988)

Now that the decision had been made to boycott the buses, it was important to win the support of the wider African American community who were not members of the NAACP or the WPC. The people who could mobilise the necessary mass support were the ministers of the segregated churches. Nixon realised that he needed the support of black preachers such as Ralph D. Abernathy, secretary of the Baptist Ministers' Alliance. And it was Abernathy who told Nixon to call the young minister at the Dexter Avenue Baptist Church, Martin Luther King Jr.

Martin Luther King Jr and the Boycott

The boycott was already in advanced planning when King was called and even then he hesitated. He had already declined a request to lead the local NAACP branch because of other commitments but, after Abernathy called, he eventually acquiesced to a meeting at his church which was attended by 70 black leaders. It did not augur well for the success of the boycott because the meeting was disorganised and confused but Abernathy, supported by Jo Ann Robinson, took over the meeting and those who were still present voted to support the boycott. They decided that a mass meeting should be called for the Monday night, and after the meeting, King and Abernathy issued new leaflets urging people to attend the Monday meeting as well as boycott the buses. Over 200 volunteers distributed the new leaflet and black taxi drivers agreed to carry passengers on the day of the boycott at a standard charge of 10 cents.

E. D. Nixon told Montgomery *Advertiser* reporter Joe Azbell about the planned protest and urged him to get a leaflet and interview people in the community because it would be a good story for the Sunday paper. And as Nixon hoped, the newspaper duly featured the story, which in turn led to local television interviewing the racist City Police Commissioner Clyde Sellers, who charged that the boycott was going to be enforced by black 'goon squads.' He was confident that the black community would not be intimidated and that the boycott would fail. The white-owned newspapers and television had ensured that any African American who had not read the leaflet or listened to the sermons that Sunday morning appealing to everyone to stay off the buses would either have seen the headline in the paper or heard Sellers on television. It was not the first time, and certainly not the last, when white folks would give unwitting support to the movement (Garrow, 1988; Branch, 1989).

On the Monday morning, 5 December 1955, the boycott was more successful than the leaders had dared to hope and later, in an unprecedented display of solidarity, several hundred blacks went to the court house to witness the case against Rosa Parks. The hearing took only five minutes and she was fined ten dollars. Following the trial the boycott organisers proposed that the bus company should allow seating on a first-come, first-served basis with blacks filling the bus from the back and whites from the front. Under this system no one would have to give up their seat or be forced to stand over an empty seat. The second demand was simply that drivers should be polite to African American riders at all times and that any driver who was rude or assaulted a black passenger should be disciplined or fired. The last, put by Ralph Abernathy, was about the hiring of black drivers because it was the black community which made up 75 per cent of the passengers. And if these modest demands had been met, nothing more would have been heard about the boycott. However, the white council's determination to resist any change ensured that the boycott would continue. The city commissioners chose resistance rather than accept modification of the segregation ordinance and the one-day boycott was transformed into a year-long struggle in which the black community would only accept total desegregation.

The boycott leaders were aware that existing groups could not coordinate the campaign and that a new organisation was needed. The NAACP did not have the mass membership, the WPC leaders could not openly organise the movement because they were employees at Alabama State College and would be dismissed, and the Interdenominational Ministerial Alliance was not appropriate because the Reverend L. Roy Bennett was unsuitable as a leader. As in any mass community action movement, there were divisions about who would best be suited to lead the new organisation that they called the MIA. All the factions did agree that the ideal leader would be Martin Luther King Jr who had only recently arrived in the city, who was minister at one of the most prestigious black churches in the town and who had been educated at Boston University in the North (Garrow, 1988). The pattern that was established in 'the walking city' would be recreated throughout the history of the civil rights movement. As J. Mills Thornton has pointed out, there is a danger that King's role 'may be very easily overstated. In Tallahassee, Tuskegee and Greensboro, it is only his example with which we are dealing. . . . In Albany, Birmingham, St. Augustine and Selma, he and his organization came into the city in response to the invitation of local black leaders to assist them in effecting goals of local importance, whatever may have been the national implications of their decision to do so.' Thornton stresses, 'In Montgomery . . . King's role was even more completely than elsewhere a function of local circumstance. He played no significant part in creating the Boycott' (Thornton, 1989). In a recent study it is suggested that King was not reluctant to take leadership of the boycott and saw it as a wider assault on capitalism (Jackson, 2007).

The black community leaders in Montgomery joined forces with the Alabama Council on Human Relations (ACHR) which was holding a meeting in Montgomery. A member of the ACHR board, Thomas Thrasher, a Montgomery minister, set up talks between the MIA and the city commissioners. The talks failed. The Chicago company National City Lines, which controlled the Montgomery bus service, refused to send an arbitrator as requested by MIA. And the resistance of the white community grew, with threats against the alternative transportation service the African American community had established. King called his friend Jemison in Baton Rouge who told him about the free ride service they had organised in their boycott and King followed his friend's advice, making the necessary arrangements at a second mass meeting.

White Resistance

The refusal of city commissioners to compromise encouraged more extreme elements in the city. Obscene and threatening telephone calls were received by MIA leaders. City police commissioner Clyde Sellers was the first to join the Citizens Council and was later followed by Mayor W. Gayle and commissioner Frank Parks. It was estimated by local newspapers that membership in the Council had grown from 6000 at the beginning of February 1956 to 12,000 by the end of the month (Thornton, 1989). This growing white resistance resulted in the harassment of the black community and led to the first arrest of King, on 26 January 1956, for speeding at 30 miles per hour in a 25 mile per hour zone. Four days later his house was bombed and his father and father-in-law pleaded with him and his wife to leave the city. To many it seemed the segregationists were united in their response. But they were not. The boycott 'revealed conclusively that segregationists at the grassroots and municipal levels were . . . . . . unsure of their tactics' (Lewis, 2006).

However, Martin Luther King Jr later recalled the vehemence with which southern whites sought to defend segregation and how he was so fearful of the hatred that surrounded him that he almost quit leadership of the boycott. He had not done so because he had prayed.

And it seemed at that moment that I could hear an inner voice saying to me. 'Martin Luther, stand up for righteousness. Stand up for justice. Stand up for the truth. And lo I will be with you, even until the end of the world.' I heard the voice of Jesus saying still to fight on. He promised never to leave me alone. No never alone. No never alone. (Garrow, 1988)

The bombing of his home now only made him more determined to fight on and not merely to make segregation more pleasant for the African American community. He agreed with the proposal of Clifford Durr and E. D. Nixon not just to challenge segregation on the Montgomery bus system but rather to end the Jim Crow system itself. The segregationists' response was to attempt to bomb Nixon's home.

The city commissioners resorted to law, not the bomb, in their efforts to break the boycott. Alabama had an anti-boycott law and in February 1956 the city fathers were determined to use it and 100 members of MIA were charged by the grand jury whose members asserted that: 'We are committed to segregation by custom and law and we intend to maintain it' (Garrow, 1988). But their determination to resist the demands for justice only strengthened the resolve of the black community and all those indicted reported en masse to the court determined to demonstrate that they would not be intimidated. As King would tell a mass rally:

There are those who would try to make this a hate campaign. This is not a war between the white and the Negro but a conflict between justice and injustice. This is bigger than the Negro race revolting against the white. We are not just trying to improve the Negro of Montgomery but the whole of Montgomery. (Garrow, 1988)

The genius of King was his ability to articulate the African American struggle in terms that were immediately understood by millions of Americans, white and black. Later his determination to follow the example of Gandhi, who had also inspired young Melba Pattillo and her grandmother in Little Rock, would transform municipal struggles over segregated buses or later student protests against segregated lunch counters into a great crusade for democracy in America. He would force black and white Americans, northerners and southerners, to challenge the system they had never questioned. The white resisters of Montgomery and other southerners who simply said 'segregation now and segregation forever' only made King and other black leaders more determined to triumph. The tragedy was that most

Americans ignored or refused to listen to King's appeal for economic justice; the message was too radical (Jackson, 2007).

The resistance from the white South in the form of the mass indictments for the first time stirred the indifferent northern public and press. As a direct result of the mass indictment, MIA received $12,000 collected in the North. Both of the leading New York papers, the *Times* and the *Herald Tribune*, carried front-page stories of the events in Montgomery and King's address to the mass rally was his first to get national coverage. On network television, which limited news coverage to 15 minutes, ABC compared the Alabama protesters to Gandhi and the Montgomery city officials to the British trying to shore up their empire. Such a comparison would have delighted Martin Luther King Jr and it was a theme he took up in the first of his many speeches about the boycott in a northern city. Addressing an audience of 2500 at Brooklyn's Concord Baptist Church, he reminded them that Gandhi had brought down the British rule in India with passive resistance. The major source of inspiration for the movement was Christian. As he told a reporter, 'I have been a keen student of Gandhi for many years. However, this business of passive resistance and nonviolence is the gospel of Jesus. I went to Gandhi through Jesus' (Garrow, 1988).

'Not a One Man Show'

This was not just a protest led by a charismatic leader but rather, as Jo Ann Robinson correctly described to a black reporter at the time, it was a mass movement. 'The amazing thing about our movement is that it is a protest of the people. It is not a one man show. It is not the preachers' show. It's the people. The masses of this town, who are tired of being trampled on, are responsible. The leaders couldn't stop it if they wanted to' (Garrow, 1988).

Although Robinson's assessment was correct, the leadership of King was increasingly emphasised especially by sympathetic outsiders such as the African Methodist Episcopal (AME) Church, the National Council of Churches and the American Fellowship of Reconciliation (AFOR). Bayard Rustin, the African American pacifist, and the Reverend Glenn Smiley, a white officer of AFOR, came to Montgomery from New York to speak with King and other black community leaders. Smiley, a Texan and fellow southerner, was profoundly influenced by the nonviolent direct action teachings of Gandhi but found that although King admired the Indian leader, he had admitted that he did not know very much about him. After the interview Smiley wrote that, 'King can be a Negro Gandhi, or he can be made into an unfortunate demagogue destined to swing from a lynch mob's tree' (Garrow, 1988). King would choose to follow Gandhi and not the role of demagogue chosen by his white political opponents.

King had to face the court and not the lynch mob. He was the first indicted boycott leader to be tried, found guilty and fined $500 with another $500 in court costs or 368 days in jail. His conviction was appealed and all other cases were held over until the appeal court had ruled. Meanwhile the suit challenging the constitutionality of the city bus segregation ordinance had been filed on 1 February 1956 and on 5 June the federal district court ruled in *Browder v Gayle* that segregation on the buses was unconstitutional. The city commissioners were not willing to accept the ruling and they decided on two further steps: first they appealed to the federal Supreme Court, and second, on 13 November, they filed for an injunction to end the car pool. But it was too late. The Supreme Court on the same day upheld the lower court ruling. It was agreed at a mass meeting on 14 November that the boycott should be called off as soon as the desegregated buses started to move. After over a year, on 21 December, the first African American to climb aboard a Montgomery bus was Martin Luther King Jr.

The victory at Montgomery was based on a mass movement of the black community that practised nonviolent direct action combined with the NAACP strategy of using the courts to overthrow the Jim Crow system. As the first tentative steps to challenge segregation met resistance from the white community, so the goals were changed from amelioration of the system to its overthrow and just when blacks were determined to fight for justice, the white resisters would turn to violence and threats of violence. On 10 January 1957 two homes, including the home of Ralph Abernathy, and four black Baptist churches were bombed. Later that month a bomb made of 12 sticks of dynamite was found on the porch of Martin Luther King's home and was defused (Garrow, 1988).

White Sympathisers

One of the houses bombed that 10 January was the home of the Reverend Robert Graetz, the white minister at the black Lutheran Church in Montgomery who was the only white person to openly provide support for the boycott. The deeds and words of a few white people played a part in the success of the movement. It was all very well for King and Abernathy to talk of a multi-racial democracy but in the segregated world of Montgomery, very few blacks had any reason to believe that there were whites who shared their dream. Robert Graetz and his wife by their daily actions were living proof that such white people existed. And they were not alone. The Texan Glenn Smiley of FOR did much to persuade King that Gandhi provided the role model that he was searching for. Clifford and Virginia Durr gave advice and help throughout the boycott and they were two southerners who contributed to its success. It was not only people who had long been associated with the struggle for civil rights who gave encouragement to black protest leaders. In Montgomery several white citizens wrote to the *Advertiser* supporting black complaints against the bus system. In such a rigidly segregated society, letters from citizens such as Mrs I Rutledge, who said that she did not know one white person who thought it was 'right that a Negro may be made to stand that a person may sit', must have reassured those who participated in the boycott. Miss Juliette Morgan compared the boycott to Gandhi's salt march. She was convinced that: 'Passive resistance combined with freedom from hate is a power to be reckoned with' (Garrow, 1988).

Even in the darkest moments there were other whites who supported the black struggle for justice. Two years later in Little Rock, Arkansas, the 15-year-old schoolgirl Melba Pattillo, along with nine other African American teenagers, had to face the bayonets of the National Guard and the fury of the white racists as they attempted to integrate Central High School. She drew strength from brave women like Rosa Parks and the calm self-assurance of Thurgood Marshall. The extent of her and other young black people's ignorance of whites can be seen in the beliefs of her friend Marsha. 'She said white people didn't perspire, so I had to be certain I didn't let them see me perspire. I was petrified on that first morning I was to go to school.' Her fear was increased by the actions of the mob and their threatening attack on her friend Elizabeth Eckford. "The next Sunday the newspaper had an advertisement showing the white mob with the 'twisted, scowling faces with open mouths jeering.' The advertisement had been paid for by a white man from a small Arkansas town and it read: 'If you live in Arkansas study this picture and know shame. When hate is unleashed and bigotry finds a voice, God help us all'." As she recalled, 'I felt a kind of joy and hope that one white man was willing to use his own money to call attention to the injustice we were facing. Maybe the picture would help others realize that what they were doing was hurting everybody.' And during her time at Central High, she was helped by a white student named Link who took great risks but managed to prevent her from being attacked on many occasions. Her grandmother and mother were worried. 'Although I, too, was undecided about trusting Link, I continued to defend Link as both of them came up with dozens of reasons why I shouldn't trust this white boy. Still, there was something inside me that said he had taken a big risk giving me his car that day' (Beals, 1994).

It was not only individual acts of courage and statements of support that made African Americans aware that there were white Americans who shared their dream. White southerners played a leading role in the Southern Conference Education Fund (SCEF), an organisation which had fought for civil rights and equality during the 1940s and 1950s when the white majority sought to retain segregation. Aubrey Williams, president of the SCEF, came from an old southern family in Birmingham, Alabama, and graduated from Maryville College in Tennessee. After a short time as a minister he went into social work, worked with FDR and his New Deal programmes and while at the Works Progress Administration was made aware of racist practices. He fought hard to combat them and became a good friend of A. Philip Randolph and Mrs Roosevelt. Forced out of his job in 1943, he returned to the South to work with the National Farmers Union in Alabama where he edited a farming journal and built homes for black families. Throughout the post-war period Williams warned that the poor whites of the South, who had been so badly mistreated, were 'the likeliest material in the country for the lumpen proletariat, the mass base for a racist, fascist movement.' Because of the Depression millions of them had left the South and they took their virus with them. The poor white 'is a very dangerous man, and he must be cured, and during the process of cure he must be guarded from destroying others' (Klibaner, 1989).

Williams, despite his isolation from the majority of white southerners, influenced people like James Dombrowski, a Tampa Florida native and graduate from Emory University in 1923. In graduate school in the North he became interested in labour history and Christian socialism and published his dissertation in 1936, *The Early Days of Christian Socialism in America*. A founder member of the Highlander Folk School in 1932, he served as its staff director until 1942 when he joined the Southern Conference for Human Welfare. He worked for SCEF for 30 years advocating nonviolent change in the South and he persuaded many black and white clergymen to commit themselves to the organisation's work (Klibaner, 1989).

Williams also persuaded Carl and Anne Braden to stay in the South and offered them positions as field secretaries for SCEF. Carl Braden was a Kentucky native whose father, a railroad worker, was a socialist. Carl's socialism was profoundly influenced by his mother's Catholicism. Although he had gone to seminary, he turned to newspaper reporting and while at the Louisville *Courier-Journal*, he met and married Anne. Unlike Carl, Anne Braden had never experienced grinding poverty but rather came from a middle-class family and was brought up in Mississippi and Alabama. She had attended a series of private schools and after graduating from an exclusive college she worked as a journalist in Birmingham and Louisville. 'For Anne, Carl's world was a shattering, albeit liberating experience. The emotional and intellectual walls that segregation and years of indoctrination in white superiority had built around her crumbled under the impact of sharing social, political, and simple human experiences on an equal basis with black people.' In 1954 they agreed to help a black friend, Andrew Wade, who wanted a better home and so they bought a house in an all-white neighbourhood and sold it to him. The racial tension was inflamed by the belief that Braden was a communist. Found guilty of conspiracy, he served eight months of a 15-year sentence until the Supreme Court ruled that the state law was unconstitutional (Fosl, 2002).

All those active in the SCEF realised that people of goodwill, both black and white, needed encouragement. They organised meetings and the Fund became 'a nerve center of inter and intra-racial communication in the South.' As part of that effort to improve communication, Carl and Anne edited the *Southern Patriot* and later helped students in SNCC establish their own paper *The Student Voice* (the forerunner of the alternative media, known as the 'underground press,' published by white anti-war, feminist and gay and lesbian radicals in the later 1960s and 1970s). Their activities they believed would also bring pressure on the federal government. The Fund members turned their semi-annual meetings into workshops which involved the wider community and in 1958, for example, a workshop was held at the black Fisk University in Nashville, Tennessee, which was addressed by Aubrey Williams. Fisk students would play a major role in the campaign of the 1960s.

Frequent trips by King to the North led to friendships with other whites who sympathised with the aims of the boycott leaders in Montgomery. Rustin introduced King to Harris Wofford, the first white man to graduate from Howard University Law School, the premier black university in the United States. Wofford was also a friend of E. D. Nixon of the MIA. Rustin also introduced King to Stanley Levison, a New York lawyer who, working with Ella Baker, had raised funds in that city for the MIA. All were agreed that now was the time to organise a regional group that would bring an end to segregation in the South. As the bombs were being planted in Montgomery on 10 January, Rustin drew up the plans to challenge bus segregation throughout the South but he knew also that they meant to challenge 'the entire social, political and economic order that has kept us second class citizens. . . . Those who oppose us understand this.' The two weapons chosen to win the war were voting power and mass direct action. The new organisation, the Southern Leadership Conference, later called the Southern Christian Leadership Conference by Martin Luther King Jr, was set up in 1957. Although the Conference had had Medgar Evers of the NAACP on its committee as it became SCLC, Evers agreed with Roy Wilkins of the NAACP that he, Evers, would resign from the committee. NAACP officials worked with King but this did not overcome the deep distrust between the two organisations.

Although often distrustful of one another, the leaders of these groups presented a united front when in negotiations with any administration. Wilkins, King, Randolph and Lester B Granger of the National Urban League met with President Eisenhower to stress the concerns of the black community. The four men agreed that Randolph would make the opening statement and the other three would address three points each. In the meeting, Eisenhower defended his administration and refused to give any promises about further action. And the pressure at a local level seemed even less successful with the city of Montgomery refusing to respond to demands for desegregation of schools or even parks. The city commissioners did not feel any urgency and the MIA was divided by factional disputes over issues such as which organisation spoke for black America.

Following a short visit to India, King took part in the second march on Washington to demand school desegregation. The march on 18 April 1959 was reasonably successful, with an estimated 26,000 participating. King, Tom Mboya of Kenya and Roy Wilkins were the three main speakers. The consequence of this rally was a meeting for King with the Vice President, Richard Nixon. King was very impressed with the Vice President's support for the civil rights movement and added: 'If Richard Nixon is not sincere, he is the most dangerous man in America' (Garrow, 1998).

Despite their efforts, Rustin, King, and Levison had not created an effective national lobbying organisation. With the increasingly acrimonious feelings between King and E. D. Nixon, the MIA had become moribund and King decided to leave Montgomery and go to Atlanta. Despite the success of the mass boycott in integrating the bus service and the contribution such grassroots activism had had on drafting the civil rights acts of 1958 and 1960, white southerners had shown they were just as determined to resist the burgeoning movement as African Americans were prepared to struggle for justice. Perhaps in King's gloomiest moments he recalled a visit he had made with Ralph Abernathy to the Highlander Folk School in Tennessee in 1957 where they heard Pete Seeger sing the old union song 'We Shall Overcome.' As King had said to Anne Braden, 'There's something about that song that haunts you' (Garrow, 1988).

3

THE STRUGGLE INTENSIFIES: JFK AND A NEW FRONTIER?

Despite the sit-ins and boycotts of the late 1950s which sought to capitalise on the success of the Montgomery boycott, it was not at all clear as the new decade began whether the African American community would still be singing 'We Shall Overcome' at the end of the decade. Martin Luther King Jr had moved with his family to Atlanta where he had the advantages and many disadvantages of being close to his strong-willed father. As he started a new career in the unofficial capital of Dixie, southern Democrats were pleased that a young senator whom they had promoted for the vice presidency in 1956 was preparing his assault on the executive office. When King met with John Fitzgerald Kennedy (JFK) on 23 June 1960, privately he was not impressed with the young senator from Massachusetts. The black preacher was convinced that the senator's voting on the 1957 Civil Rights Act was determined by his desire to win southern support for his presidential campaign rather than any set of principles.

The Greensboro Sit-in

While Kennedy was campaigning for power in the Democratic Party, and Martin Luther King Jr dreamed of winning control over the National Baptist Convention, four black students in Greensboro, North Carolina, entered the Woolworth's store and went to the whites-only luncheon counter. They sat at the counter on the afternoon of 1 February 1960 and promised to return at ten o'clock the next day. This was not the first of the sit-in protests. As Branch has pointed out, 'In the previous three years similar demonstrations had occurred in at least sixteen other cities. Few of them made the news, all faded quickly from public notice and none had the slightest catalytic effect anywhere else. By contrast, Greensboro helped define the new decade' (Branch, 1989).

The Southern Regional Council, an inter-racial group of moderates, issued a report by Leslie Dunbar a few months after the Greensboro sit-in entitled *Reflections on the Latest Reform of the South*. He wrote: 'Almost from the beginning the sit-ins have been referred to as a "movement" . . . No one ever speaks of the "school desegregation movement." One accomplishment, then, of the sit-in was to achieve, almost from the start, this recognition' (Laue, 1989). During the summer of 1960, 79 sit-in demonstrations were led by students, 78 of which were in the South and border states, with North Carolina (18), Florida (12) and Virginia (10). Among the reasons given by students for their participation was not only their sense of personal frustration but also their sense of commitment and belief in justice. 'Your relationship with the movement is just like a love affair,' said one student. 'You can't explain it. All you know is it's something you *have* to do' (Laue, 1989).

Perhaps the 1960s sit-ins came to be called 'the movement' because the four students from North Carolina Agricultural and Technical College captured the spirit of the moment. It is difficult to explain the heady sense of optimism that the young generation felt – that anything was possible and no problem need go unresolved. The ageing General Eisenhower was an outspoken opponent of the military industrial complex, but sadly was better known among the young for his golf and his heart attacks. It was time for their elders, who had made so many mistakes, to move over and let the young solve the world's problems. Surely they would not repeat the mistakes of the older generation with their wars and crusades against the 'Red menace.' It was this intense idealism that motivated the black students in the South and their white supporters. Regardless of what they actually achieved, the young black Baptist minister, Martin Luther King Jr, and the young Catholic politician from Massachusetts expressed the hopes and dreams of these baby boomers.

These young people had loyally pledged allegiance to the flag each morning in school and it was in the schools across the nation that they were told of the unique promise of America. For the older generation the latest Chevrolet or Ford, with its new layers of chrome, came to represent the ideal which could be achieved by hire purchase. Conspicuous consumption and leisure were the concern of adults, but for many of the young who had been constantly reminded in high school of their fortunate status as citizens of the wealthiest democratic society on earth, the determination was to make the

American Dream a reality. The warnings about the dangers of communism had lost their impact. This was especially true for the South where the schools and churches preached white supremacy as a bulwark against communism. As Paul Goodman observed in *Growing up Absurd* in 1960, 'Now that Law and religion side against them, the Southerners are maniac with wounded conceit and sexual fear; their behavior on integration should be referred not to the Attorney General but to the Public Health Service.' He added, 'All this has come banging down on the children as the battleground. Yet, paradoxically, among all young people it is perhaps just the young people in the South, whites and Negroes both, who most find life worth living these days, because something real is happening' (Howard, 1982).

News of the Greensboro sit-in swept not only through the local community but across the South. Floyd McKissick, NAACP Youth Council leader, was told about the sit-in by one of the protesters. The following day the vice president of the predominantly white National Student Association had heard about the demonstration and had gone to Greensboro. And this was before news of the sit-in was reported in the media. By the third day of the protest the number of students involved was over 80 and the word reached Reverend James Lawson in Nashville. On that day sympathy demonstrations were held in Durham, Raleigh and other cities in the state. By the weekend over 400 students had taken part in the sit-in which was extended to other stores in Greensboro. On the following Thursday, the Reverend Fred Shuttlesworth had arrived from Birmingham, Alabama, to preach a midweek service. He was immediately aware of the historic significance of the events and telephoned Ella Baker in the SCLC office in Atlanta and told her: 'You must tell Martin that we must get with this.' He was certain that the sit-ins would 'shake up the world.' King was the first black leader to give his full support to the students when black newspapers were dismissing the demonstrations as merely student pranks. Three weeks after the sit-ins started in Greensboro, King spoke to a rally in Durham and he reiterated that: 'Men are tired of being trampled over by the iron feet of oppression.' He continued with praise for the students: 'What is fresh, what is new in your fight is the fact that it was initiated, led, and sustained by students. What is new is that American students have come of age. You now take your honored places in the world-wide struggle for freedom' (Branch, 1989).

The Nashville Sit-in

Meanwhile in Nashville, James Lawson found himself overwhelmed by volunteers to take part in similar demonstrations. Approximately 500 students, mainly from the city's four black colleges – Fisk, Tennessee State, Meharry Medical and the Baptist seminary – insisted they should hold their own demonstration. Lawson tried to dissuade them pointing out that only 75 of them had completed training at Highlander in nonviolence. In addition, he said they did not have bail money and many would be arrested by the Nashville city police. Despite his reservations, the students were determined to act and he gave them a crash course on nonviolence. As one historian has written, 'The Nashville students – destined to establish themselves as the largest, most disciplined. and most persistent of the nonviolent action groups in the South – extended the sit-in movement into its third state. Their success helped form the model of the student group – recruited from the campuses, quartered in the churches, and advised by preachers' (Branch, 1989). A Fisk student, Marion Barry Jr, was elected chairman of the SNCC which was set up at a meeting sponsored by the SCLC at Shaw University, Raleigh, North Carolina, on 17 April 1960 (*The Student Voice*, June, 1960).

Only 12 days after the students had made their protest in North Carolina, the students in Nashville, whose leaders included Chicago native Diane Nash, sat-in at lunch counters in the dime stores in the city. The protesters were attacked and in the weeks that followed almost 150 were arrested. Nash told the judge that she and 15 others would go to jail rather than pay the fines because if they paid, they 'would be contributing to and supporting the injustice and immoral practices that have been performed in the arrest and conviction of the defendants' (Branch, 1989). On hearing her remarks, 60 others also chose to be jailed. By 10 May the downtown stores capitulated, lunch counters were integrated and African Americans were hired in non-menial positions for the first time. On 7 March in Knoxville, Tennessee, the black students from Knoxville College and white students, such as Harry Wiersema Jr, from the University of Tennessee (UT) held a series of sit-ins and eventually the counters were integrated (Proudfoot, 1990). In Chattanooga white shoppers rioted rather than integrate (*The Student Voice*, August 1960; Proudfoot, 1990). At a SNCC meeting held at Atlanta University from 13 to 14 May 1960, the students adopted a statement of purpose drawn up by the Reverend James Lawson of Nashville. They would be motivated by nonviolence because they declared:

Through nonviolence, courage displaces fear; love transforms hate. Acceptance dissipates prejudice; hope ends despair. Peace dominates war; faith reconciles doubt. Mutual regard cancels enmity. Justice for all overthrows injustice. The redemptive community supercedes [sic] systems of gross social immorality. (*The Student Voice*, June 1960)

Although many kept to nonviolence, it was not easy. Mrs Annie V. Rankin of Mississippi chose passive resistance when she sat-in at a store in Natchez and did so through a long career in the struggle. But when a black man was murdered in Jefferson County in 1967 because he voted for a black candidate, she wrote to friends that 500 were waiting for the white killer who had fled. They were determined that 'if he shows up he is a dead duck' (Rankin Papers, Mississippi Digital Library, Tougaloo College).

But for SNCC founders, nonviolence was the road. It was a choice supported by others at the meeting including Ella Baker and the Reverend Wyatt Walker of SCLC, the Reverend Edward Brown of Atlanta Congregational Churches, Max Heirich of the American Friends Service Committee (AFSC) and Len Holt of CORE. The committee of SNCC was divided into three subcommittees for co-ordination, communication and finance. It was agreed to have an office in Atlanta, hold regular monthly meetings and raise funds for their work. They sought close co-operation with the NAACP and its Legal Defense Fund. Recognising the importance of good communications, they decided to publish a newsletter to be distributed to every group and cover action throughout the South. They stressed the need for a 'system of flash news to alert the nation of emergencies and serious developments' (*The Student Voice*, June 1960). They arranged for press releases, public relations pamphlets and interpretative statements for the outside press. Carl and Anne Braden, of SCEF, used their skills as professional journalists to help the students.

The sit-in movement was a mass protest organised by African American students from black campuses but it had support from a few white southern students. Those whites who participated were mentioned in the SNCC newsletters. In October a story was headlined 'PARKER STILL JAILED.' Richard Parker of Florida State University was in the Duval County Jail, Jacksonville, with a broken jaw. He was sentenced to 90 days for inciting a riot in Jacksonville. He took part in the Jacksonville sit-in on 25–26 August and was arrested three days later and had lost 25 pounds since his imprisonment (*The Student Voice*, October 1960).

From the very beginning the sit-in was more than just asserting the right to be served at previously all-white lunch counters. For the students, 1 February 1960 was Freedom Day. In an editorial in *The Student Voice* in August 1960 entitled "Politics and the Student Movement", the editors complained: 'The political ramifications of the student protest movement are often underestimated and glossed over.' But as the movement gained strength they should widen the battle and 'it is imperative that we look into the possibility of engaging in political activity on all levels, local, state, and federal.' They had to inform politicians of their views 'forcefully.' 'Elections are coming in November, and we have done our part in seeing that both parties have included in their platforms the strongest civil rights planks ever written.' But this was not good enough and students were urged to drama-tise 'the most blatant denial of civil rights that exists in this country today – the denial of the right to vote to millions of citizens of the South.' The edi-torial called on students North and South to hold protest rallies and pickets on election day. 'As citizens working for the betterment not only of our com-munities, but of the country and the world, again we are called to witness that we are willing to do that which is often unpopular to see that neither we nor our fellow-citizens are forced to endure second-class citizenship.'

King Meets Kennedy

The members of SNCC were following a policy originally set out by union leader A. Philip Randolph and by Martin Luther King Jr of SCLC. On 9 June, Randolph and King jointly called on voters to picket the Demo-cratic and Republican national conventions. They attacked the Civil Rights Act of 1960 as inadequate and pointed out that millions of Americans were still second-class citizens. They argued that marching on the conventions would force the political parties to act. Harlem Congressman Adam Clayton Powell stridently opposed their campaign and denounced King as the 'cap-tive of socialist interests.' Although the row with Powell eventually forced Rustin to resign as coordinator of the New York office of SCLC, the visit to New York resulted in King having a breakfast meeting with presidential candidate John F. Kennedy. The two men agreed that firm executive lead-ership was needed and that urgent action was required to ensure the right to vote and to end discrimination in housing. Despite King's private doubts whether the young man was a politician of principle, after the meeting he stated publicly, 'I was very impressed by the forthright and honest manner in which he discussed the civil rights question. I have no doubt that he would do the right thing on this issue if he were elected President' (Garrow, 1988).

At a second meeting in mid-September, Kennedy was better briefed. Again Kennedy reassured the Atlanta preacher that he supported strong measures to ensure the right to vote. King refused to endorse Kennedy but the presence of Harris Wofford in the Kennedy campaign must have influenced King. Although King's campaign with Roy Wilkins was called a 'Nonpartisan Crusade to Register One Million New Negro Voters', most involved knew it was an attempt to register more Democratic voters.

King had more immediate things on his mind such as the determination of African American students at the five black colleges in Atlanta to be part of the crusade for freedom. The students were impatient with the store-owners, especially Richard H. Rich, owner of the biggest downtown store. Despite meetings with them, Rich refused to integrate his facilities and three student leaders – Lonnie King, Herschelle Sullivan and Julian Bond – persuaded King that he had to join their sit-in. On 19 October, starting at 11 a.m., 75 students from the five colleges moved on to the stores and the first arrests were made at the Magnolia Room of Rich's store 30 minutes later. King was arrested and like the students he refused to post bond and spent his first night in jail (*The Student Voice*, October 1960). He was unaware that he had broken the conditions of a probation order and when the students were released King was transferred to DeKalb County handcuffed and guarded by a large police dog. Despite appeals from many people, King was sentenced to four months for violating his probation. Having avoided prison in Alabama on trumped up charges of tax evasion, King now found himself in prison for the first time (Garrow, 1988).

News of King's imprisonment was sent to Vice President Richard Nixon on the campaign trail but he refused to send a telegram because he and his advisers were aware that Eisenhower had broken into the previously solid Democratic South and Nixon wanted to retain the recent white converts to the Republican Party. Nixon's press officer Herb Klein pocketed the drafts of telegrams drawn up by campaign staffer E. Frederick Morrow. While Nixon ignored the advice of black Atlanta Republican John C. Calhoun, King's wife Coretta called her friend Harris Wofford who was working for the Kennedy campaign. John Kennedy called Mrs King. Robert Kennedy was furious and accused Wofford, 'You bomb throwers probably lost the election. You've probably lost three states . . . the civil rights section isn't going to do another damn thing in this campaign.' But he was also angry with the judge whom he telephoned, arguing that it was a constitutional right for defendants to post a bond. The next day King was released. Although John Kennedy denied any deliberate attempt to win the African American vote (Schlesinger Jr, 1979), the Democrats issued a small flyer in black precincts which read ' "No Comment": Nixon versus a Candidate with a Heart, Senator Kennedy: The Case of Martin Luther King' (Garrow, 1988). King spoke of Kennedy's 'moral courage' and Daddy King, a Republican voter, was more enthusiastic: 'I'll take a Catholic or the Devil himself if he'll wipe

the tears from my daughter-in-law's eyes. I've got a suitcase full of votes –
my whole church for . . . Senator Kennedy' (Schlesinger Jr, 1979).

Executive Action

Although the election of JFK was largely due to the African American vote,
his appointment of his brother Robert as Attorney General did not augur
well for those involved in the civil rights movement. Although Robert knew
action was necessary, he was not the most distinguished graduate of Harvard
or of Virginia Law School. As one historian has noted: 'he had not known
many black people, knew little about segregation, and had not considered
the federal role in promoting desegregation' (Bernstein, 1991, Arsenault,
2006). However, he did make an excellent choice of Assistant Attorney General by appointing the Tennessean Harris Wofford, who did know a lot
about the civil rights movement. And it was Wofford who urged the Justice Department to support the policy of voter registration that had been
adopted by the students in SNCC, as well as SCLC, and the NAACP. In
addition, he advised Kennedy to use executive orders rather than rely on
the conservative Congress to advance civil rights. The Civil Rights Commission, renewed in the Civil Rights Act of 1960, was to be continued
and the President appointed more African Americans to senior posts and
avoided segregated meetings. As Irving Bernstein points out: 'The Kennedy
policy on civil rights in 1961 called for a minimum of legislation and a
maximum of executive action' (Bernstein, 1991, Arsenault, 2006). Civil
rights activists such as Roy Wilkins of the NAACP became increasingly
frustrated at Kennedy's lack of action, especially his failure to desegregate federally funded housing, something he had promised to do during
the campaign with 'one stroke of the pen.' As the days passed the White
House received thousands of pens emblazoned with the famous phrase.
Kennedy refused to act because he was aware that segregation in housing
was a national issue with the North having the potential for great violence
and that 'Any governmental intrusion of race into housing was certain to
arouse deep emotions' (Bernstein, 1991, Arsenault, 2006). Eventually, in
November 1962, after the Congressional elections, Kennedy did sign the
executive order but it was a symbolic act with no effective enforcement
powers.

In federal employment, the President ensured the integration of the Coast
Guard Academy and set up a CEEO with the Vice President, Lyndon
Baines Johnson, as its chairman. Although based on the FEPC principle

as operated by FDR and Truman, Executive Order 10952 drawn up by Johnson and signed by Kennedy for the first time combined federal employment and government contractor agencies under such a commission. And Johnson pointed out that it was not good enough simply to forbid discrimination. 'It is necessary that affirmative action be taken to make equal opportunity available to all who, directly or indirectly, are employed by the nation' (Bernstein, 1991). Although the CEEO had the power to refuse contracts to companies that had discriminatory policies, this sanction was rarely used although there were notable successes such as the integration and promotion of African Americans at the Lockheed plant in Marietta, Georgia. Following the Lockheed agreement, Johnson announced 'Plans for Progress.' But, despite the great publicity, these produced very poor results and a Southern Regional Council study demonstrated that in the Atlanta area only three out of 24 companies were in compliance. Only rarely did the federal government threaten to bar companies from competing for federal contracts but it is possible that the publicity surrounding two firms, one in Arkansas and the other in Illinois, may have persuaded others to end discrimination.

Employers frequently, and with justification, complained that they were simply complying with demands from their workers for segregated facilities. Randolph had been campaigning for years against the racist practices of American labour unions. In November 1962, Johnson, President George Meany of the AFL-CIO, and the officials of 116 unions signed an agreement to end discrimination on the basis of race, creed, colour or national origin in hiring, apprenticeship training and promotion. 'While gains were made in this program, some unions did not sign on and a few, particularly in the building trades, did no more that affix their signatures' (Bernstein, 1991).

Although John and Robert Kennedy sought to bring about gradual change largely through executive action, they were under constant pressure from activists in SNCC and CORE, in addition to the traditional lobbying of groups such as the NAACP and the Urban League. As one commentator on the 1960s has observed:

> The Kennedy emphasis on the young, the bright, the chic and the tough was enormously appealing: it dampened criticism by its very style, and so begged for a while the questions of substance which must inevitably come. A program like the Peace Corps seemed to say that one could change the world a little for the better and have an exciting time doing it. It could also shake up establishment liberalism, which had become shop-worn. (Knight, 1989)

Whatever the intentions of the Kennedy administration, the students in
SNCC and in CORE were certainly not prepared to accept merely gesture
and style. Throughout 1960–61, students participated in voter registration
drives. Lane College students registered the black voters in Fayette and
Haywood Counties in Tennessee and 861 African Americans voted in Haywood County for the first time in 1960. The response of the wealthy white
landowners was to evict their black tenants who were organised into a 'Freedom City' by SNCC workers (*The Student Voice*, November 1960). In addition
to voter registration, students were involved in church kneel-ins, and theatre
stand-ins.

The Freedom Rides

The events which gained international news coverage were the Freedom
Rides organised by James Farmer of CORE who explained later:

> We planned the Freedom Ride with the specific intention of creating a
> crisis. We were counting on the bigots of the South to do our work for
> us. We figured that the government would have to respond if we cre-
> ated a situation that was headline news all over the world, and affecting
> the nation's image abroad. An international crisis that was our strategy.
> (Bernstein, 1991)

Certainly at the time, CORE made it clear to the President that they
were seeking an international crisis. Following the bombing of the Freedom
buses and the violent assault on Freedom Riders in Birmingham, Alabama,
Edward B. King, administrative secretary of SNCC, sent a telegram to
Kennedy in which he stated: 'At a time in the history of our great nation
when we are telling the people of Asia, Africa, Latin America and the free
world in general that we desire to be their friends Negro Americans continue
to be assaulted by the Southern reactionaries' (Bernstein, 1991).

The aim of the Freedom Riders was also to test Kennedy's willingness to
support civil rights through executive action. As early as 1946 the Supreme
Court had ruled in *Morgan v Virginia* that enforcement of state segregation
laws on interstate transport was a burden on interstate commerce and therefore was unconstitutional. In 1960 in the case of *Boynton v Virginia* the Court
had also ruled that segregated bus depots were illegal. The Riders, six black
and six white (the first of 450 who would take part in rides), left Washington
DC on 4 May 1961 to test these rulings and 'bring nonviolent direct action

to the forefront of racial injustice' (Arsenault, 2006). It is claimed that all future protestors shaped their action on the precedents set by the Freedom Riders. On 14 May after several minor incidents, the Greyhound bus pulled into Anniston, Alabama, 60 miles from Birmingham and was met by the KKK.

After their first attack on the bus they followed it out of town and when it was forced to stop because of a puncture the mob set the bus on fire. The students continued in another bus to Birmingham where the racist chief of police, Eugene 'Bull' Connor, told his men to take the day off and visit their families because it was Mother's Day. A howling mob armed with baseball bats, lead pipes and bicycle chains assaulted the students. Although FBI informer, Gary Thomas Rowe, one of the mob, had told Hoover about the planned attack, nothing was done. A group of students from Fisk University, led by Diane Nash, insisted on completing the journey. Governor John Patterson of Alabama, a friend of Kennedy, refused to give the now 21 riders, only three white, protection and they were badly beaten by a mob in Montgomery. They were attacked again in Jackson, Mississippi. All of this was carried on the national and international news just as Kennedy was preparing to meet Khrushchev shortly after his humiliation in Cuba. The rides 'reveal the differences that existed with the heterogeneous world of massive resistance supporters' (Lewis, 2006). But as Farmer knew, the lawyers in the Justice Department could no longer ignore the failure of southern states to uphold the law and by September 1961 the Interstate Commerce Commission had issued regulations ordering the end of segregation on interstate transport. However, as African Americans were only too well aware, it was one thing to issue orders and another for them to be obeyed. Years later, when the author arrived at the bus station in Selma, Alabama, in 1966 at three in the morning, there were no 'whites only' signs anywhere but the bus station was rigidly segregated. Therefore it is not correct to suggest, as Bernstein does that, 'By the end of 1962 James Farmer's Freedom Riders and Robert Kennedy's lawyers had abolished Jim Crow in interstate transportation' (Bernstein, 1991).

The Integration of 'Ole Miss'

The very confrontation that Kennedy wanted to avoid was brewing in Mississippi. It would make the events at Little Rock seem quiet by comparison. The son of a Mississippi sharecropper and an Air Force veteran, James Howard Meredith, applied to attend the University of Mississippi

('Ole Miss') at Oxford. The Democrats who ran the state were divided between moderate racists such as John Coleman and rabid segregationists such as Governor Ross Barnett. They were supported by equally racist judges who upheld the right of the University to refuse Meredith admission. Judge Sidney Mize argued that Mississippi was not racially segregated, even though no African Americans either studied or taught at the University.

After a series of appeals, Supreme Court Justice Hugo Black, a native of Alabama, ordered Meredith's enrolment. Ross Barnett went on television and threw down the gauntlet. The people of Mississippi had a choice: either they submitted to the tyranny of the federal government or they acted like men and resisted. In his determination to defend white supremacy, the governor called on the arguments of his ancestors who had fought to keep slavery: 'Mississippi, as a Sovereign State, has the right under the federal Constitution to determine for itself what the federal Constitution has reserved to it.' He would interpose the authority of the state between the people of Mississippi and federal government tyranny.

Attempts to enrol Meredith peacefully were futile. The Board of Trustees of the University surrendered their authority to Barnett. On several occasions the Governor and his deputy played out the act of interposition on the University steps. As the days dragged by, the students became more agitated and Kennedy realised that he would have to use force. The Cabinet agreed that the army should be kept in reserve and that federal marshals and prison staff should be used to minimise the risk of violence. The extreme right-wing General Edwin Walker called for volunteers to protect the University. As Barnett postured in front of the students at a football game, he failed to realise the changing situation in Washington. Initially reluctant to have a repeat of Little Rock, Robert Kennedy cynically sought political advantage from the crisis. He told his assistant Nicholas Katzenbach: 'If things get rough, don't worry about yourself; the President needs a moral issue.'

On Sunday, 30 September, Meredith was flown into Oxford with 170 federal marshals. A mob of students, joined by outsiders, started to riot throwing bricks and setting fires. The highway patrol was withdrawn, not strengthened, and this was the green light for major violence. The use of tear gas only made matters worse. The students were too busy rioting to listen to the appeal of John Kennedy in which he vainly flattered the state for its prowess on the battlefield and gridiron. By nine o'clock that evening the first fatality occurred when Paul Guilhard, a reporter for Agence France Presse, was shot in the back. An Oxford resident was killed and many others were wounded either from rocks or gunshots. The rioting lasted through the night and order was not restored until nearly seven that morning. Ross

Barnett and 'Ole 'Miss' gave the President the moral issue he had been looking for and also gave him and his brother Robert the tactics they would need later to beat George Wallace of Alabama.

Internal Divisions and External Pressures

The Kennedy brothers had not made any commitments on civil rights. The students had won the support of King and direct action tactics had proved successful despite the deep reservations of the NAACP. Roy Wilkins and the older leaders resented young leaders like Martin Luther King Jr. The latter had to stop Wyatt Walker at SCLC from introducing individual membership because it would have meant direct competition with the NAACP. However, the New York lawyer Stanley Levison and Jack O'Dell raised hundreds of thousands of dollars by direct mailing and King raised an equal amount with his speeches.

However, because of Levison's former connection with the Communist Party, Robert Kennedy gave the FBI the authority to wiretap telephone calls and even burgle the lawyer's office. The Bureau, under J. Edgar Hoover, was increasingly concerned about the communist influence in the civil rights movement. Levison warned King that O'Dell also had been a member of the Communist Party and a report of this conversation was sent to the Attorney General. In a further effort to weaken King the FBI informed newspapers, such as the *New York Times*, that O'Dell was a communist. King was embarrassed by this revelation and publicly claimed O'Dell had resigned when he, and the FBI, knew that O'Dell was still working for the SCLC (Garrow, 1988).

It was not only the FBI that caused problems for King. The students in SNCC were increasingly restive about their lack of funds. They believed that it was their direct action that had brought in money from sympathisers around the world but was now being used by Wyatt Walker to promote SCLC. While SNCC, under the formidable and inspirational leadership of men such as Robert Moses, faced great danger as they struggled to register voters in Mississippi, it was King and SCLC who got the celebrity status in New York. The fact that Ella Baker was now working for SNCC following her replacement at SCLC by Walker did not make for easy relationships between SNCC members and the older leaders of SCLC (Garrow, 1988). Ironically it was King and his supporters who were viewed as the young upstarts by the even older leadership of the Black Baptist Convention. Whereas King as vice president of the Convention had supported the sit-ins, the autocratic president, the Reverend Joseph Jackson, had openly criticised them. King was too young to challenge Jackson but a friend of his did. The election saw the triumph of the autocrat and King lost his position as vice president. From then on the black Baptist church would remain deeply divided and the Convention not only refused formal support to SCLC but actively opposed King (Branch, 1989).

The Albany Movement

These divisions within the civil rights movement help to explain the failure in Albany, Georgia. Charles Sherrod, who worked with Robert Moses in Mississippi, decided to tackle the repressive regime in southwest Georgia. He chose to organise the young African Americans in Albany, especially the students at Albany State College, by-passing the older black leadership, all of whom were active in the NAACP. Administrators at the college were alarmed at the activities of the students and tried unsuccessfully to remove SNCC organisers from the campus. The efforts of the students are generally assumed to be a failure, despite the support of King and Abernathy, who were both arrested. Certainly the police chief Laurie Pritchett made many claims about his understanding of Gandhi, and newspapers reported that he defeated nonviolent direct action with nonviolence, such as ensuring that all protesters were treated courteously when arrested. In turn the establishment press provided Pritchett with details of the students' intended demonstrations and targets, something which was to lead to deep misgivings about journalists by students in the movement. They needed publicity but the distrust planted in Albany would result in the banning of journalists from mass meetings and led to an alternative newspaper system. Pritchett, when he did not have the press giving him information, relied either on older members of the black community to report to him or even used paid informers. His much vaunted nonviolence relied on journalists who were too lazy to investigate jails outside Albany where student demonstrators were taken and subjected to Georgia's old-fashioned brutality. The city fathers knew that the student protests had been effective; business was seriously affected and their concern was evident when they insisted that King should be released from jail. But the most shocking revelation for many in the movement has been described by King's biographer:

> It was a painful irony to movement activists, who concluded accurately that the national public had taken little offense at Albany's establishment of what one observer termed "an efficient police state." So long

as the Laurie Pritchetts of the South succeeded in maintaining segregation in a fashion that eschewed public violence and brutality, it seemed
that the Kennedy brothers would be content to leave civil rights on the
back burner. (Garrow, 1988)

Fortunately for Martin Luther King Jr, the movement and the United
States, there were very few Pritchetts enforcing white supremacy in the
South. Much more typical, and well known to members of the movement,
was the violent racist police chief in Birmingham, Alabama, Eugene 'Bull'
Connor. So when white racists bombed the Bethel Baptist Church, King
was able to use the incident to insist on action from the President. African
American leaders on a visit to the White House demanded improved relations with the newly independent African countries and called on Kennedy
to take a stronger stand on the civil rights issue at home. The President
refused to give any promises and argued that legislation on civil rights was
bound to fail in Congress. It would take one more action in the struggle
for justice, which would be met with violent white resistance, to force the
Kennedy brothers to act.

King and Birmingham, Alabama

King went to New York and informed the singer Harry Belafonte of their
plans for a march and he agreed to raise money for those who would be
jailed and gave substantial sums himself. Meanwhile in Birmingham things
did not go well at first with few taking part in the marches. The newspapers
were eager to print attacks on King but 'Bull' Connor and the police showed
unexpected restraint in the early days of the demonstrations. However, the
internal divisions at Birmingham, Wyatt Walker's disputes with James Bevel,
have been exaggerated. While King explained the need for action with black
preachers and urged businessmen to negotiate, Connor's patience snapped
and he showed how he intended to deal with the continuing protests. On
Monday, 8 April 1963, a small group of demonstrators led by A. D. King
were stopped by snarling German shepherd dogs. The dogs' assault on
a demonstrator was captured by a news photographer and the picture
appeared throughout the world.

As a result of the police brutality, King decided to march on Good Friday
despite the state court injunction against them. His arrest, with Abernathy,
meant that the administration could no longer duck the challenge of the
movement. With King in solitary confinement, the President called Coretta
King to reassure her that everything would be done to protect her husband.

White Christian clergymen and Jewish rabbis published a statement in the Birmingham *News* and suggested that the demonstrations were unwise, complained that they were organised by outsiders and praised the police for their restraint. Using a copy of the newspaper, toilet paper and a pen smuggled into the prison, King sat in his cell and wrote an eight-page rebuttal, 'Letter from Birmingham City Jail.' His answer to the charge that he was a minister from Atlanta, an outsider stirring up trouble, was blunt: 'Injustice anywhere is a threat to justice everywhere.' Business and local politicians refused to negotiate and demonstrations were forced on the African Americans because the city refused to negotiate and the action was not 'untimely' because they had waited '340 years for our constitutional and God-given rights.' The time for waiting was over. A creative tension 'in society . . . will help men rise from the dark depths of prejudice and racism to the majestic heights of understanding and brotherhood.' By defying unjust laws they were not criminals and he wrote: 'One has not only a legal but a moral responsibility to obey just laws. Conversely, one has a moral responsibility to disobey unjust laws.' He claimed the moral high ground for the movement and pointed an accusing finger.

Instead of supporting the movement, white ministers, priests and rabbis in the South had opposed and misrepresented the leaders and, 'all too many others have remained silent behind the anaesthetized security of stained-glass windows.' And although he accused, he also reassured. It was the non-violence that he and his followers espoused that would redeem America and his reaction to their silence and 'laxity' were 'tears of love. There can be no deep disappointment where there is not deep love' (Washington, 1991).

Published as a pamphlet by the AFSC, it was reprinted in journals 'with almost a million copies circulating in the churches and other copies finding their way to Robert Kennedy, Burke Marshall and others in Washington.' Stephen Oates has rightly stated: 'The "Letter" became a classic of protest literature, the most eloquent and learned expression of the goals and philosophy of the nonviolent movement ever written' (Oates, 1994).

His absence while in jail gave James Bevel, who had married co-worker Diane Nash, control of the Birmingham protest. It was Bevel who realised that the movement had never fulfilled its commitment to fill the jails and he was also aware that the students at Miles College were not willing to be jail bait. He knew that high school students were eager to join the protests and had been held back by adults. Bevel had no such doubts. Ignoring the protests of their teachers and parents, thousands of high school students took to the streets. The police were fooled by diversionary marches and Bevel, Andrew Young and other volunteers armed with walkie-talkies organised march after march. On 3 May the police used dogs and fire hoses on the teenagers and 250 students were arrested. Three days later this had increased to 1000. By 7 May the jails were full, with 2500 arrests. Birmingham was a mass movement and one the administration could not ignore. Despite the criticisms of the Birmingham settlement by David Garrow, Adam Fairclough is correct when he writes: 'The success of Birmingham should not be judged according to its impact on Congress: the initiative for the civil rights bill came from the administration, not the legislature. And the evidence strongly suggests that SCLC's demonstrations played a decisive role in persuading the Kennedy administration to introduce legislation' (Fairclough, 1987).

The Attorney General had for two years sought to defuse black protest and the Kennedy brothers were seriously alarmed about the possibility of all-out race war. However, to John Dittmer, the eagerness of JFK and his brother Robert to seek compromise only 'demonstrated once again that in the short run, at least, they preferred order to justice' (Dittmer, 1995). This fear of a race war was heightened following Robert Kennedy's meeting with black intellectuals, novelist James Baldwin, sociologist Kenneth Clarke, playwright Lorraine Hansbury and with singers Lena Horne and Harry Belafonte, plus CORE activist Jerome Smith, who was in New York for medical treatment following one of his many beatings. Smith and Baldwin were furious with Kennedy's apparent indifference. Smith told Kennedy about the abuse he had received in the South and warned him: 'When I pull the trigger, kiss it good-bye.' When asked by Baldwin if he would fight for the United States, Smith shouted, 'Never! Never! Never!' Kennedy was shocked and angered but as his friend and biographer writes: 'He began, I believe, to grasp as from the inside the nature of black anguish. He resented the experience, but it pierced him all the same. His tormentors made no sense; but in a way they made all sense. It was another stage in his education' (Schlesinger Jr, 1979).

The March on Washington

Another part of his education were the efforts of SNCC, CORE and SCLC throughout the summer of 1963 to register voters, and the failures to do so in any number in Gadsden (Alabama), Danville (Virginia) and Plaquemine (Louisiana) underlined how easy it was for southerners to maintain white supremacy. For the Attorney General it became obvious that the courage alone of civil rights workers would never bring democracy to America. For

Martin Luther King Jr these individual failures could not be allowed to destroy the faith that had made the challenge possible in the first place. Taking up an idea first proposed by A. Philip Randolph, King decided that a march on Washington, if they could get a hundred thousand, would be sufficient pressure to demonstrate a mass demand for jobs and justice. Fairclough argues that the march on Washington had minimal impact on the legislative process. It is difficult to be certain. This underestimates the amazing scene of at least 250,000 demonstrators in front of the great American icon, the Lincoln Memorial. For the first time leading representatives of the major religions and denominations were united behind the civil rights cause. Tens of millions of North Americans watched on television and heard a young Baptist minister articulate African American demands for justice in terms of the American Dream, a dream all Americans shared. It was a familiar speech to many who had heard King before but it was a revelation to millions who had not realised the aims of the movement. However, few noticed his attacks on the economic system that perpetuated poverty and unemployment. For King, Randolph and Rustin the march was for 'Jobs and Freedom.' Most prefer to see it as a civil rights march for black people only (Jackson, 2007).

Despite the success of the march, the FBI still spent most of its time trying to undermine SCLC which J. Edgar Hoover saw as merely a communist front organisation. Although some believed Robert Kennedy had acquired a greater understanding of African American grievances, he outraged young people in the movement with the federal indictment of the 'Albany Nine' who were accused of obstructing justice. However, this concession to the segregationists did not stop the racists and their violence. Just three weeks after the march on Washington, four young black girls were killed by a bomb at Birmingham's Sixteenth Street Baptist Church. This was the seventh bomb in the last six months, and since 1956 there had been 17 bombings in that city alone. Hoover knew from an informant the names of the KKK men who had carried out the bombings. In 1971, reporters from the *New York Times* and the *Los Angeles Times* went to the Justice Department and threatened to publicise the non-cooperation of the FBI. As a result, evidence was revealed and in 1977, Robert Chambliss was convicted of murder. The Bureau did not admit that it held more evidence in the form of tape recordings and it was almost 38 years after the bombing that Klansman, Thomas Blanton, was convicted on four counts of murder. As *Newsweek* reported it was belated, inadequate justice and 'broader accountability non-existent. So the result of the Blanton conviction is not reconciliation, but relief (that Blanton was not set free) and weary resignation' (*Newsweek*, 14 May 2001). This 'weary resignation' is reflected in the remarks of Birmingham's Mayor, Bernard Kincaid, after the trial of Blanton's accomplice and fellow Klansman, Bobby Frank Cherry, who was also found guilty and sentenced to life in prison in May 2002. Mayor Kincaid hoped the city would 'put the infamous chapter behind us and turn our attention to the future' (NBC13.com/News/ 22 May 2002).

However, at the time of the bombings, southern politicians were content to remind southerners of the Civil War and appealed to interposition and nullification. Governor George Wallace stood in the doorway of the University of Alabama vowing to keep segregation for ever and these actions fuelled the violence of the resurgent Klan. 'And the very notion of couching the confrontation as a constitutional issue was precisely in keeping with Wallace's strategy: an abstract struggle between "states' rights" and the "central government" ' (Carter, 1995). But Kennedy did not want a repetition of the violence at 'Ole Miss.' Instead, Wallace's racist appeal to southern white nationalism was met by John Kennedy's televised address to the nation in which he committed himself to a civil rights bill providing a federal remedy to integration of public accommodation (Dalleck, 2003). Only seconds after the President had stopped speaking a shot rang out in the humid Mississippi night in Jackson. Mrs Medgar Evers ran out to find her husband, the head of the state NAACP, dead on the front porch (Garrow, 1988).

The very violence that southern politicians had encouraged and which the FBI had done nothing to stop was further aided by the indifference of the northern newspapers and network television. It was in such a climate of fear, hate and violence that the President went to Dallas, Texas. The murder of the young President plunged the nation into mourning and into a period of great uncertainty. Blacks and liberals were worried about the obvious popularity of politicians such as Goldwater and Wallace. There were dire predictions that if the supporters of these two men joined forces, then the United States was on the brink of becoming a fascist state.

4

TRIUMPHS AND TRAGEDIES: LBJ, THE GREAT SOCIETY AND THE LIMITS OF LIBERALISM

As Lyndon Baines Johnson took the oath of office aboard Air Force One, Jacqueline Kennedy stood next to the Texan, her husband's dried blood still clinging to her pink suit. It was the sort of tragic scene that many in the civil rights movement knew all too well. The terrible events in Dallas, Texas, would not be the last time that the Kennedys would be the victims of political assassination, just as the death of Medgar Evers, whose killer Byron D. La Beckwith was convicted only in 1994, would not be the last death among those who fought for justice in America. The next four years, especially, would see important triumphs but also terrible tragedies.

For some writing about the civil rights movement in later years, the extraordinary union of massive black struggle with white liberal forces in the United States in 1963 also had its dangers. According to one African American: 'The central dilemma of the first stage of the black freedom movement emerged: the existence and sustenance of the civil rights movement neither needed nor required white aid or allies, yet its success required white liberal support in the Democratic Party, Congress and the White House' (West, 1993). According to Allen Matusow, John Kennedy, a traditionally conservative politician, had 'inadvertently helped arouse among millions a dormant desire to perfect America' and as a consequence he became 'the reluctant champion of Martin Luther King.' He continues, 'Only later, during Lyndon Johnson's term as president would the limits of liberal goodwill become apparent and the flaws of liberal reform be exposed' (Matusow, 1986). This view conforms with the majority opinion that the liberalism of the 1960s was limited: it not only failed to achieve its limited goals but did positive harm to the United States as well as to the people it sought to help.

The very existence of liberal goodwill was in doubt when LBJ took office. Despite his insistence that he was a national leader from a western state, many in the North viewed him as a vulgar Texan from the Deep South. There are parallels with 1945 after the death of FDR, when Truman was little known and deeply distrusted by northern voters, especially African Americans. Despite his limitations, FDR had done a great deal for black Americans and he was the champion of the liberal cause. Although Truman's achievements for African Americans were limited, he was the first president of the United States openly to attack the evils of discrimination in American society.

To appease southerners, LBJ made judicial appointments (Navasky, 1971) which only increased his white liberal critics' distrust. John Kennedy came to be viewed as the liberal president who championed the 1963 Civil Rights Bill which sought to enfranchise blacks by strengthening voting rights. It also proposed that the Justice Department could initiate desegregation suits and thus overcome massive resistance to school desegregation. Discrimination in public places was to be illegal. The President wanted power to cut funds to state programmes that discriminated. Although the majority of Americans supported his civil rights stand, Harris poll findings showed that in 1963, 6.5 million Americans who had voted for Kennedy in 1960 said they would not vote for him in 1964, and 4.5 million of these indicated that it was because of his stand on civil rights (Matusow, 1986). The question that worried African Americans and their liberal supporters was how would the accidental President act? Would he be true to his region, would he simply push through the Kennedy legislation or would he be an enthusiastic supporter of the civil rights movement? Many Americans remembered the uncertainty after FDR died. But now they had to cope not with the sudden death of a president but with his assassination. Many worried about their country's future and doubted the Texan about to take power.

The Civil Rights Act, 1964

Initially, Johnson overcame these doubts and the Civil Rights Act of 1964 has rightly been 'heralded as one of the great achievements of Lyndon B. Johnson and his presidential administration.' Segregation was banned in all public facilities in America. It also 'raised the issue of "public" versus "private". Contrary to conservatives, the administration supported the view that any privately owned enterprise that accepted tax-payers' funds or business was public' (Anderson, 1995). The federal government could withhold money from private companies that discriminated. The Equal Employment Commission was set up. Passage of the Act paved the way, in part, to the very important Voting Rights Act of 1965 and the Housing Rights Act of 1968 (Loevy, 1980). Johnson had supported the Bill as Vice President; therefore when he took office black leaders in the nation trusted him to get it passed. He did 'a masterful job of using the publicity powers of the presidency to press for the Civil Rights Bill.' He took the lead in opposing George Wallace's campaign for the Democratic nomination in 1964 and LBJ used Wallace's vehement opposition to the Bill to persuade Everett Dirksen, the leader of the Senate Republicans, to support the legislation.

Although Hugh Davis Graham accepts Robert Kennedy's claim that he told Johnson that he needed Dirksen to get the votes, it is very unlikely that such a master manipulator of the Senate as LBJ would have even asked Robert Kennedy for advice (Graham, 1994). Johnson was a political master. Johnson said he had helped JFK because the Ivy Leaguers 'don't know any more about Capitol Hill than an old maid does about fuckin'' (Woods, 2006). In fact, the search for a bi-partisan approach to ensure the Bill's passage was first outlined by Vice President Johnson to Assistant Attorney General Norbert Schlei on 3 June 1963. Johnson had taken part in planning meetings and joined JFK when he met civil rights leaders. His actions were ignored by many commentators: 'As a southerner, Lyndon Johnson was mainly concerned with winning political support in the north. He would have to run for re-election in 1964, and he had less than a year to convince sceptical northern and western liberals that a southerner was an acceptable leader of the national Democratic party.' To achieve this end and stop the worst racist abuses, Johnson actively worked with Congress, civil rights leaders and the media to ensure the passage of the legislation. In his State of the Union address in 1964 he declared: 'As far as the writ of Federal law will run, we must abolish not some but all racial discrimination. For this is not merely an economic question – or a social, political or international issue. It is a moral issue – and it must be met.' He linked his battle for civil rights to his battle against international communism. 'Today Americans of all races stand side by side in Berlin and Vietnam. They died side by side in Korea. Surely they can work and eat and travel side by side in their own country' (Loevy, 1980). Although Johnson shared many of the prejudices of his fellow southerners and he was certainly ambitious, he was also driven by a desire for social justice. As one biographer, argues:

> With the single exception of Lincoln, he was the greatest champion with a white skin that they had in the history of the Republic. He was to become the lawmaker for the poor and downtrodden and the oppressed. He was

to be the bearer of at least a measure of social justice to those whom social justice had so long been denied, the restorer of at least a measure of dignity to those who desperately needed to be given some dignity, the redeemer of the promises made to them by America. (Caro, 2002)

Johnson succeeded in getting stronger legislation than that conceived by Kennedy and to do so achieved an historic first by stopping a filibuster of the Bill in the Senate with a two-thirds vote for a closure motion. This success was achieved because Johnson had had a long career as an outstanding legislator (Woods, 2006) and he believed laws could obliterate racial discrimination. But to achieve this legislation required a consensus across party lines.

Unfortunately for LBJ, his search for consensus would become increasingly difficult. His dream of a 'Great Society' to complete the unfinished business of the New Deal was defeated by the failure of this 'consummate legislator' to win the support of Martin Luther King Jr and the young leaders in SNCC as much as by the increasing difficulties he would face in Vietnam. For a president worried about 'the burden of national unity', Johnson was concerned that only days after signing the Civil Rights Act, riots broke out in Harlem and Brooklyn in New York City. In the following days Rochester, New York and Jersey City, Paterson and Elizabeth, New Jersey, were torn by riots (Johnson, 1971). The predominantly white student body at the University of California at Berkeley rebelled against the paternalistic regime and demanded the right of free speech and assembly – a rebellion led by students who had been active in CORE and SNCC during the Freedom Summer (Blum, 1991).

The Mississippi Freedom Democratic Party

For Johnson and the civil rights leaders the main aim of 1964 was the electoral victory of the Democratic Party under the leadership of LBJ against the challenge of Alabama Governor George Wallace in the party and from Senator Barry Goldwater the ultra- conservative Republican from Arizona. Meanwhile in Mississippi Robert Moses, a student from New York, had been working with SNCC to register voters. A black woman attended one of the meetings arranged by Moses. Fanny Lou Hamer, at 44 the youngest of 20 children of black sharecroppers, had grown up in Sunflower County not knowing that she had the right to vote (Asch, 2008). She volunteered to go to the court house and register. As she said: 'The only thing they could do to me was kill me and it seemed like they'd been trying to do that a little bit at a time ever since I could remember.' Dismissed from the plantation because she refused to give up her efforts to register, there were attempts to murder her and she was brutally beaten in Winona – a beating that left her permanently injured. This did not stop her and many more from fighting on and she joined SNCC in 1963 (Mills, 2007). Hamer and many African Americans struggled to bring democracy to Mississippi and, ironically, their arch enemy, Senator James Eastland, fought them using the language of freedom (Asch, 2008) and warnings of race-mixing. And Mrs Hamer knew all about the South and 'mongeralization.' Her grandmother had been raped by many white men and 20 of her 23 children were born because of these assaults (Lee, 2000).

Undaunted by Eastland's demagoguery, they formed the inter-racial Mississippi Freedom Democratic Party (MFDP) and challenged LBJ. Others in the civil rights movement did not support this tactic. Andrew Young considered it 'unnecessarily dangerous' because 'there was no protection for civil rights workers' and he believed rural black people were too practical to support such an impractical scheme. Although he believed northern radicals abused the students' idealism and the students manipulated local black leaders, he admits the MFDP 'did transform politics in Mississippi, by planting seeds that would be harvested later' (Young, 1996). When the MFDP failed to unseat the Mississippi delegates at the convention they challenged the seating of five Congressmen. Those testifying were all women (Mills, 2007). Others who were beaten by local police and MFDP members are less well known. Mrs Annie Rankin was in Washington. She was active in the movement in 1961 sitting-in at a 10 cent store in Natchez, Mississippi, and sought to register for the vote in 1964. A teacher in the Freedom Schools, she worked with Mrs Hamer and other organisers (Rankin, undated).

Men and women, black and white, participated in the Voter Education Project supported by several civil rights groups. To avoid disputes over funding, the groups had united under an umbrella organisation entitled the Council of Federated Organizations (COFO). Moses was director of voter registration and Aaron Henry of NAACP was elected president. Voter registration was concentrated in the areas of both the highest black population and largest number of white Citizens Councils. And the students, many from segregated institutions, used the all-black churches and black newspapers to make links with residents and their other organisations such as youth groups (Carson, 1981). As Julian Bond, a SNCC activist, recalled a few years later: 'The biggest change in SNCC came in '63–'64 when we decided to build political organizations as well as just try to get people to register to vote' (Stoper, 1989).

The Freedom Summer was designed to register voters to support the MFDP which had been formed in April. It was also used to expand the freedom school programme, an idea of Charles Cobb. It was Cobb who suggested recruiting northern college students to come to Mississippi (Carson, 1981). On 13 June the first white volunteers started training at Western College for Women. Although subject to tough scrutiny and psychological tests, Oxford, Ohio, was paradise compared with Oxford, Mississippi. As David Dennis, Robert Moses' assistant, told an interviewer ten years later. 'We knew that if we had brought in a thousand blacks, the country would have watched them slaughtered without doing anything about it. Bring in a thousand whites and the country is going to react.' Young African Americans had already been beaten and murdered but there was no protection provided by federal forces and no publicity in the major newspapers. Similar attacks on white students would force the FBI to protect civil rights workers and the newspapers and television would report every assault. As Dennis admits, it was SNCC's 'sorta cold' assessment that to achieve justice in Mississippi 'the death of a white college student would bring on more attention to what was going on than for a black college student getting it' (Raines, 1977).

Eight days later two whites did 'get it.' Three COFO workers left Meridian, Mississippi, to investigate the burning of a black church. They disappeared. Two CORE members, James Chaney, a black Mississippian, and Michael Schwerner, a white social worker and CORE member from New York, along with Alan Goodman, one of the first student volunteers in Ohio, were reported missing to the Justice Department (Mills, 2007). As usual there was no immediate response on the part of the FBI. Not that this came as any surprise to SNCC workers. Bob Zellner, a white student from Alabama and SNCC staffer, recalled the FBI's response when a McComb, Mississippi, mob tried to murder him. After the assault in which his assailants sought to gouge his eyes out, Zellner was imprisoned. Then three or four men arrived to take pictures of him and reassured him that he had not been alone; they had taken notes throughout. This was his first experience of the FBI and 'I realized they were a bunch of gutless automatons. . . . This guy thought it would *comfort* me to let me know that he was out there recording my death' (Morrison, 1987).

Prior to the disappearance of Chaney, Schwerner and Goodman, there had been over 150 cases of violence and intimidation against black civil rights workers and local residents who supported the movement. The federal authorities took no action in any of these cases. In contrast, the news of the disappearance of the three men 'immediately focused national attention on the Summer Project' (Carson, 1981). And this was despite appeals to Robert Kennedy by the parents of Goodman and Schwerner. Twenty four incidents were reported between 21 and 26 June despite the presence of FBI agents and the international press (*The Student Voice*, 3 June 1964). A further 39, including bombings and shootings, occurred between 26 June and 10 July (*The Student Voice*, 15 July 1964).

The federal government drafted in 200 naval personnel, Justice Department officials and 150 FBI men to search for the three civil rights workers. After paying informers, the bodies of the three men were found on 4 August 1964 in an earth-filled dam near the town of Philadelphia (Carson, 1981). Ella Baker told MFDP delegates: 'The symbol of politics in Mississippi lies in those three bodies that were dug from the earth this week' (Mills, 2007). CORE leaders, despite their anger, knew that demonstrations against the President would exacerbate the situation and help the conservative Goldwater. In early August James Farmer assured administration officials that they would not picket Johnson on a visit to Syracuse, New York. Farmer persuaded CORE members to petition the President's staff instead. Relations between Farmer and federal officials became increasingly strained. None of the 20 men arrested by federal authorities, including the sheriff of Neshoba County, were charged with the state offence of murder. They were accused of the federal offence of depriving the men of their civil rights. LBJ preserved his liberal consensus. Three years later seven men were convicted and sent to prison (Carson, 1981). It took an Englishman to tell their story in an error-strewn film *Mississippi Burning* (Portis, 2008).

As the three bodies were discovered SNCC leaders and their supporters were planning a major challenge to unseat the delegates selected by the segregated Democratic Party of Mississippi. They were confident that an inter-racial group who, unlike the regular party, were all dedicated to the election of Johnson would see the replacement of the old order with the new. Ella Baker would claim four years later that she had never been optimistic about the challenge to the regular delegation. She argued: 'The fact that liberals and most of the black civil rights leadership were committed first to elect Johnson was crucial' (Stoper, 1989). Her assessment was correct but at the time SNCC and their supporters lobbied hard in the convention to win (*The Student Voice*, 5; 19 August 1964). LBJ, the man they were struggling to support, does not even mention the MFDP in his memoirs but rather recalls 'happy, surging crowds and thundering cheers. To a man as troubled as I was by party and national divisions, the display of unity was welcome indeed' (Johnson, 1971).

This unity was bought at a high price. Johnson used Hubert Humphrey, an acknowledged leader of liberal Democrats and Joe Rauh, to get the MFDP to accept the Reverend Ed King, the white chaplain from Tougaloo College, and Aaron Henry, head of the Mississippi NAACP, as delegates.

Johnson 'pretended to negotiate with the MFDP' (Young, 1996) but preferred to listen to southern Democrats and the threat from Governor John
Connally of Texas that, 'If those baboons walk onto the convention floor we
walk out' (Burner, 1994). Robert Moses' biographer points out: 'The administration and the party in this critical juncture lay bare their inability to
understand not only the moral premise on which the creation of the MFDP
rested but also the very real and dangerous physical battle the delegates
had fought to be there' (Burner, 1994). Humphrey and Walter Mondale
were instrumental in appeasing the racists from Mississippi and it was an
appeasement that would prove costly to both men in their later presidential
ambitions (McAdam, 1988; Burner, 1994).

Significantly, LBJ was supported by Martin Luther King and SCLC,
Roy Wilkins of the NAACP and Whitney Young of the National Urban
League, a group dedicated to helping African American business development. Although his relationship with King has been correctly characterised
as 'volatile' King supported the administration compromise and urged the
MFDP to reach a consensus with the liberals. Jim Forman and Cleveland
Sellers of SNCC were furious at what they believed was King Jr's betrayal
and Alabama activist, John Lewis, told Andrew Young, 'Andy, we have shed
too much blood in Mississippi to accept a compromise.... People were murdered in Philadelphia, and there is no punishment. When we try to register
to vote, we get sent to jail, we are beaten, we are threatened. We can't back
down, we've come too far' (Young, 1996). King argued that a coalition of
unions, liberals and blacks would deliver progressive reform and that the
coalition's influence would grow as white southerners left and joined the
Republican Party (Jackson, 2007). He was correct only in his view that very
many southerners would shift their party allegiance. A white activist from
Mississippi, Bill Higgs, present at the meeting, recalled Moses' response:
'We're not here to bring politics into our morality but to bring morality into our politics.' And as he reflected later, one of the major reasons
for their defeat was not solely race: '[the] Democratic Party has organized
around the middle class. And we were challenging them not only on racial
grounds ... but we were challenging them on the existence of a whole group
of people who are the underclass of this country, white and black, who are
not represented' (Burner, 1994; Jackson, 2007).

The 1964 Campaign

The campaign by Johnson and Humphrey against a bitterly divided Republican Party led by the conservative senator from Arizona, Barry Goldwater,

resulted in a landslide victory for the Democrats. Significantly the traditional base of the Democratic Party in the South was beginning to crumble. Of the six former Confederate states that supported the party, four, Arkansas, Florida, Tennessee and Virginia, did so solely because of the African American vote. Only in Johnson's home state of Texas did the majority of white voters support the party. As the editors of *The Student Voice* of 25 November 1964 pointed out: 'The rejection of Negroes from the traditionally integrated Republican party, the lack of support the Democratic ticket received from local and state Democratic party figures in the deep South, and the clear delineation of Senator Barry Goldwater's position favoring states rights and "local option" of segregation all contributed toward a Democratic victory.' Goldwater's southern strategy failed but Republicans would not give up trying.

Following the election and despite his later protestations (Johnson, 1971), President Johnson was reluctant to push for further legislation, preferring to wait for the South to implement the Civil Rights Act. But the experience of SNCC, CORE and SCLC volunteers trying to register voters made them determined to force the issue. The mass movement of African Americans and their white supporters forced a showdown in Selma, Alabama. The nation was once more forced to witness the violence of the 'genteel South' fighting to preserve white supremacy. Out of a possible five million black voters in the South only two million were registered. In Mississippi only 6.4 per cent of potential African American voters were registered despite the efforts of Robert Moses and others.

The Challenge at Selma

The situation was just as dire in Alabama. In the city of Selma, African Americans were a majority of the 29,000 population but only 3 per cent of the electorate. The sheriff of Dallas County, including Selma, was Jim Clark, a violent racist demagogue who had attacked blacks in 1963 when they tried to register to vote. With support from a racist judge and indifferent federal officials, Clark almost succeeded in destroying the voting rights drive. James Bevel of the SCLC knew that dramatic action was required and called on Martin Luther King Jr to defy the ban on black marches and meetings. King and 15 black groups in Selma decided to challenge Clark and his paramilitary forces and force the federal government to act.

The Selma white community was divided between those who supported Clark, the 'stupid segregationists', and those who backed the Director of

Safety, Wilson Baker, the 'smart' racists. According to one white resident: 'The trouble is, too many of our people fear the white man more than they do the Negro and won't speak up against Clark' (*The Student Voice*, 26 March 1965). Despite Baker's 'smart' racism with the detention of American Nazi Party leader, Lincoln Rockwell, on 19 January, the 'stupid' segregationist Sheriff Clark arrested 67 blacks who were trying to register to vote. Six days later surprised whites saw one black woman retaliate against the sheriff, knocking him down twice after he had hit her. Immediately dragged to the ground by three of Clark's deputies, Annie Lee Cooper found the sheriff was willing to ignore the newsmen, sit on her stomach and club her senseless. As one historian has put it: 'The sound of the clubbing could be heard through the crowd that had gathered in the street. By the next day the political echoes of the beating had resounded through the country' (Weisbrot, 1990).

Even as Johnson was instructing the new Attorney General, Nicholas Katzenbach, to draw up legislation giving federal protection to those registering to vote, Clark defied federal court rulings. With hundreds in jail, he moved quickly to imprison the two men he believed were communist agitators – Martin Luther King Jr and Ralph Abernathy. From his prison cell King wrote a letter to the American nation demanding federal protection for those who wanted to vote.

'Bloody Sunday' and the March to Montgomery

Nearby towns held marches in support of the Selma campaign. On 18 February in Marion, state troopers shot and wounded Jimmie Lee Jackson. Refused treatment in the local white hospital, he was taken to Selma where he died. His death was just one of many in the South that were not prosecuted. William Moore, a postman, had been shot and killed and the man responsible was freed. Four girls were blown up in the 16th Street Baptist Church and the three white men arrested were freed for lack of evidence. A 13-year-old boy, Virgil Ware, was shot and although his killers confessed, they were only charged with manslaughter and after a few days in jail were released on probation. Police in Birmingham shot and killed Johnny Brown Robinson, aged 16 (*The Student Voice*, 26 March 1965). There were no convictions and despite pleas from the black community, J. Edgar Hoover claimed that the FBI had no jurisdiction but instead he went to enormous lengths discrediting King and other civil rights leaders.

This failure to act makes 'Bloody Sunday' of 7 March 1965 seem inevitable. King planned a march from Selma to Montgomery to provide mass support for the Voting Rights Bill proposed by Lyndon Johnson and supported by Republican Everett Dirksen. Hosea Williams of SCLC and John Lewis of SNCC led 600 marchers from the AME Church towards the Edmund Pettus Bridge where they were met by state troopers wearing Confederate badges, sheriff's deputies, and mounted men armed with clubs and electric cattle prods. Although given two minutes to return to their church, the charge of the troopers came in less than a minute. John Lewis, who had bowed his head but refused to retreat, was the first to be struck, suffering a fractured skull. Five women were also among the first to be beaten, including Amelia Boynton who was clubbed and tear gassed. With blacks fleeing for safety, Sheriff Clark unleashed his mounted paramilitary forces who later took part in the riot attacking innocent people in the city's black section.

Pictures of the beatings were broadcast around the world as well as across the nation. The majority of Americans were horrified by what they saw and liberal senators such as the Republican Jacob Javits of New York denounced the reign of terror. As Lyndon Johnson recalled: 'The Alabama state troopers took matters into their own hands. With night-sticks, bullwhips, and billy clubs, they scattered the ranks of the marchers. . . . The march was over. But the struggle had just begun' (Johnson, 1971). But while the vast majority of whites in America were united in their horror at Selma, for those involved in the movement it was a crucial turning point. Many young members of SNCC were eager to retaliate. As Julian Bond recalled a few years later, the problem with nonviolence was that many African Americans in the Deep South 'carried guns for self-defense as a matter of custom' (Stoper, 1989).

Nonviolence may have been a way of life for John Lewis; it was not for most African Americans. King flew in from Atlanta and the divisions between him and the majority of SNCC members came into the open. King had agreed to lead a symbolic march to the bridge. State troopers and Sheriff Clark waited on the other side and then seemed to leave the road open inviting King to lead a march past the troopers on the road to Montgomery (Carter, 1995). Cleveland Sellers and James Forman wanted King to march. Ralph Abernathy, King's associate in SCLC, recalled that SNCC workers 'felt betrayed' and thought King lacked courage. 'It was the first time that such accusations would be made, though not the last. Soon, very soon, the advocates of violence would be saying that Martin was too timid to lead the movement, and then that he was too cowardly' (Abernathy, 1989). King refused either to defy a federal court injunction or to walk into the trap and led the marchers back to the church where James Forman argued that the only reason they had not been attacked was because white folks were in the march. Sellers, Forman and Stokely Carmichael were increasingly restive with the tactic of nonviolence, and bitter that the suffering of African Americans was barely noticed whereas the slightest injury to whites was widely reported.

Despite the killing and maiming of many blacks, it was the assault by a white mob on four marchers, all white Unitarian ministers, that galvanised the President into action. The Reverend James Reeb of Boston, a 38-year-old father of four, was savagely beaten and died two days later in hospital (*The Student Voice*, 26 March 1965). Johnson immediately telephoned Mrs Reeb to express his sympathy but refused to send in federal troops because he believed that it would jeopardise the Voting Rights Bill. Instead, he met George Wallace at the White House. Johnson was angry and demanded, 'Why are you fucking over your president?' (Woods, 2006). But he also feared the demonstrators would accuse him of lack of action. And typical of southern politicians he bemoaned that: 'Once again my Southern heritage was thrown in my face. I was hurt, deeply hurt. But I was determined not to be shoved into hasty action' (Johnson, 1971). The President told Wallace to protect the rights of African American citizens. Wallace claimed he lacked funds to protect the marchers who had been given authority to march by federal Judge Frank Johnson. LBJ federalised the state troopers and sent Ramsey Clark, the new Attorney General, to take control. When the marchers reached Montgomery, King assured them that 'segregation is on its deathbed in Alabama' and concluded, perhaps seeking to answer his young critics as to how long it would take:

How long? Not long, because no lie can live forever.

How long? Not long, because you still reap what you sow.

How long? Not long, because the arm of the moral universe is long but it bends toward justice.

How long? Not long cause mine eyes have seen the glory of the coming of the Lord, trampling out the vintage where the grapes of wrath are stored. He hath loosed the fateful lightning of his terrible swift sword. His truth is marching on.
(Abernathy, 1989)

The fateful lightning struck the next day when Mrs Viola Liuzzo was ferrying several marchers back to Selma. A white woman driving with a black man Leroy Moton, Mrs Liuzzo was breaking one of the sacred southern codes of 'honour.' She had been subject to various attacks during the day, and now a car sped past and three shots were fired. Shortly after King's speech, Mrs Liuzzo was killed. Moton stopped the car and in trying to revive her was covered in blood. Her blood saved his life. When the assassins came up to the car they assumed Moton was dead also (Abernathy, 1989). FBI head, J. Edgar Hoover, told LBJ that Mrs Liuzzo was a drug addict and Nicholas Katzenbach that 'she was sitting very, very close to the Negro in the car. . . . It had the appearance of a necking party' (Woods, 2006). Despite Hoover's lies, unlike most murders in Mississippi, this one did not take long to solve because an FBI agent, Gary Rowe, was one of the killers.

While the consensus among SNCC, SCLC and CORE was breaking down at Selma, LBJ struggled to maintain unity with liberal Republicans and Democrats to meet the crisis. Initially reluctant to take precipitate action, LBJ agreed with Congressional leaders to address a joint session on the evening of 15 March. In his address Johnson linked the violence in Selma with the opening skirmishes of the American Revolution and the end of the Civil War. Then 'in a Texas version of the southern Baptist rhythm and tenor that Martin Luther King had mastered' (Woods, 2006), Johnson stated: 'There is no issue of states' rights or national rights. There is only the struggle for human rights,' and he ended with the words of the movement: 'Their cause must be our cause too. Because it is not just Negroes, but it is all of us who must overcome the crippling legacy of bigotry and injustice. And . . . we . . . shall . . . overcome' (Johnson, 1971).

The Voting Rights Act 1965

Four months later, on 6 August 1965, Johnson signed the Voting Rights Act. The strain between some of the civil rights leaders and the man from Texas was evident even at this ceremony. James Farmer of CORE was invited to the signing ceremony but LBJ sought to snub Farmer and only reluctantly acknowledged him. Julian Bond of SNCC commented in 1968 that, 'The '64 and '65 Civil Rights Acts took the pressure off the country. People weren't as concerned about civil rights because they figured they'd done what they should do for it' (Stoper, 1989). This view is underlined by LBJ in his memoirs where he writes that: 'With the passage of the Civil Rights Acts of 1964 and 1965 the barriers to freedom began tumbling down. At long last the legal rights of American citizens – the right to vote, to hold a job, to enter a public place, to go to school – were given concrete protection' (Johnson, 1971). In Alabama in 1964 fewer than 22 per cent of African Americans were registered voters and by 1968 it was 57 per cent and in Mississippi from 7 per cent to 59. The number of black voters had tripled (Sitkoff, 1993). And LBJ also knew that once African Americans had the

vote all parties would need their support (Woods, 2006). But not everyone
does understand.

During the years of triumphant conservatism, politicians and scholars
have tended to deride the liberal response to the challenge of the civil rights
movement. The very stridency of these attacks against liberals, federal government power, and the conservatives' attempts to repeal the Voting Rights
Act, or to dismantle the Great Society programmes, suggests rather that liberals were successful. In the 11 southern states 430,000 blacks registered to
vote in 1966. 'It was,' one South Carolinian observed, 'more than anything
else that occurred during the movement years, an expression of the will to
citizenship and responsibility of the mass of Negro Southerners – the under-
lying strength of the people that had given rise to the movement in the first
place' (Watters, 1971). Gradually segregation and denial of the vote would
become part of history. These liberal reforms brought about a quiet revolution in the South. In 1965 a white woman was murdered because a black
man was a passenger in her car but thirty years later an African American
would write a book to explain to his children that before the Civil Rights
Acts they would not have been allowed to stay in the same hotel as their
white mother (Gates, 1995). He did not tell them that in most southern
states, their parents' marriage would have been illegal, and that their daddy
might have been lynched for marrying a white woman.

Civil Rights and the Anti-Vietnam War Movement

Despite these long-term gains, the tensions between LBJ and groups such
as SCLC, CORE and SNCC were evident in 1965. Howard Zinn, the history professor and SNCC member, criticised NAACP leader Roy Wilkins
and James Farmer, leader of CORE and spokesmen of the Urban League,
for attacking SNCC's opposition to the United States intervention in Vietnam. Zinn argued: 'Movement people are perhaps in the best position to
understand just how immoral are this nation's actions in Vietnam. . . . They
understand just how much hypocrisy is wrapped up in our claim to stand
for "the free world".' Just as civil rights workers were labelled 'outside agitators' in the South, so those who fought American imperialism were dubbed
communist, a term which was the same as 'nigger,' because both were labels
which denied a person's individuality. 'SNCC always prided itself on a special honesty, on not playing it "safe", in saying exactly what it felt like saying.
Shouldn't it now say, at this crucial moment, that FREEDOM NOW must
be international?' (*The Student Voice*, 30 August 1965).

In the same month that Zinn posed the question, 'Should civil rights workers take a stand on Vietnam?', Martin Luther King Jr urged the President to stop the bombing of North Vietnam and seek negotiations with the Viet Cong. King was increasingly concerned about the under funding of Great Society programmes. He was determined to attack the problems of poverty in northern ghettos. King preferred to privately urge Johnson to change his policy in Vietnam, and he did not become a leader in the anti-war movement until 1967. It was King, not Johnson, who then broke off relations. King refused invitations to the White House.

While King left the leadership of the anti-war movement to the Students for a Democratic Society (SDS) who used the methods of sit-ins and teach-ins from their days in the civil rights movement, he still found himself at odds with LBJ over another issue – the problems of the inner cities. Johnson saw this as yet another unfair criticism of his efforts. But the Atlanta minister was determined to heighten awareness of the plight of those in the ghettos of the North. The first announcement that SCLC intended to 'close down' the city of Chicago in 1966 was made by James Bevel at Northwestern University, two weeks after the march on Selma. Five months later King and Andrew Young announced that SCLC would work with the Coordinating Council of Community Organizations and attack discrimination in housing and problems of urban poverty. Most historians have judged their efforts a failure and a defeat. Adam Fairclough shares the view of King's critics that 'white exclusiveness was an unshakeable reality, [and] to confront it head-on, from a position of political isolation was self-defeating.' It also made white liberals question 'the viability of nonviolent tactics' (Fairclough, 1987).

King Goes to Chicago

Certainly, by challenging the mayor of Chicago, Richard Daley, SCLC were taking on one of the most powerful men in the Democratic Party and threatening the liberal desire for consensus. Johnson needed the Irish American's support because it was widely believed that Daley had rigged the election of John Kennedy. In addition, challenging housing discrimination in Chicago with nonviolent protests led to white mobs and a white backlash that many liberals feared. Racial violence by white and black in the city only intensified the distrust between the city officials and the leaders of SCLC. The white residents, angry at liberal efforts to integrate their neighbourhood, stoned Martin Luther King Jr as he led a nonviolent march through Gage Park. The marchers were called 'cannibals', 'savages' and 'niggers' and one sign read, 'The only way to stop niggers is to exterminate them.' The veteran of so many struggles in the South, King told the press that he had 'never seen as much hatred and hostility on the part of so many people.' For those who knew the city's long history of racial violence, the scenes were reminiscent of the riot in 1919. And the hostility was not limited to whites. Daley, the master political tactician, announced his own poverty programme and proposals for Chicago and used 'patronage to enlarge his potent outposts in the black community. He felt strong enough to suggest that King go home to Georgia, and seven Negro ward committeemen seconded him' (Oates, 1994).

In the political fallout, a liberal congressman who had voted for the Civil Rights Act struggled for re-election and Senator Paul Douglas, who had supported fair housing legislation, was defeated by Republican Charles Percy. The beneficiary of the white backlash would be George Wallace in his 1968 campaign. The Catholic Church was divided and the Archbishop John Cody did not like King. A white supremacist priest even defied his cardinal and was elected as a city alderman.

Did the Chicago Freedom Movement make any gains? SCLC received four million dollars from the Housing and Urban Development Department, working with the Community Renewal Foundation, to rehabilitate housing in Chicago. The federal Office of Education provided a $100,000 grant for a scheme to improve the skills of Lawndale residents. There were several community groups which did effective work for several years, especially Operation Breadbasket, organised by Jesse Jackson. But the resistance of the Daley machine to the nonviolent strategy persuaded most African Americans in the city, and some whites, that the machine could not be reformed. And in 1983, activists of 1966 supported the successful challenge for mayor by the African American Harold Washington (Ralph, 1993).

The FBI and Martin Luther King Jr

The SCLC in Chicago and in Cleveland in 1967 was increasingly faced with the institutional racism of northern cities. King realised that African Americans and the poor of the cities, just as much as in the rural South, fought each other for scraps from the table. His experiences in Chicago radicalised him and he stressed the need for dramatic change in the economic structure and advocated Christian socialism (Jackson, 2007). His socialism took him further from the liberals and confirmed the view of J. Edgar Hoover of the FBI that King and his followers were a communist menace. And Hoover needed no persuading. Although he protected KKK terrorists, such as the bombers of the Birmingham 16th Street Baptist Church (see Chapter 3), Hoover was concerned only with discrediting civil rights leaders. He told the press that Bayard Rustin was a convicted homosexual and a former communist labour leader (Branch, 1998). Black Congressman, Adam Clayton Powell supported Hoover and claimed King and Rustin were sexual partners, forcing Rustin's resignation from the SCLC (D'Emilio, 2003). But King continued to work with Rustin and considered him a friend despite pressure from supporters who were concerned that the media would use these charges and Rustin's homosexuality to destroy King (Garrow, 1988). Ironically, Roy Wilkins of the NAACP did not show the trust in King that King showed towards Rustin. Instead, Wilkins fed Hoover's paranoia about King, members of SCLC, SNCC and CORE. When FBI documents were released years later, Wilkins angrily denied he had collaborated in Hoover's plan to smear King. Both of King's advisors who had had connections with the Communist Party, Rustin and Levison, did not want him to take his campaign into the northern ghettos.

In 1964, Hoover described King as a 'most notorious liar' shortly after it was announced that the Atlanta minister had been awarded the Nobel Prize, and William Sullivan of the FBI sent a letter to King describing the civil rights leader as 'a dissolute, abnormal moral imbecile' who was guilty of 'incredible evilness.' King was urged to commit suicide: 'You are done. There is but one way out for you. You better take it before your filthy, abnormal fraudulent self is bared to the nation' (Garrow, 1988). It is hardly surprising that King and his supporters had little faith in the FBI or an administration that failed to appreciate his awareness of the problems posed by ghetto poverty. He was accused of fomenting trouble. If Johnson had trusted King and his supporters, he would have been aware of the pending violence. As it was, in 1967 presidential assistants visited the major cities in the North and West and were oblivious to the dangers. After visiting cities like Detroit in May 1967 they failed to find any evidence that the situation was so bad that a massive riot would occur only two months later or that the Black Panthers even existed in Oakland, California.

The Black Panther Party, Malcolm X and Black Power

Dismissed by some as gun-toting youths the Black Panther Party was organised by Huey Newton and Bobby Seale in the Oakland, California, ghetto but took its name and symbol from rural nonviolent movement of Lowndes County Freedom Organization which registered voters in Alabama. The Panthers believed they would never 'pierce the present white power structure,' so they decided to form their separate party and elect blacks to public office (*The Student Voice*, 20 December 1966). Although the rhetoric of Black Power distressed King and alarmed many white Americans, the demands of these young men and women were not that far removed from those of King. Both believed in the institutional nature of racism in America; both believed that only massive expenditure would eradicate the endemic poverty in many parts of America; both believed that socialism provided a constructive alternative to American capitalism (Marable, 1997).

Black nationalists and black power advocates, however, disagreed with King, and others, who supported integration, about the role of the churches; they disagreed over the redemptive power of nonviolence. Black power advocates learnt from the rural black communities of Mississippi and Alabama that weapons were needed in self-defence. Their arguments were the same as those put by the National Rifle Association. The difference, as King realised, was that white folks had more guns and would be prepared to use them. And King was right when he wrote: 'Beneath all the satisfaction of a gratifying slogan, Black Power is a nihilistic philosophy born out of the conviction that the Negro can't win' (King, 1967). In addition, just as some African Americans questioned Martin Luther King Jr's appeal to nonviolence, there were an increasing number who questioned the prevailing Christian world view of the black community. The most charismatic man to challenge the SCLC's faith in nonviolence was Malcolm Little, better known as Malcolm X.

Both of his parents, Earl and Louise Little, were involved with the black nationalist movement of the 1920s headed by Marcus Garvey. This involvement led to their being driven from their home in Omaha, Nebraska, and in 1929 a white hate group torched their home in Lansing, Michigan. Malcolm would claim later that his father had been lynched by a white mob but there is no evidence for this. On the other hand there is much evidence from Malcolm and others that he was subjected to harsh punishment by his father. Despite claims about the profound influence of Garveyism on Malcolm Little, there is little evidence for this and Malcolm's youth was spent in petty crime, robbery, drug abuse and pimping. During a stay in prison he met a member of the Nation of Islam, or Black Muslims, and was converted. He dropped his 'slave name' Little and replaced it with X.

Although a small sect founded in 1930, the Nation of Islam grew in the northern cities in the 1950s. The religious views of the Muslims were based on the arguments of its leader, Elijah Muhammad. Unlike the teachings of the Koran, Elijah Muhammad argued that Allah had made all people black and that it was the evil acts of a black chemist that created the white race. Allah in his anger swore that his chosen black people would be enslaved by the white devils but at the time of judgement the whites would be destroyed. It has been suggested that the fact that Malcolm X 'used vituperative language against whites did not mean that he hated whites or that he was trying to make blacks hate them. Rather his purpose was to wake up blacks to the need to love each other' (Cone, 1993).

Whatever his intentions were when he was a disciple of Elijah Muhammad, his attacks on white devils and his demand for segregation not only frightened and angered white conservatives – they had the same effect on white liberals. Additionally, the strong anti-Jewish attacks, a central theme of the Black Muslims, was accepted by the wider black nationalist movement. It re-enforced the old anti-Jewish belief held by many black (and white Christians) that all Jews were 'Christ-killers.' Cultural black nationalists such as Ron Karenga and LeRoy Jones (Imamu Imiri Barraka) shared these anti-Semitic views and the alliance of Jewish Americans and African Americans was severely damaged as a result. Malcolm X's call for black segregation was espoused by the 500 members of the Republic of New Africa who demanded that five states should be handed over to the black people of the United States (Tugaloo Digital Collection, 2009).

Before he was assassinated in 1965, Malcolm X visited Mecca where he discovered that Muslims came in every colour. It has been suggested that Malcolm was reluctant to leave Elijah Muhammad (Cone, 1993), but upon his return from Mecca he set up his own mosque based on Sunni Muslim belief. He argued that black and white Americans should struggle to overcome the oppression of racism. In comparing African Americans and Jews, Malcolm X maintained: 'The biggest difference between the parallel oppression of the Jew and the Negro is that the Jew never lost his pride. He knew he had made a significant contribution to the world, and his sense of his own value gave him the courage to fight back. It enabled him to act and think independently, unlike our people and our leaders' (Dyson, 1995). And eventually Malcolm even apologised for his bitter assaults on Martin Luther King Jr. His murder, probably by fellow Muslims, means that we will never know if he could have worked with King and the SCLC. Unfortunately in recent years it is the early Malcolm that is heard in the speeches of Louis Farrakan, the current head of the Nation of Islam, and not the Malcolm of reconciliation who returned from Mecca.

Black Nationalism and Black Women

Black nationalism emphasised the secondary status of women. It was the conventional view of historians and sociologists that the black male had suffered the most from the institution of slavery. The male slave's leadership in a patriarchal society had always been denied because the institution of marriage was forbidden. The ultimate power always rested with the master not the slave. Black Nationalists took particular exception to this view as expressed in the 1965 report on the *Negro Family* authored by Daniel Patrick Moynihan. 'In essence the Negro community,' according to Moynihan, 'has been forced into a matriarchal structure which, because it is out of line with the rest of American society, seriously retards the progress of the group as a whole and imposes a crushing burden on the Negro male and, in consequence, on a great many Negro women as well.' As Davis argues: 'The controversial finale of the Moynihan Report was a call to introduce male authority (meaning male supremacy of course!) into the Black family and the community at large' (Davis, 1994). Paula Giddings points out, 'The Moynihan Report was not so much racist as it was sexist' (Giddings, 1984).

It was not only white sociologists such as Moynihan who advocated a black patriarchy in the later sixties. Exponents of Black Power in SNCC and other organisations such as the Black Muslims were also sexist. Angela Davis was criticised by black cultural nationalist leader Ron Karenga in San Diego for taking an active role in organising a rally in 1967: 'A woman was supposed to "inspire" her man and educate his children.' She recalls that when she had a prominent role with SNCC in Los Angeles this caused resentment: 'By playing such a leading role in the organization, some of them insisted we were aiding and abetting the enemy, who wanted to see Black men weak and unable to hold their own' (Davis, 1988).

Pauli Murray, black activist, academic, lawyer, lesbian-feminist, poet and Episcopal priest, was alienated by black power advocates at Brandeis University and she saw her white colleagues' willingness to have a Black Studies programme as cynical and an all-black teaching staff as intellectually wrong. Although alienated by the 'coercive power' of young militants, she admits: 'the black consciousness movement was the transformation of a people robbed of a prideful past, the retrieval of a communal history that had long been ignored, the affirmation of a positive identity after centuries of denigration, and the flowering of a racially inspired art, music, literature and scientific achievement.' And she recognised, 'my barely disguised hostility toward the Black Revolution was in reality my feminist resentment of the crude sexism I perceived in many of the leaders of that movement' (Murray, 1989). A founder member of the National Organization for Women (NOW), she was an activist until her death in 1985.

Paula Giddings shows that Black Muslims 'in an era of male revolt' insisted that black women should be 'submissive' and that black men should not allow black women on the streets alone because Elijah Muhammad, the spiritual leader of the Muslims, maintained females are 'given to evil and sin while men are noble and given to righteousness.' She attacks the views of Baraka who demanded that black women should be submissive to the 'wiser' black man. According to Giddings, 'It was but a short step from this sort of thinking to advocate that women remain politically barefoot and literally pregnant' (Giddings, 1984). As Davis discovered during her work for SNCC in Los Angeles: 'It was a period in which one of the unfortunate hallmarks of some nationalist groups was their determination to push women into the background' (Davis, 1988).

Many black men who were not nationalists resented the role played by black women in the movement. A King co-worker stated, 'Martin ... was absolutely a male chauvinist' (Oates, 1994). In part, this was due to the tradition in which many black women were encouraged to get a good education because black families believed that daughters suffered less discrimination in employment than their sons. Black women's role as major breadwinners resulted in tensions with the women's movement. The latter failed to understand black women were *relatively* successful when they were faced with the double discrimination of being black and women and 'the failure effectively to challenge Moynihan's solution [black patriarchy], with all its implications, retarded both movements' (Giddings, 1984). Black women later rebelled against black male patriarchy. President Johnson's response to the challenge of Black Power was to say that he was 'not interested in black power or white power.' As he reflected later, it was an easy remark for a white person to make and he acknowledged: 'Black power had a different meaning to the black man, who until recently had had to seek the white world's approval and for whom success had come largely on white people's terms. To such a man, black power meant a great deal more in areas that mattered the most – dignity, pride, and self-awareness' (Johnson, 1971). It is a pity he did act on this sensitivity when he was in the White House. But assailed by many for his policies in Vietnam, Johnson could not take criticism from people who did not share his liberal beliefs and values (Woods, 2006).

The President was even more aggrieved when his National Advisory Commission on Civil Disorders reported on the cause of the urban riots. Headed by Otto Kerner, the Democratic governor of Illinois, the Commission was carefully selected to reflect Johnson's desire to maintain a consensus between the two main parties. The appointment of Roy Wilkins of the NAACP and black Republican Senator Edward Brooke also reflected his faith in moderate leaders. His anger was thus the greater when the report blamed the riots on white racism and recommended a massive federal spending programme. Johnson claimed that to meet the report's recommendation would have required an additional '$30 billion, in addition to the $30 billion plus already in the budget for the poor.' Such a figure he believed was unrealistic and he argued later: 'Setting such an unattainable goal could easily have produced a negative reaction that in turn might have endangered funds for the many invaluable programs we had fought so long to establish and were trying so hard to strengthen and expand' (Johnson, 1971).

Whatever the doubts and grievances felt by the President, King believed Johnson was responsible for America's tragic involvement in the Vietnam War which was undermining the triumphs of the movement. After his first criticism of the war at a press conference in 1965, he spoke to an anti-war meeting at the Riverside Church in New York City in 1967. 'A few years ago there was a shining moment in that struggle. It seemed as if there was a real promise of hope for the poor – both black and white – through the Poverty Program. There were experiments, new beginnings.' However, as the war escalated these initiatives were 'eviscerated as if it were some idle political plaything of a society gone mad on war.' It was the poor regardless of race who were the cannon fodder of the war and yet they still could not go to school together and so long as their own government was 'the greatest purveyor of violence in the world today' he could not criticise violence in American ghettos (Oates, 1994). King decided to fight the backlash from conservatives and black nationalists by highlighting the fact that it was the poor, black and white, who suffered disproportionately on the battlefields of Vietnam. Poverty and discrimination were not just problems for African Americans.

Politicians and the American affluent middle class had to be made to understand that the majority of the poor and illiterate in the United States were white, brown and red. The liberal Great Society reforms with all their strengths and weaknesses were not programmes to benefit blacks only. King planned another march on Washington but this was to be a rainbow coalition of the disadvantaged. The Poor People's Campaign would involve Native Americans, Mexican Americans and poor whites as well as African Americans and they would live in Resurrection City in the capital until legislators acted.

Murder in Memphis

King never led the march. Flying to Memphis, Tennessee, at the request of his friend the Reverend James Lawson, King gave his support to striking garbage workers. On the second visit on 3 April 1968, he recalled how he had almost died in 1959 after he had been stabbed while on a visit to New York. He referred to a letter he had had from a young white girl who wrote: 'I read in the paper of your misfortune and of your suffering. And I read that if you sneezed you would have died. And I'm simply writing you to say that I'm so happy that you didn't sneeze.' And King continually reiterated that he was pleased that he did not sneeze because if he had, he would not have seen the advances they had made. As for the future, they would triumph despite 'the difficult days ahead.' He only wanted to do God's will. 'And He's allowed me to go up to the mountain top. And I've looked over. And I've seen the promised land. And I'm happy tonight. I'm not worried about anything. I'm not fearing any man. Mine eyes have seen the glory of the coming of the Lord' (Washington, 1991).

The next morning, standing on the balcony of the Lorraine Motel, Martin Luther King Jr was assassinated. America had lost the greatest black spokesman of the century, a man who could explain with a calm passion the meaning of the civil rights struggle to many indifferent Americans in speeches that would transform the lives of many of them and who also could speak with the emotional fervour of an Old Testament prophet that would galvanise black congregations to follow the nonviolent road to justice. Everyone who heard his last sermon was certain, that like Moses, he had been to the mountain top and seen the promised land.

But even many supporters agreed with Bayard Rustin's harsh assessment. 'I knew Martin very well... but he did not have the ability to organize vampires to go to a bloodbath' (D'Emilio, 2003). However, the lack of formal structure in the SCLC had its advantages as Adam Fairclough has argued but it also meant King was continually reacting to unexpected local demands for his time. He went to Memphis to help an old friend, Reverend Lawson, who was engaged in a bitter battle with that cities authorities who refused to recognise the right of sanitation workers to form a union. King realised that to achieve his ambition he had to go further and transform the struggle from civil rights to human rights and unite with labour (Honey, 2007; Jackson, 2007). But it also meant he could not concentrate on his major project the Poor People's Campaign. Recent scholarship has emphasised the role of local individuals and groups and has criticised the 'top down approach' (Payne, 1996). However, local activists were frequently divided by personal feuds, battles for federal assistance and often turned to outsiders for help. Although Medgar Evers reluctantly succumbed to pressure from Roy Wilkins to exclude SCLC from Mississippi, Evers and other NAACP local activists were inspired by King. Mississippi groups, such as the Poor People's Corporation, sought to liberate the black community with cooperative farming but 'poverty was so endemic that only the federal government had sufficient resources to combat the problem' (Dittmer, 1995). These squabbles, the economic poverty of grassroots' activists and lack of formal SCLC organisation meant a lack of preparation and King was often exhausted. A reluctant leader, King exposed the hypocrisy of American democracy but he had witnessed a revolution.

Despite appeals for calm, rioting swept across the United States. For a week 100 towns and cities saw major riots, with 46 killed, 3000 injured and 27,000 arrested. It took 21,000 federal troops and 34,000 National Guardsmen to restore order after $45 million worth of property had been damaged. Congress, which earlier had defeated a minor budget measure for rat control in the slums (sneeringly dubbed a 'civil-rats bill'), did pass a weak fair-housing bill following the assassination. Although discrimination in renting or buying houses was made illegal, it was up to individuals to act. The legislation included a clause to appease whites because incitement to riot was now listed as a serious federal offence. It was a far cry from the early years of the administration when 60 education acts, including the Headstart programme, and the Medicare and Medicaid legislation which did so much to help in the education and health of some of the poorest citizens in America were enacted.

One student of the Johnson presidency has assessed LBJ's support for the civil rights movement. On the question of racial justice, he writes that: 'No president, not even Abraham Lincoln, had so forthrightly identified himself with the Constitution, and with the values of the country with the cause for equal rights for African Americans' (Woods, 2006). However, it was not simply disillusionment and anger that alienated so many from a president who had sought to do so much. Many who had benefited from the liberal reforms turned to Johnson's arch enemy, Robert Kennedy. As the New York Senator's friend wrote later: 'He [Johnson] had always known that, as in the classic Hollywood western, there would be the inevitable walk down through the long silent street at high noon, and Robert Kennedy would be waiting for him' (Schlesinger, 1979). Robert Kennedy believed he could re-unite the country, end the violence and heal the rift between white and black. His conviction was born in a belief that John was the martyr for civil rights and nurtured by a hatred for LBJ that dated back to the ferocious fight to win

JFK's nomination and LBJ's refusal to offer Robert the vice presidency in 1964 (Woods, 2006).

Despite triumphs such as the Voting Rights Act, tragedy struck again. For many millions of the disadvantaged, especially African Americans, Robert Kennedy was the last white politician they felt they could trust. He had seemed genuinely interested in their plight, wanting to renew their faith that the American Dream could become a reality. When he broke the news of King's assassination to a black crowd in an Indianapolis ghetto, he said he understood that some would hate white people but reminded them that a white man had killed his brother. In the dark cold night he looked down from the back of a flatbed truck and said: 'My favorite poet was Aeschylus'. He wrote: 'In our sleep pain which cannot forget falls drop by drop upon the heart until in our own despair, against our will, comes wisdom through the awful grace of God.' He moved on to campaign in California. At a victory rally in Los Angeles after winning the primary he said, 'We are a great country, an unselfish country and a compassionate country. I intend to make that my basis for running' (Schlesinger Jr, 1979). Moments later he was assassinated and in his last speech he failed to credit LBJ's achievements. On 12 December 1972, shortly before his death, Johnson told a meeting: '[To] be black in a white society is not to stand on level and equal ground. While the races may stand side by side, whites stand on history's mountain and blacks stand in history's hollow. We must overcome unequal history before we overcome unequal opportunity' (Woods, 2006).

Johnson's quiet revolution had had dramatic effects, especially on his beloved South, despite his fears that his war on racism and poverty might result in resurgent conservatism.

5

THE NEW RIGHT AND CIVIL RIGHTS

For those caught up in the civil rights movement, 1968 seemed to be the year the rule of the old elite was coming to an end. In Northern Ireland, France, Germany and Japan students seemed to be in the vanguard of a major revolution that would sweep away the old liberal and conservative establishments. Johnson had refused to seek re-election, the Democratic candidate and liberal Vice President Hubert Humphrey campaigned on the 'politics of joy' and the voice of the new conservatism was the deeply distrusted former Vice President, Richard M. Nixon. Humphrey had to rely on LBJ and the boss of Chicago, Mayor Richard Daley, at the Democratic convention in Chicago. After Robert Kennedy's murder in Los Angeles, the first senator to challenge LBJ, Eugene McCarthy of Minnesota, was still in the nomination race and his popularity was rising. But he failed to win over the Kennedy supporters and behaved more as a spectator of events rather than someone trying to shape and mould them and as a result many delegates supported the anti-war senator from South Dakota, George McGovern.

Chicago, 1968

At the Democratic Party convention, millions of American viewers saw the ruthless assault on anti-war protesters in the convention hall by Daley's lieutenants and in the streets by his police force. The most trusted man in America was CBS newsman, Walter Cronkite, who watched helplessly while one of the CBS news team was beaten up in the convention. Cronkite deplored what he called 'fascist' tactics. Under pressure from his bosses, he gave Daley an easy time in an interview the next day in which Daley claimed that the police were upholding law and order in response to violent assault from hippies and others. For many Democrats, such as Senator Abraham Ribicoff, the tactics of Daley were reminiscent of the Gestapo. The majority of Americans, however, would have agreed with LBJ about the radicals. The President had wanted, in his own words, 'to get them by the balls.'

George Wallace of Alabama was determined to appeal to the growing numbers of voters who were alienated by the civil rights movement – not just southerners but blue collar workers in the North. He ran for the presidency as an American Party candidate. Eager to attract sufficient support to throw the election into the House of Representatives, Wallace combined his racism with a populist assault on banks, Wall Street and federal government bureaucrats. Unfortunately for Wallace, he chose as his running mate the outspoken retired Air Force General Curtis LeMay. The general's desire 'to bomb the North Vietnamese into the Stone Age' scared some Wallace supporters, and the general's support for civil rights, citing the armed services as the ideal integrated society, angered others. Disillusioned Wallace supporters either drifted back to the Democratic Party or turned to the man who had returned from the politically dead – Richard Nixon.

Nixon had been defeated in 1960 by the narrowest of margins by John Kennedy, and his hatred for the Kennedys was deep and lasting (Kutler, 1998). In 1962 he lost his bid for governor of California; the disgruntled candidate told the press: 'You won't have Nixon to kick around anymore.' But whatever pleasure the journalists may have gained from writing his political obituary, Nixon never gave up his quest for the presidency (Ambrose, 1989). He hoped the party would turn to him in 1964, but they preferred Goldwater, and following the defeat of the conservative cause, those same journalists were writing the obituary of the party itself.

Meanwhile Richard Nixon methodically travelled the 'rubber chicken and green pea circuit,' talking to American Legion groups and frightened suburbanites. As the civil rights marches continued and young Americans protested against the war in Vietnam, Nixon spoke to angry and scared white people and reassured them that they were the 'silent majority' and that civil rights workers, communists and radicals should not take the law into their own hands.

For Nixon the great achievement of Martin Luther King Jr was that 'he worked to resist extremists in the movement, those who wished to resort to violence to reach their goals.' Nixon was confident that it was pressure from these 'extremists' that 'sometimes caused him [King] to be more extreme in his public views than he otherwise would have been' and in his memoirs the disgraced former President admitted that King's 'death left black America without a nationally recognized leader who combined responsibility with charisma.' And while others might be 'reasonably effective' he was sure that 'none could match his mystique and his ability to inspire people – white as well as black – and to move them' (Nixon, 1978). But he did not condemn the failure of southern states to fulfil their constitutional duties and their reluctance to protect the lives and rights of African American citizens. And the reason is given by his closest advisor, Bob Haldeman, who noted in his diary after a meeting with President Nixon in 1969, *'Went through his whole thesis re: blacks and their genetic inferiority'* (Perlstein, 2008).

Nixon's Southern Strategy

Whatever qualified praise he had for King in later years, Nixon knew that opinion polls which excluded Wallace showed the vast majority of the Alabama governor's supporters preferred him to be president. The southern strategy adopted by the Republicans was not to attack George Wallace, as Humphrey did, but to argue that a vote for Wallace was a wasted vote. While Nixon was prepared to concede the Deep South states to the Alabama governor, he was determined to win the border states of Tennessee, Kentucky and Virginia as well as the Carolinas and Florida (Nixon, 1978). To ensure the success of his southern strategy, Nixon chose the Governor of Maryland, Spiro Agnew, as his vice presidential candidate because the Governor, after the Baltimore riots in 1968, had denounced the black leadership as 'Hanoi-visiting...caterwauling, riot-inciting, burn-America-down type of leaders.' When informed about this outburst Nixon's response was: 'That guy Agnew is really an impressive fellow. He's got guts. He's got a good attitude' (Ambrose, 1989).

Leaving Agnew to attack Humphrey as 'soft on communism' and 'soft on crime,' Nixon wrapped himself in the American flag and appealed to the wounded nationalism of the American electorate. He told a cheering crowd in Springfield, Ohio: 'We must gain respect for America in the world. A burned American library, a desecrated flag, a ship captured by international outlaws on the high seas – these are the events which in effect squeeze the trigger which fires the rifle which kills young Americans.' As Humphrey gained in the polls, Nixon attacked the Great Society programmes' attempts to deal with poverty – poverty which Democrats believed was a major cause of crime. Johnson's 'war on poverty was not a war on crime' according to Nixon, 'and it was no substitute for a war on crime' (Nixon, 1978).

Central to Nixon's law-and-order strategy was an attack on the Supreme Court. He attacked the 1966 *Miranda v Arizona* decision in which the court insisted that suspects must be notified about their rights upon arrest. For Nixon the mid-sixties was a time when a 'new liberalism was fashionable, in which there appeared to be more concern for the rights of the accused than for the protection of the innocent' (Nixon, 1978). In addition, in an appeal to southerners, Nixon argued that the Court should follow a strict construction of the Constitution, an argument that southerners had used against the earlier rulings of the Court such as *Brown*. He assured southerners and northerners opposed to integration of schools that he would not withhold federal funds from school districts that were slow in complying with the court ruling (Blum, 1991). As a student of massive resistance to civil rights has argued, 'the façade of unified southern resistance crumbled into its constituent parts, leaving only those that were sufficiently subtle in their approach, or that had chosen to encode overtly racist appeals in such a way to make them palatable to a broader, non-sectional audience to continue their work and to merge almost imperceptibly into a steadily evolving national landscape' (Lewis, 2006).

And Nixon knew this audience. In 1968 after the black athletes' protest at the Mexico Olympics and riots in New York, Los Angeles, Detroit and Newark, black efforts to highlight their problems were portrayed as attacks on patriotism and law and order. In a national radio address, Nixon warned that 'we face the prospect of war in the making on our society. We have seen the gathering hate, we have heard the threats to burn and bomb and destroy.' The riots were the beginning of an 'insurrection' and force should be met by force. Nixon said the nation understood the 'resentments' and 'grievances long suppressed. But that lesson has been learned.' He claimed that further disturbances 'could engulf not only the cities, but all the racial progress made in these troubled years. . . .' The carefully crafted speech made the white nation believe they had 'given' blacks their rights. Nixon had not denounced riots in the South, the Klan and its murders, riots by whites in Chicago and Boston. In the coming race war 'Richard Nixon cast himself as the white side's field marshal' (Perlstein, 2008). With the apparent triumph of the southern strategy, later Republicans and their advisors, Lee Atwater, Carl Rove and Bush father and son used less coded ways to link law and order and race.

Despite Humphrey's remarkable fight, Nixon was elected. In the popular vote Nixon received 43.4 per cent and Humphrey 42.7. George Wallace got

13.5 per cent and all the polls indicated that if he had not been a candidate, most of his vote would have gone to Nixon. The result therefore was not as close a decision as it seems, but rather reflected a marked shift to the right in which blue collar workers in the North deserted the Democratic Party despite the efforts of union leaders in the AFL-CIO.

Nixon as President, although serious and intelligent, was an isolated figure who had passionate hatreds for intellectuals, dissenters and critics, especially the press and television. Barry Goldwater, the Republican presidential candidate in 1964, claimed that Nixon was the most dishonest person he had ever known and that Nixon would readily lie to his wife, family, the Republican Party, the American people and even the world. And his attitude towards African Americans was not promising. During his campaign in 1960, he had complained that he would have to give a speech on 'all that welfare crap' and in 1967 he wrote in the *Reader's Digest* that America 'far from being a great society, ours is becoming a lawless society.' According to Nixon the cause was the tolerance of lawlessness, not by Mississippi sheriffs, but rather civil rights groups which were aided by universities 'where civil disobedience may begin and where it must end' (Ambrose, 1989).

SCLC and the Charleston Hospital Workers' Strike

And Nixon's southern strategy was tested early in his presidency when South Carolina officials in Charleston refused to settle a hospital workers' strike for a wage increase from $1.30 an hour. Although there was a history of civil rights achievements in South Carolina, especially the voter registration work of Septima Clark, the state and the city were obdurate in the face of change. It was to be the battleground for the last success by African Americans using the methods of early struggles such as in Montgomery. As Andrew Young, a long-time civil rights worker, has admitted, 'In 1969, the increasingly contentious staff at SCLC was saved from the jaws of total disintegration once again by the timely strike of black hospital workers in Charleston, South Carolina' (Young, 1996).

The action was co-ordinated by the local churches and labour unions using boycotts and publicity to advance the claims of the hospital workers for union membership. With no local union to help, they turned to a branch of the Retail, Wholesale and Department Store Workers Union (AFL-CIO), based in New York. And as soon as the Medical College administration found out on 20 March 1969, they dismissed the 12 leaders who were recruiting staff to join the union. As a result 450 walked off their jobs and were fired.

Financial assistance came from the northern union and union leaders such as Walter Reuther, of the United Auto Workers. Meetings were held in the Morris Brown United Methodist Church under the leadership of the Reverend John Goodwin, and Septima Clark was on the local committee to help the strikers. Boycotts of downtown Charleston hurt local businessmen – an estimated $15 million in tourist income alone – and textile leaders grew alarmed that union organisation might spread to their non-unionised plants. On 26 June 1969 union recognition was granted, employers introduced a dues check off system and the dismissed workers were re-instated. 'As in Memphis, the strength of the Charleston movement relied upon a coalition between workers and churches, with the clergy sharing leadership roles with the spokespersons for the workers.'

> But sadly, Charleston was the first and last partnership of this type, and the last major campaign waged by SCLC. We had hoped that Charleston would be the beginning of something new; but it turned out to be the end of the direct-action phase of the movement for us, and of the application of direct-action techniques developed in the sixties. (Young, 1996)

Although this might be true for SCLC and the black civil rights movement as defined by the 1960s, African Americans were active in the anti-Vietnam War demonstrations and sit-ins. White and black civil rights workers knew only too well that it was the poor and the black who suffered the highest casualties in the American army. The killing of students at Kent State by the Ohio National Guard and at Jackson State University in Mississippi by state troopers led to a nation-wide strike by university students. Mass protest did not die in 1969.

Nixon and Abernathy

Nixon's first meeting with one of the leaders of civil disobedience was not auspicious. Ralph Abernathy, the new leader of SCLC following the murder of Martin Luther King Jr, had first sought a meeting with Nixon when the President was on a trip to South Carolina. Abernathy was helping the Charleston hospital workers and when Nixon declined the meeting, Abernathy sent students to demonstrate and heighten awareness of the workers' problems. The students were arrested. On 13 May 1970, Abernathy flew to Washington for a meeting with Nixon at the White House. It was disastrous.

In his memoirs Nixon ascribes the failure of the meeting to Abernathy and his associates. Nixon calls it a 'shambles' because the black minister was 'either unprepared or unwilling, or both, to have a serious discussion. Instead he postured and made speeches. He began by reading a list of demands and spent the rest of the time restating them in more colorful ways. Nonetheless he seemed pleased that we had made the effort and at the end he thanked me profusely for taking the time to meet with them' (Nixon, 1978). To be fair to Abernathy, Nixon's own racist views influenced his recollections of the meeting. In an early White House tape, Nixon says about hiring blacks: 'With blacks you can usually settle for an incompetent because there are just not enough competent ones. And so you put incompetents in and get along with them, because the symbolism is vitally important. You have to show you care' (Summers, 2000). Perhaps his concern for 'symbolism' later persuaded him to appoint the first black Assistant Secretary of the Navy, a black admiral and another African American as chairman of the Federal Communications Commission (Summers, 2000).

Certainly, Nixon was not amused when Abernathy left the meeting and told the press that it was one of the most 'fruitless' he had ever attended. According to Nixon, he (Nixon) reassured his advisor Daniel Patrick Moynihan that it was actions not words that would demonstrate his sincerity. He does not refer to the note he sent to his advisors John Ehrlichman and H. R. Haldeman in which he wrote: 'This shows that my judgement about *not* seeing such people is right. No more of This!' (Ambrose, 1989). As for Abernathy, he writes that he was convinced that Moynihan and others were 'full of earnest resolve and high blown rhetoric.' But he was not fooled. 'They had been so certain that their economic double-talk had mesmerized all of us' (Abernathy, 1989).

Following the meeting with Abernathy, Moynihan wrote to Nixon: 'The time may have come when the issue of race could benefit from a period of "benign neglect". The subject has been too much talked about.' For Moynihan the debate was controlled 'by hysterics, paranoids and boodlers on all sides. We need a period in which Negro progress continues and racial rhetoric fades' (Ambrose, 1989). Nixon said the phrase 'benign neglect' was taken out of context by his critics in the media and Congress. And in his own defence, he points with pride to his affirmative action programme (Nixon, 1978).

Nixon and Affirmative Action

Although opposed to quotas in job hiring he was determined that all federal contractors would hire more minority workers. Each contractor had to set a goal for affirmative action and federally funded construction projects in Philadelphia were targeted with the intention of increasing minority workers from 4 per cent to 26 per cent. Conservatives argued that Title VI of the Civil Rights Act prohibited affirmative action. The proposals as laid out in the Philadelphia Plan violated the Act which stipulated that no one could be denied the benefits of federal financial assistance based on race, colour or national origin. According to Nixon he was attacked by Congressional conservatives, and Everett Dirksen informed him bluntly: 'As your leader in the Senate of the United States, it is my bounden duty to tell you that this thing is about as popular as a crab in a whorehouse.' The proposal would split the Republican Party and as party leader in the Senate he could not support it (Nixon, 1978).

Nixon ignored his advice. Affirmative action was introduced in October 1969 at a federally funded hospital project and was extended to building trades unions in New York, Pittsburgh, Seattle, Los Angeles, St. Louis, San Francisco, Boston, Chicago and Detroit. Nixon fought off opposition in Congress and from George Meany, the leader of the AFL-CIO. By 1972 the plan was extended beyond the construction industry to over 300,000 firms. Nixon recalled his disappointment with the 'luke warm support from most of the national black leaders who tended either to minimize the results we had achieved, or to complain that we had not gone far enough.' His response to this criticism was 'to wonder whether the black leadership was not more interested in dramatic tokenism than in the hard fight for actual progress' (Nixon, 1978; Graham, 1994).

Why would a conservative president dramatically expand a policy first outlined by the liberal LBJ in an executive order in 1965? According to one scholar it is not as paradoxical as it appears. 'Faced with growing urban violence, government leaders sought to fend off social chaos by launching benefit programs with quick and visible payoffs.' However, it was not just the pressure of civil rights groups or the courts which prompted Nixon to act. One of the main reasons was his desire to punish organised labour which had led the opposition to his nomination to the Supreme Court of Judge C. F. Haynsworth of South Carolina. In addition, he wanted to break the coalition of the AFL-CIO and civil rights groups because unions would seek to maintain their seniority system and control over labour contracts, whereas African Americans would support his programme as a way of breaking down institutional racism. In the process Nixon would destroy the New Deal alliance which had maintained the Democrats as the majority party. By advocating black capitalism he was confident that he would build a black middle class that would return to the Republican Party. But most important of all was the intent to ensure Republican control of the Congress, the White House and the federal judiciary (Graham, 1994).

Supreme Court Nominations

Nixon used Supreme Court appointments as part of his southern strategy and not merely to appoint more conservative justices. He described liberal Supreme Court judges with what he admitted was 'colorful language' and particularly disliked Thurgood Marshall, appointed to the Supreme Court by LBJ. Three he considered 'real boobs', and 'Marshall was just there because he's black' (Kutler, 1998). With the defeat of Haynsworth, Nixon decided 'to settle for an incompetent' and defied the advice of many leading lawyers and law professors and submitted the name of Judge G. Harrold Carswell for the vacancy on the Court. Without doubt he was the worst nominee to the Court in history. A life-long segregationist, Carswell's rulings on the circuit court in Florida reflected his racism and most of his decisions had been overruled by the Supreme Court. Even a sympathetic biographer of Nixon admits, 'his qualifications for the high court were simply nonexistent' (Ambrose, 1989). Nixon supporter Roman Hruska (Republican senator from Nebraska) declared in Carswell's defence that because many Americans were mediocre, they should have a representative on the Court!

Nixon continually denied Carswell was a racist and despite warnings from his party, pushed ahead in April 1970 with the nomination knowing it would be defeated. When it was, the President called a news conference and lashed senators for voting against good southerners and intelligent conservatives. 'When you strip away all the hypocrisy, the real reason for their rejection was their legal philosophy ... and also the accident of their birth, the fact that they were born in the South.' He was determined he would never nominate another southerner because it was not fair they should face such 'character assassination.' And he concluded: 'I understand the bitter feeling of millions of Americans who live in the South about the act of regional discrimination that took place in the Senate yesterday.' Nixon always defended his nominee, dismissing Carswell's support of segregation as 'youthful indiscretions' and maintaining that he still believed that 'Carswell would have passed muster by the standards of other times' (Nixon, 1978). As Nixon's biographer rightly points out, it was the South that was insulted by the nomination of Carswell, as if this fourth-rate judge was the best the South could offer. Senator Albert Gore Sr of Tennessee voted against Haynsworth and Carswell because they were totally unqualified. He considered Carswell's nomination as 'an assault on the integrity of the Senate' (Ambrose, 1989). Consequently, Gore was one of the first casualties of the southern strategy. Nixon illegally funnelled large sums of money to Gore's opponent, William Brock, who exploited Gore's liberal positions, especially on civil rights.

The nominations of strict constructionist and right-wing judges and his opposition to making Martin Luther King Jr's birthday a national holiday were all part of Nixon's gestures to win over southern white voters. It was the politics of symbolism. On reading the proposal for a national holiday, Nixon wrote, 'No! Never!' Stephen Ambrose argues, 'the South wanted more than symbolic defiance' (Ambrose, 1989). Nixon was soon given the opportunity to advance his appeal to the South and at the same time continue his efforts to discredit the Supreme Court.

School Desegregation

His first attempt to deliver tangible benefits for most white southern politicians failed disastrously. The Secretary of Health, Education and Welfare (HEW), Robert Finch, had approved a plan for the desegregation of Mississippi schools which, if the state failed to comply, would result in loss of federal funding. Senator John Stennis of Mississippi demanded that the policy be reversed and Nixon forced Finch to go to the courts and request a delay of the plan. Faced with continued non-compliance, the Supreme Court in *Alexander v Holmes County Board of Education* ruled that *Brown II*, requiring compliance 'with all deliberate speed', no longer applied and ordered the immediate end of the dual school system. The solution for Nixon's dilemma came from the Attorney General of the United States, John Mitchell, who argued that desegregation should be left to the judicial process 'because seeking injunctions and bringing lawsuits was not only a slower, more careful procedure but would place the onus of enforcement on the courts instead of the White House.' The wrath of southerners would be deflected onto the hated federal courts (Greene, 1992).

This proved to be valuable advice. The federal courts were impatient with the tardy compliance with its rulings on desegregation, were determined to speed up the process. Whites in the South had maintained virtually segregated schools by devices such as allowing families to choose their children's school and this 'freedom of choice' was ensured by bussing white children to white schools. In 1970 a North Carolina federal judge ordered bussing across Charlotte to ensure compliance with *Brown*. In 1971 the Supreme Court upheld the ruling in *Swann v Charlotte-Mecklenburg*.

Nixon opposed bussing of school children between school districts in order to achieve desegregation. Of course, millions had been bussed in every American state for years, and it was viewed as a positive benefit because it allowed for consolidation of schools, especially in rural areas, which enabled bigger schools to offer a better education for their pupils. Now bussing was associated with race and the slogan was, 'No forced bussing.' In the Department of HEW, which had responsibility to enforce the *Brown* rulings under the 1964 Civil Rights Act, there were many who were eager to support the courts but felt that the administration and Nixon in particular were preventing them from achieving the goal of desegregation. One hundred and twenty-five HEW workers resigned and in response in March 1970 Nixon issued a statement supporting desegregation but opposing bussing (Ambrose, 1989). In his memoirs he reiterates statements he had made as President: 'I felt obliged to uphold the law; but I did not feel obliged to do any more than the minimum the law required, while hoping that the Court would eventually see how its well-intentioned ruling was both legally and socially counterproductive' (Nixon, 1978).

Throughout the next few years he reassured conservatives such as John Tower of Texas, Strom Thurmond of South Carolina and Richard Russell of Georgia that he would do everything possible to curtail the activities of HEW officials and in a memo to John Erlichman on 28 January 1972 he wrote, 'I believe there may be some doubt as to the validity of the Brown philosophy that integrating education will pull up the blacks and not pull down the whites.' But on another issue there was no doubt 'that education requiring excessive transportation of students is definitely inferior.' He insisted that his views on race were 'ultraliberal' and he was correct in opposing 'forced integration of education and housing.' He maintained he was not motivated by politics and that he directed $2.5 billion towards improving schools (Nixon, 1978). He fails to point out that he proposed a 'moratorium' on court orders requiring bussing until 1973 and that many of his attempts to fund schools were efforts to support the various segregationist academies that had sprung up over the South as the wealthier whites withdrew from the public education system.

The immediate result of the Court's rulings and Nixon's inability to thwart them resulted in the rapid integration of southern schools. When Nixon came into office 68 per cent of African American school children were attending segregated schools in the South. By the time he was forced to leave the White House in 1974 it was only eight per cent (Greene, 1992). And it is the courts that should get the credit, because, as Nixon planned, it was they who took the blame.

Bussing and Desegregation in Northern Schools

The courts came under assault in the North as well as the South. And efforts by the court to break *de facto* segregation in northern cities failed. The desegregation of schools became a major issue in the election campaign of 1972 and would help Nixon's plan to destroy the New Deal coalition shaped by Roosevelt in the thirties.

Ironically, in June 1974, when Richard Nixon was fighting for his political life in the Watergate crisis, a federal judge attacked the public school system of Boston, Massachusetts, as segregated because blacks were confined to inferior schools which were poorly equipped and staffed by inadequate teachers. Black students were to be bussed into South Boston. The consequences were similar to those of Little Rock in 1957. South Boston was an area of mainly Irish American working-class who had always been staunch supporters of the Democratic Party. Whatever the liberals, like Senator Edward Kennedy, may have preferred, they were not going to comply with the law. The students, parents and city officials were overwhelmingly opposed to bussing of black students from the Roxbury neighbourhood. The riots in Boston gladdened the hearts of southern segregationists.

While the courts sought to tackle segregation in Boston, a similar attempt was being made in Detroit, but in this case the court sought to overcome white flight to the suburbs by linking the suburban schools with the inner-city schools. The Governor of Michigan, Henry Milliken, opposed the plan. Obviously so long as African Americans and other minorities were prevented from moving into the suburbs because of restrictive covenant clauses, the school systems could never achieve the objective as laid down in *Brown*. One of the consequences of the judge's Detroit plan was to ensure the triumph of George Wallace in the 1972 Michigan primary.

In 1974 the Supreme Court in *Milliken v Bradley* overturned the Detroit bussing plan by a five-to-four majority, with the majority arguing that the suburbs were not responsible for the segregation and so should not be used to resolve the problem. All four of Nixon's appointees to the Court ruled with the majority. One of the four was William Rehnquist who had been nominated because of his conservatism. He had been approved by the Senate following the bitter battle over Carswell, but Rehnquist's record on civil rights was no better. In the 1950s Rehnquist had argued in favour of the *Plessy v Ferguson* ruling of 1896, which upheld segregation as long as facilities were separate but equal, and he had maintained that 'it is about time that the Court faced the fact that the white people in the South don't like the colored people.' In addition, in 1964 he advocated the use of racial zoning covenants for private businesses (Greene, 1992).

Shirley Chisholm: The First Black Woman
to Seek the Presidency

The disputes between black women and white feminists surfaced again during the 1972 presidential election campaign of the African American Shirley Chisholm. As the first black Congresswoman, Chisholm of New York symbolised the new politics of the 1970s. As an early member of the NOW and the National Women's Political Caucus, it seemed as though she had certain constituencies at her command. Although her failure was partly due to finance, disorganisation and lack of preparation, it also 'revealed the shortcomings of the Black and feminist movements, shortcomings that would be fundamentally damaging to both.' Eventually NOW supported her. 'But the belated support for Chisholm was too slight to have any impact. The lesson that could be learned was that Black women also figured slightly in the priorities of the women's movement' (Giddings, 1984; Marable, 1997).

Not only did many women fail to support Chisholm, black political leaders such as Julian Bond, Richard Hatcher, Mayor of Gary, Indiana, Jesse Jackson of Chicago, and Clarence Mitchell, Mayor of Atlanta met with other men, such as the black nationalist Imiri Baraka, and they considered three options: to run 'favourite son' candidates in several states, to support George McGovern or to back a black male candidate. None of those present at the Chicago meeting supported Shirley Chisholm. Her defence of Angela Davis, in prison on charges of 'murder, kidnapping and conspiracy', did not win her support either. Ironically, given its extreme sexism, the male-dominated Black Panther Party was the only major group in the black community which endorsed her candidacy. 'She concluded that the failure of her campaign was due more to sexism than racism, and the realization was demoralising.' In 1983 Chisholm did not seek re-election to the House of Representatives (Giddings, 1984).

Many black women accused the women's movement of not helping Chisholm because white feminists saw the right to control reproduction by abortion as paramount. Black women were more concerned by the revived eugenics movement, largely motivated by racism, whose members argued in favour of sterilisation. Angela Davis maintains the campaigners for abortion should have included 'a vigorous condemnation of sterilization abuse which had become more widespread than ever.' And she cited evidence from the Director of Population Affairs that estimated the federal government had funded between 100,000 and 200,000 sterilisations alone (Davis, 1983). African Americans knew more about the influence of eugenics on the American medical profession which had deliberately sought to prevent black, ethnic and poor women from reproducing. Abortion was legalised in the 1973 *Roe v Wade* decision (Garrow, 1994). The pro-choice victory was a victory for white women and gave many conservatives an emotive campaign issue which weakened support for wider civil rights for blacks.

Radical black, lesbian feminist, Cherl Clarke, explained: 'What drew me to politics was my love of women, the agony I felt observing the straight-jackets of poverty and repression I saw my own family in.' She criticised the early feminist movement as 'exclusive and reactionary' but she argued for a coalition. Heterosexual men, black and white, had 'colonized' women's bodies but lesbians, by denying men their power, were free. Lesbian feminists, she contends, 'can be compared to the civil . . . rights activist of the 1960s who was out there on the streets for freedom, while many of us viewed the action on television' (Moraga and Anzaluda, 1983). Davis's feminism and Clarke's lesbianism were, in part, a response to black male machismo. In later years, as African American men searched for a new leader, African American women increasingly looked towards white women for support. And black women, like Fanny Lou Hamer, became 'a revered figure in the women's movement as well' (Dittmer, 1995).

The Politics of Euphemism

Bussing was all part of the politics of euphemism as practised by Nixon and the right. Opposition to 'forced bussing' was the code used to reassure conservatives in the North and the South that he would never support the goals of the civil rights movement. The persistent demand for 'law and order' was not meant as a rebuke to the southern states for failing to provide equal protection and rights for all their citizens, but rather an attack on any form of dissent whether expressed by civil rights groups, anti-war demonstrators, environmentalists or consumer groups. Nixon's 'New Federalism' was a way of attacking liberal social welfare reforms by transferring power to state programmes. By doing so he was simply supporting the contention of southern politicians who, in their resistance to the civil rights movement, had continually defended state sovereignty. His bitter personal attacks on federal civil servants were also an assault on the Great Society programmes. Although the vast majority who benefited from these schemes were white, it was the popular perception that they were designed only to benefit African Americans and other people of colour. And LBJ watched helplessly from his ranch in Texas as his 'beautiful woman,' the Great Society, was taken apart by Nixon. 'It's a terrible thing for me to sit by and watch someone else starve my Great Society to death,' Johnson complained. 'Soon she'll be so ugly that the American people will refuse to look at her; they'll stick her in a closet to hide her away and there she'll die' (Kearns, 1976). While federal and state politicians either bled or exploited the welfare programmes of the Great Society, people like Fanny Lou Hamer fought to expose the corruption in Medicaid and poverty schemes in Mississippi (Dittmer, 1995).

Black Capitalism

Nixon's dislike of the Great Society programmes and welfare was shared by many, including his Democrat advisor on minority affairs, Daniel Patrick Moynihan. Instead of getting government handouts, 'Nixon believed in government hand-ups, and he was convinced that the best way to help disadvantaged groups was with capitalism rather than welfare which he believed was "creeping socialism".' Nixon notes in his memoirs, 'minority enterprises were getting only $8 million of business through government contracts. By 1972 they were getting $242 million. In the same period the total of all government grants, loans and guarantees directed toward helping minority business enterprises had jumped from $200 million to $472 million.' He points out that two-thirds of the top one hundred black companies had been set up during his administration and that 'receipts of . black-owned businesses jumped from $4.5 billion in 1968 to $7.2 billion in 1972' (Nixon, 1978).

Federal government assistance to black business was a method followed by subsequent presidents and supported in Congress. An African American Democratic congressman from Baltimore, Maryland, proposed, in an amendment to the 1977 Public Works Employment Act, an appropriation of $4 billion to stimulate the economy and that 10 per cent of each grant should be for minority business. The set-aside programme was approved with virtually no discussion and no committee hearings. The programme of 1967, which had had no racial basis and designed to aid Disadvantaged Business Enterprises, had now become set-asides for minority business enterprises. 'The set-aside model for federal grants and contracts proved attractive in the 1980s not just to liberal Democrats in Congress but also to Republican presidents Ronald Reagan and George Bush. Like President Nixon, they attacked racial quotas but supported affirmative-action programmes that encouraged entrepreneurship' (Graham, 1994). Ironically, affirmative action, severely criticised by the New Right in the 1990s, was developed and defended by presidents who gave birth to and represented the New Right majority.

If Nixon's policy was to build a black middle class which would support the Republican Party, it did not pay dividends in the short term. In his re-election in 1972 African Americans stayed loyal to the Democratic Party. Following the attempted assassination of George Wallace, which took the Alabama governor out of the presidential race, Nixon saw the triumph of his southern strategy – all the former Confederate states voting overwhelmingly for the Republican Party. But the Democrats still controlled Congress because 'Nixon completely wrote off local races, telling Erlichman that the Republicans had raised the "worst crop of candidates in history" ' (Greene, 1992).

The failure to win African American support was not a surprise to Nixon. Although Stephen Ambrose stresses that in the 1950s Nixon 'was the only one who would go into the South and tell southerners that segregation was morally wrong', it is also true that he became very quiet on the issue. It is evident that he had more sympathy for white southerners and their resistance to integration than he did for African Americans in their struggle for justice. He refused to support Robert Finch at HEW and followed John Mitchell's advice: 'Do only what the law requires, not one thing more.' Nixon was certain that they would never gain credit from the African American community and he wanted to keep 'as low a profile as possible' on desegregation. As Ambrose admits, 'he passed on his best opportunity for greatness.'

The opportunity was to complete the task for which LBJ had shown true presidential leadership – solving the civil rights question. Nixon failed to provide 'an enthusiastic advocacy of integration, a wholehearted acceptance of the necessity for equality of opportunity in the marketplace, a compelling commitment to decency in race relations in all areas.' Ambrose confesses, 'Richard Nixon did not want to be the nation's leader. He only wished the problem would go away' (Ambrose, 1989).

African Americans and liberals were only too aware of this lack of leadership and that the legacy of Richard Nixon would last long after he left the White House in disgrace following the Watergate scandal because of his appointments of four conservatives to the Supreme Court. The Court, which had been the ally of the civil rights movement, could no longer be relied on for support and this in turn had long-term consequences for those, such as the NAACP, who struggled for justice through the legal system. Ralph Abernathy, of SCLC, recalled that in 1976, 'The civil rights movement was no longer as fashionable as it once had been.' He also believed that future battles would be smaller and complicated and would not get the media attention. 'Watergate had been a better show than anything we had managed to stage' (Abernathy, 1989). He was not surprised when he was asked in 1976 to resign from the leadership of the SCLC.

A more generous assessment of Nixon's career was made by President Bill Clinton who was attacked by 'Nixon haters' for giving a eulogy at the former president's funeral. Clinton generously writes that Nixon's contribution to civil rights was significant compared with those Republicans who came after him (Clinton, 2004).

Civil Rights and President Gerald Ford

LBJ is often quoted as saying that Gerald Ford could not 'chew gum and walk at the same time.' And this image of Ford as a bumbling, hapless president ensured he only served out the months following Nixon's disgrace and resignation. Ford had become Vice President following the resignation of Vice President Agnew who had pleaded 'no contest' to bribery charges. Ford, the House of Representatives Minority Leader from Michigan, was promoted by Nixon. Fred Emery concludes, 'Clearly, Nixon thought that Ford, generally seen as a genial but limited Republican journeyman, was also good impeachment insurance' (Emery, 1994).

Ford was a Nixon loyalist which was reflected in the sweeping pardon he awarded Nixon. In a rare proclamation, Ford pardoned Nixon for 'all offenses against the United States which he, Richard Nixon, has committed, or may have committed' (Emery, 1994). The Senate investigations into such abuses, headed by Senator Frank Church, show just how extensive those crimes were. And Nixon's tapes revealed his massive 'abuse of power' (Kutler, 1998).

Gerald Ford not only had the distinction of pardoning a president but also of having the worst civil rights record of any president since 1945. He made no public statements in support of civil rights. A political scientist has pointed out that, Ford, like Nixon, 'paid less attention and gave less support to civil rights in their public statements' (Shull, 1993). However, in 1963 following the violent attacks on civil rights workers hoping to march from Selma to Montgomery, Alabama, Ford had supported legislation to allow use of the 'maximum power of the federal government to prevent further violence and to protect constitutional rights in Selma, Alabama' (Carter, 1995). He had voted for the Civil Rights Act of 1964 and the Voting Rights Act of 1965. But when Nixon tried to weaken the voting rights legislation he had the enthusiastic support of Ford. Moreover, when Ford became

President, he never asked for or supported civil rights legislation and issued no executive orders to advance the cause of civil rights.

And Ford's dislike of liberal justices was well known. He worked enthusiastically for Richard Nixon in an attempt to remove a justice considered by conservatives to be an outrageous menace, Supreme Court Justice William O. Douglas. Nixon appointee, Will Wilson, head of the Criminal Justice Division under Attorney General John Mitchell, gave derogatory information to Ford in a campaign to impeach Douglas. Like many of the tasks he undertook, his efforts were unsuccessful and Wilson later complained, 'Ford took the material we gave him and screwed it up. Ford blew it' (Carter, 1995). And his only appointment to the Supreme Court, John Paul Stevens, a conservative, later angered many Americans when he authored a majority ruling in 1997 that the Communications Decency Act, which sought to censor internet pornography, was unconstitutional.

He did not 'blow it' for New Right conservatives when it came to his appointments to the federal district and appellate courts. In the district courts, 90 per cent of his appointments were white and 98 per cent were male. None of these judges was considered qualified by the American Bar Association. For the appellate courts he was more consistent; 100 per cent were white males. Only 17 per cent of these, in the opinion of the American bar, were considered exceptionally well qualified (Shull, 1993).

In the election of 1976, against Jimmy Carter of Georgia, Ford made no attempt to win African American votes. Increasingly the Republican Party was a white man's party. 'Gerald Ford's version of the Southern strategy delivered nearly two-thirds of the white vote to the Republicans' (Werner, 2002). And, as he had done throughout his short term in the White House, Ford used his hostility to 'forced bussing' to reassure voters that their schools would remain white and his only initiative in civil rights was an attempt to win legislation against bussing of schoolchildren to overcome segregation. Critics were right when they complained that Nixon and Ford had failed to support the gains of the 1960s. It might be contended that inaction as well as actions had set the agenda for rolling back the civil rights movement's successes.

Ironically, conservatives attacked Nixon and even Ford because they thought they were too sympathetic to civil rights groups and the liberal agenda. Pat Buchanan, who had earlier supported Nixon, now complained that Nixon had betrayed the conservative cause. In a seven-page memorandum to Nixon, Buchanan claimed that the President had surrounded himself with liberal advisors and that conservatives were 'the niggers of the Nixon Administration' (Ambrose, 1989). Nothing in Ford's short term in office persuaded him that anything had changed. To rectify this situation Pat Buchanan and California Governor Ronald Reagan decided to take up the banner of the 'moral majority' and sweep the remaining liberals and communist dupes out of Washington.

Following the single term of the Georgia Democrat Jimmy Carter (see Chapter 6), whose major achievements were the appointment of minorities and women to prominent positions and the renewal of the Voting Rights Act, the former sports commentator, movie actor, FBI agent and Governor of California tried once again for the presidential nomination of the Republican Party. Ronald Reagan, who had been a liberal Democrat as a young man, had embraced anti-communism and became in the 1950s an ardent supporter of Joseph McCarthy, who led the witch-hunt against American communists with his United States Senate interrogations. Reagan was an enthusiastic convert to new conservatism and to the dubious campaign tactics of William Casey, his campaign manager, who stole Carter's briefing notes before the television debate.

Ronald Reagan and the New Right

An ardent supporter of Barry Goldwater in 1964, Reagan bitterly attacked liberal Republicans, such as Nelson Rockefeller of New York, as traitors to the party. When Reagan first ran for governor of California in 1966 he was careful not to repudiate members of the extremist right-wing group, the John Birch Society, because he knew that Nixon had lost conservative support in 1962 when he had attacked the Birch group. Reagan compromised to keep extreme right-wing support; he campaigned for members of the Society but issued a statement criticising Robert Welch, the founder. When he was attacked in the Republican primary by the former Mayor of San Francisco for not supporting the Civil Rights Act of 1964 he lost his temper shouting: 'I resent the implication that there is any bigotry in my nature. Don't anyone ever imply that' (Dallek, 1984). However, his first presidential campaign stop was in Nashoba County which included Philadelphia, Mississippi, near the site of the 1964 murder of the three COFO volunteers. In front of an all-white crowd waving Confederate flags he defended southern resistance in the name of 'states rights.' African American commentator, Bob Herbert, later noted that, 'Reagan was the first presidential candidate ever to appear at the [Neshoba County] fair, and he knew exactly what he was doing when he told that crowd, "I believe in states' rights." Reagan's defenders have tried 'to put this appearance into a racially benign context.'

But, 'Reagan may have been blessed with a Hollywood smile and an avun-
cular delivery, but he was elbow deep in the same old race-baiting Southern
strategy of Goldwater and Nixon' (*New York Times*, 13 November 2007).

He also supported the American Medical Association in their battle
against Medicare and argued that: 'Medical care for the aged is a foot in
the door of a government takeover of all medicine.' He even alleged that
income tax was a 'progressive system spawned by Karl Marx and declared
by him to be the prime essential of 'a socialist state.' For Reagan the threat
was not from liberalism but from the 'socialism' of the Democratic Party
which would destroy individual initiative (Boyarsky, 1981).

Reagan courted the conservative vote when dealing with civil rights
issues. A typical, and frequently repeated, story by Reagan concerned the
black Chicago woman Linda Taylor. In this tale Reagan linked African
Americans and welfare, so-called 'welfare queens', reinforcing the popular
perception that many black women exploited the welfare system paid for
by hard-working white folk. In addition, his rendering underlined his typ-
ically cavalier use of statistics. Campaigning for the presidency in 1976 he
claimed she 'has eighty names, thirty addresses, twelve Social Security cards
and is collecting veterans' benefits on four non-existing husbands... Her
tax-free cash income alone is over $150,000.' In fact Taylor was convicted
in 1977 of welfare fraud using two, not eighty, names which she used to
collect 23 welfare cheques worth $8000, not $150,000. According to the
New York Times, during this same campaign he used a typical racial epithet
to a southern audience when he complained about a 'young buck' receiv-
ing food stamp benefits (Cannon, 1991). The stream of allegations about
welfare cheats re-enforced popular perceptions that race and crime were
connected. This is reflected in the mandatory sentencing laws passed in
1986 which deal with cocaine. The sale of only five grams of crack cocaine
meant a mandatory sentence of five years imprisonment, the only mandatory sentence for possessing any drug. It takes 500 grams of powder cocaine
to trigger the same sentence. The fact that crack was largely used by young
African Americans meant a disproportionate number of them ended up in
prison. Powder cocaine was the drug of choice largely among white, affluent
Americans (ACLU Report, 21 May 2002).

Was Reagan a Racist?

It might be true that Reagan was not 'racially prejudiced' in the most viru-
lent form but he was happy to allow Lee Atwater, a young Republican from

South Carolina and protégée of the arch-segregationist Strom Thurmond, to shape his campaign. But although Reagan's support for African Americans was limited, in his early years at Eureka College he supported integration of the football team and as a sports broadcaster in the 1950s he spoke in favour of integrating black baseball players into the major league teams. After these early days he had attacked the 1964 Civil Rights Act and the 1965 Voting Rights Act, and opposed laws seeking to forbid discrimination in housing and the desegregation of schools by bussing. When running for Governor of California his constant themes were 'morality, law and order, strong leadership and traditional values. Reagan was particularly skilled in relaying this message in a non-threatening way.' He combined attacks on civil rights legislation with 'opposition to anything that smacks of bigotry and discrimination. We must make those who walk with prejudice walk alone.' But he exploited the disturbances of the 1960s and the television images of graphic pictures of race riots and demonstrating students that fed alienation, especially of blue collar Democratic voters. Combining supposed social concern with genuine conservatism ensured his landslide victory (Mark, 2007). It would be the pattern for the Republican Party of the future.

As president, he tried to win over leaders of the 1960s civil rights movements with promises of job training for inner-city youth which would break the so-called 'dependency culture' that he and they believed the welfare state had fostered. Abernathy was concerned that the Republican southern strategy was winning over whites only and he blamed African Americans because of their blind loyalty to the Democrats. In the 1980 campaign, civil rights activists, such as Ralph Abernathy, Charles Evers and Hosea Williams, endorsed Reagan rather than Jimmy Carter (Abernathy, 1989). Despite Abernathy's support for Reagan, perhaps hoping for some influence in a conservative administration, 'Ronald Reagan received the lowest percentage of the black vote of any Republican presidential candidate in history' (Shull, 1993).

Abernathy was rapidly disillusioned with the new president. Although 'honored guests' and 'treated as important celebrities' at the inauguration party, Abernathy complained that he did not get a chance to speak with Reagan. All his efforts in the coming days and weeks to meet with Reagan or his senior staff failed and he 'didn't get past a third-echelon staff member.... No one, it seems, knew or cared about the president's promises' (Abernathy, 1989). What Abernathy failed to appreciate was that Reagan was a different type of activist. 'Instead of extending civil rights, he sought to reduce the government's role' (Shull, 1993). The former leader of SCLC was not the only one who was disillusioned with Reagan. Leaders of the NAACP were offended when he refused to speak at their annual convention in 1980 because he had a prior arrangement – a riding holiday (Cannon, 1991). When he made good the error and went to the NAACP meeting in July 1981, he angered delegates when he coolly informed them that the plight of many African Americans was due to government programmes passed by liberal Democrats. Reagan asserted: 'Many in Washington over the years have been more dedicated to making the needy people government dependent, rather than independent. They've created a new kind of bondage.' He said, 'the Emancipation Proclamation freed black people 118 years ago, today we need to declare an economic emancipation' (Dallek, 1984).

Reagan's indifference is reflected in his inability to even recognise his only black cabinet officer, Charles Pierce, at a meeting of black mayors. The president alienated the civil rights leaders by his constant refrain that big government did not solve problems; 'government *is* the problem.' As Stephen Tuck points out, 'By contrast, civil leaders had long seen big government as the key to solving problems of gross inequality.' He argues that young rap singers provided a new divisiveness in the old-style civil rights movement. Combined with the rise of new conservatism the result was NAACP membership collapsed in the 1980s from 500,000 to just 100,000. He rightly contends that conservatism forced local and community groups to work together on many issues while others fought to defend civil rights legislation and defeat Reagan's opposition to sanctions against apartheid South Africa (Hudson and Davies, 2008).

And whatever his publicly professed sympathies for an equal society, Reagan promoted William Rehnquist to Chief Justice of the Supreme Court, elevating a man who had consistently opposed the 1954 *Brown* ruling which declared segregation of schools by race unconstitutional. He was 'confirmed . . . by the fewest votes ever for a successful nominee for chief justice' (Shull, 1993). Reagan further strengthened the far right influence on the Supreme Court with his appointment of Antonin Scalia. A later effort to appoint the ultra-conservative, Robert Bork, was defeated in 1987 by a coalition of 185 organisations led by civil rights, labour and women's groups.

The New Right Budget

Reagan's first budget was to be the first step in the revolution that would sweep away years of accumulated 'state dependency.' His budget director,

David A. Stockman, stated: 'The Reagan Revolution, as I had defined it, required a frontal assault on the American welfare state.' And he admitted that 'forty years' worth of promises, subventions, entitlements, and safety nets issued by the federal government . . . would have to be scrapped or drastically modified.' This 'minimalist government' would offer 'even-handed public justice, but no more.' Free-market economics would liberate the nation, and deregulation would increase 'capitalist wealth and the expansion of private welfare that attends it.' The budgets failed, according to Stockman, not because of huge tax cuts and massively increased defence spending, but because he did not 'cut welfare programmes which "are family-destroyers." They subsidize a culture of poverty, dependency, and social irresponsibility' (Stockman, 1987). In an interview with William Greider of *Atlantic Monthly*, the 'high-sounding philosophy' of supply-side economics was, according to Stockman, nothing more than the old idea of giving tax breaks to the rich in the hope that eventually the good effects might benefit the poor. He admitted, 'It's kind of hard to sell "trickle down", so the supply side formula was the only way to get a tax policy that was really "trickle down" ' (Johnson, 1991). And Stockman was not alone when he attacked the welfare state. Ralph Abernathy criticised Democrats who saw welfare as a 'benign thing rather than as a millstone around the neck of the black population' (Abernathy, 1989).

Despite Stockman's later complaints that the President failed to support his efforts, Reagan was a true believer and it was his passionate conviction which won over many doubters in both parties. Following the decision to cut taxes by 25 per cent over three years and increase military expenditure, one Republican moderate is quoted as saying, 'Pray God it works. If this economic plan doesn't jell, where are we going to get the money for anything?' They were forced to borrow and thus increase the budget deficit. Although the welfare state was not swept away by this budget or subsequent budgets, it was the poor who took the brunt of the cuts. The number of people eligible for food stamps, Medicaid, unemployment benefit, housing assistance, student loans, child nutrition programmes, public service jobs and legal aid were cut back. And the tax cuts did not benefit the people who had lost out. As Robert Dallek points out: 'The 31.7 million taxpayers making $15,000 or less a year were to receive only 8.5 per cent of the reduction while 12.6 million people earning $50,000 or more a year were to get 35 per cent of the money given up by the federal treasury.' In their determination to encourage the 'productive potential of free men in free markets' the contribution of corporations in federal taxes was reduced from thirteen cents to eight cents per tax dollar' (Dallek, 1984).

Stockman attacked conservatives such as Irving Kristol for not going far enough and thus ensuring the persistence of the welfare state. Certainly the much vaunted Reagan Revolution was merely a harsher form of policies supported by Republican and Democratic administrations. According to Congressional Budget Office statistics for 1977 to 1987, the family income after taxes in 1988 dollars, and adjusted for inflation, saw the richest 5 per cent increase their earnings by 37.3 per cent from $94,476 to $129,762. However, the poorest 10 per cent of the population with earnings of $3673 in 1977 had had their earnings reduced by 10.5 per cent in 1987 to $3286. The after-tax income of the top 1 per cent increased by 87 per cent during 1980 to 1990 (Shull, 1993).

The NAACP members' anger over Reagan's priorities in his budget was made clear by Benjamin Hooks, the head of the Association. Hooks denounced the budget plans as bringing 'hardship, havoc, despair, pain, and suffering on blacks and other minorities.' African Americans who supported his criticisms included Coretta Scott King, Martin Luther King Jr's widow, and the mayor of Detroit, Coleman Young.

The Commission on Civil Rights and the IRS

Reagan was not only activist in his budget proposals which cut the welfare state – he was determined to change the structure, personnel and mission of the United States Commission on Civil Rights. In this he was also following the example set by Richard Nixon, who had demanded the resignation of the head of the Commission, Father Theodore Hesburgh, who refused to oppose bussing for integration. Nixon appointed a Republican, Arthur Fleming, in the hope that he would be more compliant to Nixon and the demands of the New Right. He was not and was outspoken in his criticism of Republican administrations, especially that of Ronald Reagan.

Fleming was fired by Reagan and the ousted Commission member complained at a news conference that his dismissal signalled a retreat on affirmative action. A NAACP spokeswoman commented: 'What the administration is trying to do is not just put civil rights on the back burner, but take it off the stove completely.' And the man Reagan chose to help him weaken the Commission was a conservative black Republican, Clarence Pendleton of the San Diego Urban League. He was an ideal choice for Reagan in that Pendleton was a staunch believer in self-help, free markets, opposed to affirmative action and bussing to achieve integration. The President was not

concerned that: 'The increased politicization of the commission perpetu-
ates [his] image as an opponent of civil rights.' Reagan won his battle with
the liberals and transformed the Commission into a conservative body that
accepted the New Right critique of affirmative action and bussing (Shull,
1993).

It has been argued in Reagan's defence that he 'was so cut off from the
counsel of black Americans that he sometimes did not even realize when he
was offending them' (Cannon, 1991), but if that is the case then as President
he was responsible for not seeking any advice from the African American
community and it is doubtful that he was not aware of the offence he
caused. One 'glaring example' of this remoteness, it is suggested, was his
support in 1982 for Bob Jones University in South Carolina and the Golds-
boro Christian Schools in North Carolina when they challenged the right
of the Internal Revenue Service (IRS) to deny tax exemptions to segregated
schools. This IRS policy was aimed at southern schools set up to avoid integration and the policy had had the consistent support of three presidents,
Nixon, Gerald Ford and Jimmy Carter. In the case of Bob Jones University,
although it admitted a few minority students, interracial dating and marriage were prohibited by the school rules which it claimed were based on
the Bible. Later Reagan claimed: 'All I wanted was that these tax collectors
stop threatening schools that were obeying the law' (Cannon, 1991).

In the resulting storm of protest, Reagan was told that African Americans
viewed him as a traitor and he hastily sought a compromise. He suggested
that his proposed legislation would not only stop IRS bureaucrats making
social policy but also prevent schools that were segregated benefiting from
tax-exempt status. As Robert Dallek points out this was designed as 'the
politics of symbolism' that would please everybody. 'Black Americans were
supposed to accept the picture of a compassionate president opposed to discrimination, while conservatives were supposed to see his action as a victory
over arbitrary bureaucrats and for the rule of Law.' The Reagan administration had 'lined up with white suburbanites in opposition to government
insistence on equal rights for minorities.' The administration only backed
away when it seemed that it would lose moral authority but still sought to
keep conservatives reassured (Dallek, 1984). Perhaps this is a harsh judgement. There were many Republicans only too eager to court the racist
vote, but Reagan's dislike of strong federal government had been a persistent theme of his campaigning since the 1960s. Arthur Aughey points out,
'The success of Reagan in the 1980s owes much to the forms of argument
provided by conservative intellectuals in the previous two decades' (Aughey,
1992).

Renewal of the Voting Rights Act

The New Right conservatives, especially the growing numbers of south-ern Republicans, were not content with budgetary measures and symbolic gestures of opposition to school desegregation. They were particularly con-cerned about the Voting Rights Act of 1965, which had been renewed by Richard Nixon and Gerald Ford. They expected Ronald Reagan to fight the efforts of liberal Democrats and Republicans who were determined to renew the Act. The law which enabled the federal government to register an unstated percentage of voters in districts where were not registered had transformed southern politics. In Mississippi, for example, the number of African Americans registered as voters had increased from 6.7 per cent to 59.8 per cent in three years. Reagan made it clear that he was not in favour of renewal and very grudgingly accepted the revision of the Act which was designed to stop state and local officials from using registration and voting procedures that resulted in discrimination against minorities. This change ended the requirement to prove the intention to discriminate, a much harder thing to do in law (Dallek, 1984).

Reagan's opposition to the Voting Rights Act was based on a desire to strengthen Republicans in the South and among white working-class voters in the North and it was based on his reluctance 'to use federal authority in the cause of punishing discrimination of any sort.' Both were factors in his opposition to the Civil Rights Restoration Act (CRRA) of 1988. The Act resulted from a Supreme Court ruling, *Grove City v Bell* (1984) that limited anti-discrimination laws to federally aided programmes, and not to the insti-tution where the discrimination occurred (Cannon, 1991). The result of this ruling meant that a department of a university, for example, that practised discrimination would lose federal funding, but not the university that had permitted the discrimination to take place. The CRRA has been consid-ered by some as 'the most significant civil rights legislation in twenty years' (Shull, 1993). It was designed to reverse the *Grove City* ruling which dramat-ically limited the scope of four major civil rights laws. Any organisation or institution had to be in compliance with the civil rights legislation if any part of the organisation was to get federal funding. But conservatives had not given up their fight.

As a lame-duck president who had no need to court voters, he vetoed the Act in 1988. He had warned that he would do so because the legisla-tion 'dramatically expands the scope of federal jurisdiction over state and local governments and the private sector, from churches and synagogues to farmers, grocery stores, and businesses of all sizes.' According to Reagan it diminished individual citizens. His critics' rejoinder was that the Act was merely restoring the situation to what it had been prior to the Supreme Court ruling. The vociferous support of the Moral Majority and its leader, the Reverend Jerry Falwell, harmed rather than aided Reagan's cause. The fundamentalist minister was convinced that churches would be forced under the act to hire homosexuals or drug addicts with AIDS as teachers or youth workers. Even conservatives thought these attacks were nonsense and the law was passed, overriding the Reagan veto. The Republicans in Congress were deeply divided with 21 Republican senators and 52 members of the House voting with the Democrats to override the veto (Shull, 1993).

Affirmative Action

Throughout Reagan's presidency civil rights leaders had to fight just to retain the advances made in the 1960s and especially contentious was Lyndon Johnson's Executive Order 11246 which laid down that all federal contractors had to enforce affirmative action policies to ensure minority workers were hired. This policy was extended by Nixon. Reagan had joined the opposition to a consent agreement negotiated by Birmingham, Alabama's first black mayor, Richard Arrington. Now the president and his supporters sought to overturn 11246 and backed court cases that opposed affirmative action but his opponents mustered enough support to prevent this. Failing to win the battle he saw other ways to achieve his goals such as starving 'enforcement agencies of resources to leave them weak and ineffective. In addition he appointed black conservatives like the poorly qualified Clarence Thomas to the Department of Education to delay school integration and then to head of the Equal Employment Opportunities Commission described as 'the most controversial appointee of all. Thomas knew that if he wished to get ahead with these conservatives he had to oppose affirmative action' (Hudson and Davies, 2008). He did and achieved his ambition at the expense of others.

The Legacy of Ronald Reagan

Just as President Johnson caught the liberal mood of the nation in 1964 to introduce sweeping reforms in his Great Society programme and civil rights activism, so Ronald Reagan personified, and exploited, the fears of a nation transformed by the civil rights revolution. Although Jesse Jackson in

1980 and 1984 sought to rebuild a 'rainbow coalition' of the working class, minorities and women in his two bids for the presidency and demonstrated that a black man could be a viable candidate for President, it was Ronald Reagan who knew his audience better. In his efforts he was aided by African Americans who had either benefited from the civil rights movement, such as Pendleton, or by one-time leaders of the movement, such as Abernathy. In his memoirs Abernathy criticises young blacks for taking 'the past too much for granted,' forgetting the sacrifices of an earlier generation.

> Had it not been for the character and courage of these simple people, we would not have raised a generation of leaders and nothing would have changed. We would still be looking from afar at the high walls of an impregnable city. So these are the first great heroes and heroines of our struggle. (Abernathy, 1989)

And he grieves for those who died for the cause and 'in the growing twilight my heart also aches for those anonymous generations who never saw the Promised Land, even from the mountain top' (Abernathy, 1989). It only makes it all the more sad that a sick, and ageing fighter of the civil rights struggle should have campaigned for Ronald Reagan who had for so long led the resistance to the movement. Abernathy summed up the failure of a dream. SNCC workers in the 1960s believed it was these 'simple people' who should make the decisions themselves – not leaders. When Charles Payne returned to Greenwood, Mississippi, in the late 1980s 'the style of contemporary Black leadership struck me as rigorously top-down.' Although this was typical of local politics throughout the country, 'against the history of Black struggle and growth in the Delta, it seemed to have a special poignancy' (Payne, 1996). The triumph of the New Right and the apparent withering of local activism in states such as Mississippi meant that when Reagan left office the city was more impregnable than at any time since the 1950s. Despite liberal fears about the policies of these New Right years, conservatives underestimated the way in which the civil rights movement had transformed the country and especially the South.

6

TRANSFORMATION: A NEW SOUTH?

LBJ had always wanted consensus politics but by 1968 he was facing mounting opposition over his foreign policy in Vietnam from the left, and vociferous attacks on his radical legislation on civil rights and economic policies from the right. He admitted: 'There were deep divisions in the country, perhaps deeper than any we had experienced since the Civil War. They were divisions that could destroy us if they were not attended to and ultimately healed.' On his return to the ranch in Texas he walked beside the Pedernales River and reflected that as President 'I had given it everything that was in me' (Johnson, 1971).

However, as President he had shattered the broad alliance which had brought him so many legislative successes. Johnson sought to ensure continued support from a sympathetic Supreme Court after Chief Justice Earl Warren said he was to retire. LBJ persuaded his old friend and adviser, Abe Fortas, a liberal Tennessean, to be nominated as the new Chief Justice. Fortas would have been the first Jewish head of the Court. Republican Senator Dirksen and James Eastland, the Democrat senator from Mississippi, were able to block the appointment of Fortas by two votes. Eastland was angered by a speech in which Fortas had urged Jews to support the civil rights movement. According to Johnson, Eastland interpreted that statement as a conspiratorial call for Jews and Negroes to take over America (Johnson, 1971). Eastland, with his paranoid fears of a Jewish-communist-black plot to destroy America, personified the old South.

The civil rights struggle and the anti-Vietnam War movement not only influenced African American lives, it transformed the lives of many white southerners. The characterisation of the South as home only to those who are violent, racist, insular and forever reliving the battles of the Civil War is an over-simplification. Southerners have been accused of shackling themselves to a 'false image' but that image is as much an invention of northerners as of southerners. There has always been another South. Although many liberal southerners failed to meet the challenge posed by the civil rights movement, there were many who in the finest sense upheld the southern tradition of honour. It is true that some southern judges such as E. Gordon West of Louisiana refused to enforce the *Brown* ruling. William Harold Cox of Mississippi called African Americans 'niggers' and accused some of them of behaving like 'a bunch of chimpanzees.' However, these Kennedy appointments to the federal court were not typical of all southern judges. Frank Johnson, appointed to the Alabama Middle District federal judgeship by Republican President Eisenhower and to the Fifth Circuit Court of Appeal by Democrat President Jimmy Carter, struggled to preserve the rule of law in the face of southern resistance to the civil rights movement. Johnson was willing to confront his old law school associate, George Wallace. Although southern radicals have had their critics, they also played a valuable role during the repressive years of the 1940s, 1950s and 1960s when they kept alive the dream of a just South. This is especially true for James Dombrowski and Carl and Anne Braden. There was a significant minority of white southern students who took part in the civil rights and anti-war movements.

The civil rights movement transformed the South. Black southerners proved that with their courage when they challenged Eugene 'Bull' Connor and Sheriff Jim Clark. Their refusal to accept second-class citizenship and their determination to struggle for justice forced many southerners to question the received wisdom of their political, religious and educational leaders. Foremost in the struggle were the African Americans of the South – it was their battle and they were determined to make it their victory. However, it is important to remember that white politicians, such as Senator Albert Gore Sr, had the courage to face the challenge presented by the movement. Other moderates not only achieved state power but gained the ultimate prize that had eluded Gore – the presidency. Jimmy Carter was elected governor of Georgia as an anti-segregationist candidate and eventually became president of the United States. However, the challenges which produced southern liberal Democratic political leaders, such as Jimmy Carter of Georgia and Bill Clinton of Arkansas, also saw the revolution in voting in the South after 1968. Since the Civil War the vast majority of white southerners voted Democrat. Only in a few isolated areas, such as East Tennessee or northern Alabama which had supported the North during the Civil War, was it possible for a Republican to stand for election and be sure of winning. Truman, Kennedy, and even to some extent Johnson could rely on the instinctive white southern support for the Democratic Party. Richard Nixon and Ronald Reagan changed that. The South was solid Republican, a fact underlined by the sweeping gains of the Republicans in the 1994 mid-term elections and the presidential elections.

That changed in 2008. It took many years but the much derided attempts to unite white and blacks in the South paid off. Three southern states – Virginia, North Carolina and Florida – contributed to the election of the first African American President in the United States. And if more black voters in Mississippi had participated he would have won that state too.

The Senator

Albert Gore Sr of Tennessee grew up on a farm and struggled during the Depression to gain an education. He taught in a small school where he lived with a coal miner and his family whose poverty made a profound impression on him. He had wanted to enter politics since his school days and eventually, at the age of 29, he was elected as a pro-New Deal Democrat from the Fourth District of Tennessee in 1938. In 1952 he became a senator, a post he held until his defeat in 1970. He liked to be known as a 'maverick' because he believed most Tennesseans were mavericks. In a long and distinguished career he never turned to the old tactic of race baiting (Gore, 1972).

Gore describes himself as a Populist – a movement at the turn of the century which he saw as 'an outstandingly liberal movement' and a lost opportunity in which African Americans and poor whites could have been united in their opposition to the reactionary forces that dominated the South. Gore saw Democratic Party policies of the New Deal, Fair Deal, the Great Society and the party platform of George McGovern in 1972 as the eventual triumph of Populism. Although critical of some aspects of the New Deal, he became a self-confessed 'extravagant admirer' of FDR. He supported the liberal policies of Truman and opposed the 'Dixiecrat' movement led by Strom Thurmond. 'Fortunately, not enough Southerners were willing any longer to follow blindly this advance to the rear.' Politically, the significance of the Dixiecrats was the willingness of the Bourbon leaders to desert the Democratic Party *in order to maintain white supremacy* (Gore, 1972).

When the Supreme Court ruled in *Brown* in 1954 that separate but equal was unconstitutional and ordered the integration of schools, Gore admits

that he was not one of the 'political heroes.' Although he had never indulged
in race-baiting, he had not been 'a torchbearer for racial equality in my first
campaign for the Senate in Tennessee in 1952' (Gore, 1972). He had openly
solicited the votes of blacks and poor whites on economic and social issues
by confronting Memphis 'Boss' Ed Crump who had controlled the black
vote in that city for many years. Gore knew that if African Americans had a
free and independent vote then the Crump machine would be destroyed.

Following the Court ruling in *Brown*, Gore defended it and described
himself as a moderate. The powerful Georgia Democrat Roy Harris, assistant to the state Governor Herman Talmadge, contended that, 'Moderation
means gradualism and gradualism means race mixing.' Similar resistance
was mounted in Tennessee by a Citizens Council for whites, a States Rights
Council, a Federation for Constitutional Government which included Van-
derbilt University English Professor Donald Davidson, and the Tennessee
Society to Maintain Segregation. Gore knew that moderation for most
southern demagogues was nothing short of communism because, even
before the *Brown* ruling, politicians in Georgia and Mississippi had antici-
pated the possibility of integration and in Georgia, for example, had tried to
convert the public school system into a private system (Gore, 1972).

East Tennessee saw the worst violence against integration in the state.
The small town of Clinton in Anderson County had too few blacks to justify
expenditure on a separate black high school and so they had been bussed to
a segregated school in Knoxville. The efforts of local and state authorities to
prepare for the integration of the local high school failed. The white pastor
of the First Baptist Church, the Reverend Paul Turner, volunteered to take
the black children to the school and was beaten for his action. His stand did
not prevent the bombing of the school in 1958. Although there was much
violence, the segregationist Citizens Council candidates were defeated in the
Clinton elections. There were brave individuals who sought to uphold the
law (Greene, 1982).

Senator Gore admired the willingness of Governor Frank Clement to
send National Guard troops into Clinton to ensure integration, but it was
not only the Governor who was tested over implementing the *Brown* decision. Opposition was growing in the South with white Citizens Councils
'formed to intimidate the Negro and keep the whites in line.' This was
reflected in the attitudes of members of the House of Representatives and
the Senate. The aim of the reactionary southerners was to label integration
as 'subversive and un-American.' As part of this campaign, southern elected
officials were asked to sign a Declaration of Constitutional Principles, pop-
ularly known as the Southern Manifesto. This 'bit of low doggerel' as Gore

describes it, was the handiwork of Strom Thurmond of South Carolina. It was Thurmond who publicly challenged Gore in the Senate to add his name to the document. Gore refused. Later he explained: 'I regarded the manifesto (what an irritating and pretentious name!) as the most unvarnished piece of demagoguery I had ever encountered.' He was certain, 'that nothing but tragedy and sorrow could come of this open defiance of the law, this cheap appeal to racism' (Gore, 1972).

Despite Faubus' popularity resisting integration at Little Rock in the neighbouring state of Arkansas, Gore eschewed racism and continued to pursue economic reform measures that would help the working class and poor whether they were black or white. He voted for the 1957 Civil Rights Act because 'it did place Congress on the side of social justice and ... the mere passage of civil-rights legislation was itself worthy of note.' However, Gore supported segregationist Buford Ellington for governor of Tennessee. Why? Gore was a party loyalist. More importantly, Gore had presidential ambitions and he needed Ellington and the state delegates' support in the 1960 convention. This act of political expediency was not rewarded and Ellington backed Lyndon Johnson.

During the 1960 campaign, Gore worked closely with John Kennedy even though many southerners saw the Massachusetts senator as a dangerous liberal and disliked him because of his Catholic faith. After the election, Gore acted as one of Kennedy's speech writers. Gore supported Kennedy's civil rights actions, especially the integration of the University of Mississippi which the Tennessean hailed as the end of the interposition argument. However, Gore was not happy with Kennedy's tax-cutting policies which he believed helped only the rich.

Although Gore had many ideas in common with LBJ, there were important differences. 'One was that I had grown stronger in Populist leanings and had become an inveterate enemy of special privilege, while Johnson had become a bedfellow of big money, oil, and military brass.' And LBJ was aware of Gore's feelings. In a secretly taped conversation with Senator Richard Russell about a 1964 Bill favouring tax cuts, Johnson complained that the Senator was 'not being very wise in your southern strategy' and he argued that he, Senator Harry Byrd and Gore 'ought to let that damned tax bill come on out.' Gore described the tax proposals as 'a rich man's bill' (Beschloss, 1997). It was Gore's Populism, as much as his increasing opposition to the war in Vietnam, that led to his disputes with Johnson. But despite these differences both southerners fought hard for the Medicare programme providing medical assistance for the elderly and Medicaid for the poor, and for federal aid for elementary and secondary education. Gore voted for the

Voting Rights Act of 1965 and for its renewal in 1970, and the 1968 Open Housing Act (Gore, 1972).

Gore considered the 1968 presidential election 'a travesty on democracy' because all three candidates – Nixon, Humphrey and Wallace – supported the war in Vietnam. He campaigned for Humphrey as the best man to extricate America from the war. As he recalled, it was a period 'when false patriotism was prevalent, a time when frustration bigotry, recrimination, fear, and littleness of spirit and mind spread across the land like waters from a flash flood.' Gore was only too aware that liberal Democrats were the target of Nixon's southern strategy and that they would be in 'the eye of the storm.' He believed Nixon was appealing to racism and regionalism in the South and the easy thing to do would have been to trim. Gore refused. He continued his attacks on the Vietnam War and he accepted the challenge of Nixon when in 1970 the President set out to appoint southern conservative judges to the Supreme Court. Gore voted against Clement F. Haynsworth and G. Harold Carswell both of whom he believed totally unfit for such a prestigious office. As Gore writes, 'It had become the litmus test of loyalty or disloyalty to the South, of white supremacy or civil rights for blacks with no room left for moderation or reason. When my name was called I voted a firm "No," and I felt good inside.' Carswell's nomination was for Gore the absolute proof of Nixon's 'anti-black Southern strategy' (Gore, 1972). His stance against the war and the judicial nominees won him support from radical students in Tennessee (*Libra*, 22 October 1970).

There is one blemish on Gore's progressive civil rights record. He opposed the 1964 Civil Rights Bill because it gave authority to 'unspecified, middle-rank functionaries in the Department of Health Education and Welfare to withhold funding from schools that refused to follow its guide-lines on integration.' For Gore this was an arbitrary use of power. He believed cutting funding to a school system because one school failed to comply with HEW regulations was unjust (Gore, 1970). However genuine his fears of arbitrary powers may have been, he must have known that it was not merely the question of one school failing to follow the guidelines but rather entire state systems refusing to do so, as in the case of the massive resistance of Virginia.

Despite this blemish on his record, Albert Gore Sr remained true to his Populist views. Although defeated in 1970 by the Republican William Brock whose campaign exploited racial fears and religious prejudice, Gore denounced the southern strategy as a slur on southerners. "It's based on the concept that people will have enough prejudice, provincialism, intolerance, and ignorance that if the national leadership will make an appeal to it, it will win' (Perlstein, 2008). Gore was proud of his long service in Congress. He articulated the liberal critique of New Right economic policy as early as 1972: 'it had always seemed to me perfectly logical that government should play an active role in the nation's business affairs, and I had never lost faith in the government's ability to guarantee economic justice to all its people' (Gore, 1972).

The President

Jimmy Carter of Plains, Georgia, was fond of recalling his Populist background and his mother, Lillian, claimed that her father was a close friend of the Populist leaders Tom Watson and Bishop William D. Johnson of the AME Church. A Jimmy Carter biographer has commented: 'Lillian has painted her father with a golden brush' (Kaufman, 1993). Even if that is the case, Lillian's frequent and sincere claims to the contrary may have influenced the political career of her son when he was the Governor of Georgia and later President of the United States. But there is certainly little evidence that he was a Populist during the 1950s and 1960s when African Americans were struggling to achieve equality under the law.

Jimmy Carter has been called a racial paternalist who did not question segregation in Georgia. From 1959 to 1961 he was a member of the Americus and Sumter County Hospital Board and in the same years he was on the Carnegie Library Board and he accepted the segregationists' policies. During the years 1956–62, when he served on the Sumter County Board of Education and was the chairman for 1962, he failed to initiate change in the school system. Carter's explanation, that he was guilty of naïve unawareness, is questionable because he actively delayed construction of one school for blacks and never supported properly equipping the schools that were supposedly separate and equal. Certainly the school board did nothing to implement the *Brown* ruling of the Supreme Court (Glad, 1980).

Carter is also accused of failing to help a Christian inter-racial community in south-west Georgia known as Koininia. One of his neighbours, Jack Singletary, was threatened by nightriders because he had lived in Koininia for a short period and told not to attend the Plains Baptist Church. Herbert Birdsey of Macon who had sold supplies to the community had had his store bombed. Carter did not help the community although he did help in easing the boycott against Singletary. But he did not join the States Rights Council, Georgia's equivalent of the Citizens Council. Perhaps he was just being politically prudent. A biographer points out, 'If he had stood with some of his other friends against integration, he would have undermined his potential as a political leader for the entire state, and eventually for the nation' (Glad, 1980).

As a state senator from 1963 to 1966, he attacked special-interest groups and their influence in the state legislature. He 'stressed the importance of caring for the poor, the underprivileged, and the under represented in Government.' This experience in the legislature spurred him to seek the governorship in a campaign that even his own advisers would later regret. 'Carter opposed bussing to achieve racial integration, and he visited a segregated private school' (Kaufman, 1993).

Not all features of this campaign are so negative and his later moderation as a governor was not so surprising. Undoubtedly Carter wanted to win the Wallace vote but he also knew that the biggest grievance in Georgia was the inequity of the tax system. He used the Populist language of 'freedom, opportunity and equal treatment' and promised to remove tax inequalities, to obey school desegregation orders as well as reform state government. One of his aides described it as 'stylistic' Populism. 'It was more an attempt to articulate the deeper feelings and frustrations of the small people – their suspicions of the urban centers, the rich, the big interests – than a fundamental challenge to the established centers of power' (Glad, 1980).

Although Carter did not trim the power of banks and big business in Georgia, he did declare at his inauguration as Governor that the days of segregation were over. He increased the number of black Georgia state employees from 4850 to 6684, he improved services for learning disabled people, and opened over 100 health centres. He made important symbolic gestures as well such as hanging a portrait of Martin Luther King Jr in the state capitol.

His success as Governor, and his long campaign for honesty in government had wide appeal and he was persuaded to seek the Democratic presidential nomination. Carter was helped by the Watergate scandal which led to the forced resignation of Richard Nixon. In the primaries, despite strong opposition from Jesse Jackson, Carter won the majority of the black vote even in states that he lost, such as Massachusetts. His candidacy and ultimate victory demonstrated that a southerner who had a popular appeal on economic issues and who was liberal on racial matters could be elected president without having to deny his southern origin.

Ironically, it was the African American legislators who made up the Black Caucus in Congress who were the most critical of Carter. His determination to control inflation led to bitter disputes within his own party but for black legislators it meant cutbacks in programmes that were designed to help the disadvantaged. Despite Carter's conservative attitude towards the economy he fulfilled many of his promises. During the campaign he promised to increase the number of minority appointments in the judiciary. Carter appointed more blacks and Hispanics to the federal judiciary than any other president before him. The percentage of black federal judges increased from 4 per cent in 1977 to 9 per cent in 1981. He made sure that minority owned companies had their fair share of federal contracts, and that federal funds were deposited in banks owned by minorities. Unlike Nixon, and later Reagan and Bush, Carter gave additional power to the Justice Department over voting rights and strengthened the Equal Employment Opportunities Commission to help it fight against job discrimination. He had two black women in his cabinet: Juanita Kreps, vice president of Duke University, accepted the post of Commerce Secretary and Patricia Harris, the dean of Howard University Law School, Secretary of Housing and Urban Development. Andrew Young, the Atlanta Congressman and former civil rights leader, was appointed ambassador to the United Nations.

When Carter was in the White House, the Supreme Court heard the first challenge to the affirmative action policy that had been encouraged by Richard Nixon. Because of previous discrimination, businesses and universities had set up special programmes which gave priority to minority candidates and universities retained a system of minority places. Marine veteran Allan Bakke challenged these programmes at the University of California at Davis because he had not been admitted to the medical school whereas African American and other minority candidates with lower scores had gained places. He won his case in the California Supreme Court and the regents of the university appealed to the US Supreme Court.

Whatever position Carter took on *Bakke v Regents of the University of California* was bound to cause him trouble. The Jewish community backed affirmative action where it set targets, but not where it provided quotas. Organised labour, another traditional group to support the Democratic Party, were totally opposed to affirmative action, and the black community, which had given Carter 89 per cent of their votes, was totally committed to affirmative action and quotas. The advice he was given at first by the Attorney General gave no direct support to affirmative action. Following consultations the administration submitted a brief which strongly endorsed the controversial policy and the Supreme Court ruled five to four that affirmative action was constitutional but that the system of racial quotas as used by the university was unconstitutional. It was widely acknowledged in the African American community that the Justice Department's brief was 'one of the major contributions to the cause of civil rights' (Kaufman, 1993).

Although Carter may have exaggerated his integrationist sympathies before he was Governor of Georgia, it is clear that as Governor and as President of the United States he not only accepted rulings of the courts but took positive action to benefit minority groups, especially the black community. Despite these policies, civil rights leaders such as Julian Bond, Hosea Williams and Ralph Abernathy refused to support the Georgian, Williams and Abernathy preferring to back Ronald Reagan. This division in the black vote is no more surprising than white southern Baptist voters rejecting Carter, a born-again Baptist from the South, in favour of Ronald Reagan who was to become the first divorced president in the history of the country – running on a religious programme that emphasised the sanctity of the family. Unlike Nixon and Reagan, Carter became the only president to win greater national and international respect in retirement than when in office and in 2002 was deservedly awarded the Nobel Peace Price.

The Black Congressmen, the Dixie Governor and Two Mayors

The South has seen a major transformation in its politics which has increased its power on the national scene. The civil rights movement and the resistance to it, ironically, brought democracy to vast areas of the South which had only known one-party rule by the Democratic Party upheld by flagrant anti-democratic devices which denied African Americans their right to exercise the franchise. The 1965 Voting Rights Act not only resulted in moderation by Democrats, with even Senator Herman Talmadge of Georgia seeking the support of black voters, it also saw the emergence of a strong moderate Republican Party with governors such as Winthrop Rockefeller in Arkansas and Linwood Holton of Virginia. The latter state had been the centre of massive resistance to the *Brown* decision to integrate schools. However, by 1970 Holton in his inaugural address said: 'As Virginia has been the model for so much else in America in the past, let us now endeavor to make today's Virginia a model in race relations. Let us, as Lincoln said, insist upon an open society "with malice toward none charity for all".'

In the 11 states that had formed the Confederate States of America in defence of slavery, the black registered voters almost doubled from 1.5 million to 2.7 million between 1960 and 1966, and had almost doubled again by 1980 to 4.3 million. The effect was not merely on national politics but was profound at a local level. By 1980 Dixie had 2600 elected black officials. This was helped by the Supreme Court in several rulings – *Gomillion v Lightfoot* (1960), *Baker v Carr* (1962) and *Gray v Sanders* (1963) – overturning gerrymandering devices used by whites to deprive blacks of representation. Tuskegee, Alabama, had its first black mayor in 1972. Birmingham, the site of some of the worst police violence, elected the African American Richard Arrington as mayor. Atlanta, the commercial and cultural capital of the South, elected Maynard Jackson and former United Nations ambassador and civil rights leader, Andrew Young, as mayor (Cooper and Terrill, 1991).

The North Carolina city of Charlotte, the national centre of attention when the Supreme Court ruled in favour of bussing to achieve integration, elected a black mayor, Harvey Gantt. The latter's election was dependent on white voters because blacks constitute only 25 per cent of the population. Gantt was an architect and widely expected to win the Senate seat when he challenged the ultra-conservative, Jesse Helms, in 1990. Helms had never won large majorities but his race message appealed especially to the small farmers of Appalachia, a vote that would be crucial in the 2008 campaign. Helms ran ads on television showing two white hands crumpling up a piece of paper the voice over saying 'you needed that job, and you were the best qualified. But they had to give it to a minority because of a racial quota.' Ironically, Helms argued he was not racist but Gantt was because he appealed to the bloc vote of African Americans in the state. It has been suggested that this had little effect on the outcome but such a view is very debatable (Mark, 2007). Helms clung to Dixie's past and did not live to see the day when his state helped elect a black president.

The Judge – Frank Johnson

Frank Johnson was born in Winston County, northern Alabama, and grew up as a devout Baptist and Republican. The hill country had no enthusiasm for slavery and few supported the Confederacy. Its Republican politics were shaped by the Civil War experience. Although not poor themselves, the Johnsons lived in an area of Alabama where coal mining, not cotton, was the main business. Many of the miners were poor and he married Ruth Jenkins, an impoverished miner's daughter. While he was at the University of Alabama law school at Tuscaloosa, a fellow student was George Wallace, future governor. Johnson had accepted segregation as a young man because he said: 'I wasn't confronted with it like I would have been had I grown up down in the Black Belt, in Lowndes County or Macon County or someplace like that.' However, he had never accepted the prevailing belief of the majority of whites that blacks were racially inferior. His wife had openly challenged the system by being the first white woman to receive a graduate degree at the formerly all-black Alabama State College. As she stated, even in her youth, 'I was known as a "nigger lover" ' (Yarborough, 1981).

In 1955 President Eisenhower appointed Johnson to the Middle District court in Alabama and Johnson moved to Montgomery with his family. He also served on the Fifth Circuit Court of Appeals that heard cases from all over the Deep South. What surprised many was his attitude and rulings on civil rights matters. During the 1955 Montgomery boycott, Fred Gray, one of two black lawyers in the city, filed a case on behalf of Aurelia S. Browder and 11 other women challenging the city segregation ordinances that applied to transport. Frank Johnson was one of the three judges that would hear the case. Johnson and Justice Richard Rives in *Browder v Gayle* ruled in a two-to-one decision which attacked the *Plessy v Ferguson* decision of the Supreme Court of 1896. They argued 'that the separate but equal doctrine can no longer be followed as a correct statement of law.' Montgomery did not appreciate the liberal views of the judge. 'Behind his back and in the press, he and his rulings were subjected to vitriolic abuse; relations with certain employees cooled noticeably; and at times even his friends and employees were made to feel community resentment' (Yarborough, 1981).

Johnson was a judge and as such he did not need to pander to the baser instincts of the white voters. He found himself in a situation where he was confronted by politicians who realised that defying the courts was an easy way to win votes. It was not only his old law school friend George Wallace who was eagerly soliciting the segregationist vote. John Patterson, who had defeated Wallace in the 1958 Democratic primary, used the slogan 'law and order' as a means of attacking the law and the courts. Johnson was willing to confront Patterson and Wallace who sought to impede the work of the Civil Rights Commission. The Commission was meeting in Alabama following the Civil Rights Act of 1957, seeking to find information about voting discrimination in the state. When Patterson and Wallace sought to defy the Commission and prevent them from gaining access to the records, Johnson issued orders requiring the officials to comply with a subpoena that necessitated officials to give evidence. Wallace continued in his defiance and Johnson cited him for contempt of court and threatened to jail him. Wallace, playing to the segregationist sentiment, was eventually tried and found not guilty. But Johnson was concerned that the show of defiance was threatening judicial authority. Johnson commented that 'this court refuses to allow its authority and dignity to be bent or swayed by such politically generated whirlwinds' (Yarborough, 1981). As a state judge, Wallace had made many public statements about his determination to defy the federal government and courts but he had secretly assisted the Commission.

Although not sympathetic to the Freedom Riders, Johnson insisted that Alabama African Americans should have the right to vote and to attend an integrated school. In 1963 Wallace, now Governor, was determined not only to keep the University of Alabama all white but to thwart efforts to desegregate city schools in the state. The major confrontation took place at Huntsville where Governor Wallace had sent state troopers to surround the high school. The parents condemned Wallace's grandstanding and the Montgomery *Advertiser* lamented his actions and asserted: 'Alabama is not a banana republic.' Johnson was one of several federal judges who signed a restraining order against Wallace. Johnson thwarted Wallace's campaign to maintain segregation and issued orders enjoining universities and schools to obey the *Brown* decision. In November, Auburn University was ordered to admit Harold Franklin, an African American graduate student.

Johnson found himself in the national spotlight again with the March from Selma to Montgomery. The Freedom March was an opportunity for Wallace to play the race card yet again. For Martin Luther King Jr it was an opportunity to expose the denial of the vote for African Americans in the South. The violent beatings of the marchers by Sheriff Clark swept around the nation and led to national and international protests. Johnson issued an order to stop further marches. Wallace and King were party to an agreement that would allow a symbolic march in defiance of the court order. Eventually Johnson agreed with the NAACP Legal Defense Fund and approved a route for the marchers and required Wallace to provide protection. It was only because the march was seeking the right to vote that persuaded Johnson that King's tactics were right (Yarborough, 1981). Johnson argued a constitutional 'theory of proportionality.' In approving the march from Selma to Montgomery he argued that, although such a march would inconvenience the public, the right of protest 'should be commensurate with the enormity of the wrongs that are being protested and petitioned against.' And he stated bluntly, 'In this case, the wrongs are enormous. The extent of the right to demonstrate against these wrongs should be determined accordingly' (Carter, 1995).

However, Johnson was not an uncritical sympathiser. He was concerned about the wider implications of civil disobedience. He maintained: 'The philosophy that a person may – if his cause is labelled "civil rights" or "states rights" – determine for himself what laws and court decisions are morally right or wrong and either obey or refuse to obey them according to his own determination, is a philosophy that is foreign to our "rule-of-law" theory of government' (Yarborough, 1981). Governor George Wallace denounced Johnson's ruling in the state legislature. He accused his old law school associate of 'prostitut[ing] our law in favor of that mob rule while hypocritically wearing the robes and clothed in the respect built by great and honest men' (Carter, 1995).

Johnson remained in the firing line. He was the judge that presided over the trial of the murderers of Mrs Viola Liuzzo and he played a major part in ensuring that the jury would eventually convict the murderers, Collie Leroy Wilkins, Eugene Thomas and William Orville Eaton (Bass, 1993). His struggle for justice and civil rights led to a sweeping attack in 1972 on the abuses that occurred in the state mental health institutions which he denounced as 'human warehouses.' He ordered Governor Wallace to comply with strict standards for care and treatment of patients, set up human rights committees for each hospital and granted them sweeping powers to ensure the protection of patients. Also in 1972, in *Newman v Alabama*, Johnson ordered that the shocking neglect of prisoners' medical care should cease, he laid down minimum conditions for prisoners and set up human rights committees to ensure that his order was fulfilled. His strict rulings on the state of Alabama's prisons infuriated Wallace who told the press that Johnson needed a 'good barbed wire enema' (Carter, 1995).

Ignored by Richard Nixon, who was intent on pursuing a southern strategy which did not include liberal Republicans such as Johnson, it was Democrat Jimmy Carter who saw the merits of this remarkable judge. The FBI had suffered from its involvement in the Watergate break-ins and cover-up and desperately needed new leadership. Carter offered the post to Johnson. Owing to ill health and two operations, he asked Carter to withdraw his name from nomination. After he had recovered it was Carter who promoted him to the Fifth Circuit Court of Appeal. Ironically, in 1979 it was one of the politicians who had attacked the courts and Johnson's rulings, John Patterson, who praised his civil rights role and inducted Johnson into the Alabama Academy of Honor (Yarborough, 1981).

The White Students

It was African American women and men who led the struggle for justice in the civil rights movement, especially students from the state-sponsored black colleges and universities. But their struggle inspired many young white southerners to challenge the myths that their parents had elaborately woven to ensure the rule of white supremacy. Just as much as the politicians and judges, these young white southerners were prepared to challenge the South, its traditions and more importantly to question the authority of their families, religious leaders and educators. Judge Johnson's son was one such student. While at the University of Alabama, Johnny Johnson led the Young Democrats in 1968 and he and his fellow Democrats endorsed the campaign of Eugene McCarthy. George Wallace was campaigning with the aid of state officials when the Young Democrats passed a resolution that the state employees should return to their jobs and Wallace could stay away from the state for as long as he wished.

However, Johnson Jr had the example and support of his mother and father who faced constant controversy for their civil rights stand. Others had much greater challenges. They were all part of the longer tradition of southern radicals as represented by Carl and Anne Braden, James Dombrowski and Miles Horton. But these young southerners are barely mentioned by historians of radicalism. Moreover in a recent study of the movement, the reader is assured that apart from 'islands' such as Austin, Texas, New Orleans, Louisiana and Atlanta, Georgia, southern students were not merely untouched by, but were positively antagonistic, to the radical movement against the war in Vietnam, the free speech movement, women's rights and gay rights. The author of that study states: 'In 1968 two movies were popular: *The Graduate* was a hit in large liberal cities, while *The Green Berets* played to crowds in small-town America. Few southern universities witnessed demonstrations' (Anderson, 1995). White students not only participated in the civil rights movement but also many became activists in their opposition to the war in Vietnam, and extended their civil rights activity to include women, gays and any group they considered victims of repression.

The response of southern students to the struggle of African Americans for justice was just as complex as the response of their parents. The South was not solid. Students at the University of North Carolina at Chapel Hill participated in the movement and Ralph Allan was a member of SNCC. In 1961 white students at Presbyterian and Baptist seminaries were arrested for taking part in sit-ins in Louisville, Kentucky. White and black students participated in sit-in demonstration in Nashville, Tennessee (*The Student Voice*, April and May 1961). A year before, the students at the University of Tennessee at Knoxville had petitioned the trustees asking them to integrate the University and the board complied with the students' wishes. Miles Horton of the Highlander Folk School in Monteagle, Tennessee, organised a workshop on 'The Role of the Student in the Changing South.' The workshop held on 11–13 November 1960 was attended by 80 students from black and white universities throughout the South.

Bob Zellner was typical of the white students who became involved in the civil rights movement. The son of a Methodist minister, he was raised in Alabama and attended Huntington College in Montgomery, Alabama. In recalling the segregated society of his youth, he commented: 'It was just the way things were. You didn't think about it. Sometimes when you are inside the system, you can't see it very well. But children are not born racists. They are taught to have racial attitudes' (Morrison and Morrison, 1987). His interest in and sympathy for the civil rights struggle resulted in the KKK burning crosses at the College. He refused to resign from the College, graduated, joined SNCC and found himself in jail when working on voter registration in McComb, Mississippi, and took part in a march to protest against the murder of a black SNCC worker. At first Zellner did not want to take part in the planned protest. He realised that the young black students were leading the first protest march in Mississippi since Reconstruction and that if they failed they would lose everything. He joined the march and was subjected to extreme violence.

Zellner was also at the Freedom March from Selma to Montgomery. As he recalled later: 'My parents supported me, but it was very alarming to my mother. She was always pleading with me to be careful.' She had good reason: Zellner's grandfather and uncle were members of the KKK and had threatened to murder him. Later he was present at the Danville, Virginia, protest in 1963 which resulted in the hospitalisation of hundreds of activists.

Ironically, just as more young southerners were prepared to challenge the southern power structure of white supremacy, black southerners became increasingly wary of co-operating with whites. During the Freedom Summer of 1964 many blacks in the movement resented the attitude of many of the white northern students. Although Zellner was excluded from the criticism because he was a southerner and 'just one of the niggers,' it was decided to exclude whites from SNCC. As a charter member of the organisation and one who had happily taken beatings and imprisonment for the struggle, he was told he could remain on the staff, attend meetings but not vote. Zellner refused. He believed 'it was a mistake. It was playing into the hands of the enemy to have a formal exclusion of whites from SNCC.' Despite his personal disappointment he refused to be bitter (Morrison and Morrison, 1987).

The emergence of Black Power came when a significant minority of southern white students were seeking to bridge the gap and were willing to take up the challenge. Although excluded from SNCC and CORE with the rising tide of black nationalism, these white southern students participated in or were influenced by the civil rights struggle and they continued the fight for reform. After leaving SNCC, Zellner assisted Carl and Anne Braden and SCEF, working with white and black pulpwood cutters who had formed in 1967 the Gulfcoast Pulpwood Association, many of whose members earned less than $3000 a year. On 23 September 1971 in Laurel, Mississippi, Charles Evers, the African American Mayor of Fayette, Mississippi, and the independent candidate for governor, addressed a rally organised by Zellner of workers who were involved in a four-year strike against the Masonite Corporation. The president of the association was James Simmons of Forest Home, Alabama. Evers told the strikers, 'I've always known that the poor black and poor white would some day get together. Thank God, it's beginning here in Jones County.' White pulpwood worker Juston Pulliam agreed with Evers and Zellner: 'People are beginning to see that rich people are out for just one thing – more money. The only way to stop it is for all the poor people to get together, no matter what color their skin is. Black and white is brothers' (*New York Times*, 24 September 1971). The strike was broken and the union was defeated (Dorothy Zellner to SCEF, Southern Mississippi, Digital Collections).

Some southern students, like those from eastern and northern universities, adopted the tactics of nonviolent disobedience to oppose the war in Vietnam. Virtually all college campuses in the South saw a remarkable amount of dissent and it was the work of these activists that has been largely ignored. Radical activism was a feature of many campuses in the South. This included underground newspapers, co-operatives, as well as educational and social reform. In Knoxville, Tennessee, between 1968 and 1980 there were several radical student and community papers such as *Paperbag*, *The Up-Country Revival*, *Libra*, *Bad News*, *Rhapsody* and *The Knoxville Gazette*. All of them reported on women's and gay liberation and radical activities in the South and the nation. Like students in the North and West, they were in a minority but they played a significant role in many aspects of the movement in the history of 1960s and 1970s radicalism.

There were students who opposed the war in Vietnam. In 1966 UT students set up the Vietnam Education Group and many of its members had been involved in the civil rights movement in Mississippi, Tennessee and Georgia. The majority of those involved in the anti-war demonstrations were from Tennessee and other southern states. For example, John Z. C. Thomas was a graduate student from Montgomery, Alabama, and David W. Bowen was from Memphis, Tennessee, where in 1965 he ensured the integration of the city's swimming pools, and

Tom Wilson, from Mississippi, had defended the right of African Americans to attend Mississippi State University. Most of the 500 students who demonstrated against the visit of Lt General Lewis Hershey, director of the Selective Service, were Tennesseans. The protesters issued a statement not only attacking Johnson for betraying his promises of peace and a Great Society, but also failing to reform the draft which 'placed the burden of this war on the poor, the disadvantaged and the black man.' These students were joined by many more in a memorial service held in honour of Martin Luther King Jr after his assassination in Memphis in April 1968. When Ralph Abernathy led the Poor People's March on Washington through Knoxville, the students helped with the housing and feeding of the marchers.

The Free Speech Movement that had swept through the University of California at Berkeley also affected universities in the South. The response of southern university administrators was the same as those in California. The President of Auburn University, Alabama, banned the anti-war activist, Reverend William Sloane Coffin, who had been invited by the students. Tennessee banned the drugs advocate, Dr Timothy Leary. Students and faculty at both universities sued for and won an open speaker policy.

The argument over speaker policy reflected the growing concern among senior administrators at the growing radicalism on the campus. Efforts by students to establish a UT chapter of the Southern Student Organizing Committee (SSOC) were temporarily thwarted. However, a chapter was functioning by 1968 and SSOC, along with a 'hippie' group calling themselves the Big Oranges for a Democratic Society, led demonstrations against attempts by the university to enforce its *in loco parentis* policy.

Student power, the anti-war movement, and racial justice were common themes for students at UT and universities in other southern states. In 1970 Nixon ordered the invasion of Cambodia and was bitterly opposed, not only on northern and so-called liberal campuses, but throughout the South. And the killing of students at Kent State University in Ohio on 4 May 1970 saw student strikes sweep across the nation, including the South. At UT, led by Jimmie Baxter, the first black student president of a predominantly white university, 70 per cent of the students supported strike action following the Kent State killings. They protested also at the murder of six black people by the National Guard in Augusta, Georgia. At least 31 universities and colleges were hit by strikes. National Guardsmen, this time unarmed, removed student activists from the University of South Carolina campus and a 100-man police riot team quelled riots at the University of Alabama at Tuscaloosa. Classes were cancelled at three Florida campuses. Violent protests occurred at Duke and Chapel Hill in North Carolina and a strike at the University of Virginia was reported as '80 per cent effective.'

Nixon and his staff were badly shaken by the protests and the President needed to be seen on a university campus. The evangelist Billy Graham had hired the football stadium at UT, Knoxville, for a revival meeting, despite doubts about such religious rallies being held on University property (Perlstein, 2008). Graham declared the meeting of 28 May 1970 a youth festival and invited Nixon to the campus. Most anti-war activists realised the dangers of this provocation but 1500 activists attended the rally carrying signs with the commandment, 'Thou Shalt Not Kill.' Gus Hadorn, a student from Sweetwater, Tennessee, recalled, 'On that particular day, I saw a lot of people that had come to the Billy Graham Crusade with hate in their eyes' (*Esquire*, September 1970). After Nixon and his entourage and the national media circus had left town, the police set about arresting students and faculty who had participated in the protest.

Some faculty members protested against the arrests but the university lawyer announced that he was investigating them for misconduct and threatened to fire them. The student newspaper attacked the proposed witch-hunt as did the faculty senate and there were no dismissals. Dan Pomeroy on behalf of the history graduate students attacked the Board of Trustees' actions. He pointed out: 'As graduate students, we are intensely interested in working for excellence in this university and resent the fact that not only are the students denied an effective voice in working for that change, but that change in general is now suspect on this campus' (Riches, 1987). These southern students in Knoxville, Jackson. Chapel Hill and even in Oxford Mississippi stood against the prevailing mores of the South and their families on issues of peace, racial equality, gay rights, the women's movement and the rights of the poor. Their story has been ignored by historians of the civil rights movement. They shared most of the aspirations of many radical students in America. The ripples on the pond set in motion by the civil rights struggle affected all parts and all persons of the nation.

David Duke and the Old South

However, not all southerners were ready to reconsider the past. It has been suggested that, 'For those who insist that southern whites have undergone a fundamental change in their racial views since the 1960s, it should give pause that Duke received roughly the same share of the vote that a white supremacist would probably have received thirty years earlier in Louisiana'

(Klinkner and Smith, 1999). The David Duke role in that state's politics tells us more about the condition of the Republican Party in the South. When he was running as a member of the Nazi Party and the KKK, Duke made no progress at all in state politics. As the authors admit, it was only when he joined the Republican Party and advocated Republican policies of ending affirmative action, cutting welfare and a tough law-and-order policy that he won election to the state legislature in 1989. In 1990 he won 59 per cent of the white vote in an attempt to defeat the incumbent senator and 55 per cent of the white vote when he was in the run-off for the gubernatorial election. It should be noted that in the days of white supremacy in the 1960s, Duke would have won 100 per cent of the white vote in both races and with virtually no black voters would have won both. In January 2003 Duke pleaded guilty to charges that he had stolen money from supporters, partly to pay off gambling debts and he was imprisoned (*Time*, 20 January 2003).

The racism preached by Duke in Louisiana as a Republican then and in 2009 was no different from that espoused by many others in his adopted party. It is true that LBJ's empowerment of black people with the Voting Rights Act made a crucial difference, but Klinkner and Smith do not give enough credit to the change in white attitudes that explain an Al Gore Sr and his son, a Jimmy Carter or a William Jefferson Clinton. And it is also true that the white backlash against the civil rights of minorities was not just confined to the South, and is evidenced by the mushrooming of militia movements in the North. George Bush Sr and the Republicans exploited this anger.

7

WILLIE HORTON AND THE SOUTHERN STRATEGY: BUSH SR

It was the blue collar voters who flocked into groups such as Restore Our Alienated Rights (ROAR) whom the Republicans were eager to win over from the Democratic Party and in the process unravel the gains made by disadvantaged groups ever since the New Deal of Franklin Roosevelt. For fundamentalists also, whether Catholic or Protestant, the anti-abortion, anti-communism and anti-bussing crusades had a national, not merely regional, appeal. According to Howard Zinn, former SNCC activist and anti-Vietnam War protester, this new mood of conservatism which emphasised national unity had been engineered by the 'uneasy club of business executives, generals and politicos.' The elite ensured that the disadvantaged turned their anger against one another: for example, it was poor black students who were bussed into poor, white neighbourhood schools that were already substandard, while the superior suburban schools remained segregated (Zinn, 1980). The spokesman of this new conservatism was the former congressman, chief of the Central Intelligence Agency (CIA) and Vice President, George H. W. Bush in his presidential campaign.

Bush, a New Englander and Ivy League educated, had spent most of his career in Washington, D.C. However, he jettisoned his identity, eagerly portraying himself as someone who opposed the establishment. Fearing that his Democratic opponents, and right-wing forces in the Republican Party, would portray him as an east-coast 'wimp', Bush claimed to be a native of Texas and was always eager to demonstrate his skill with a gun, tossing horseshoes, as well as forcing journalists into endless hours of early morning jogging.

141

When seeking the nomination against Reagan, he had attacked his opponent's 'voodoo economics.' However, he quickly adopted the economic theories of Milton Freidman, espoused by Reaganites, in order to achieve his vice presidential ambition. He had supported the Equal Rights Amendment (ERA), women's right to choose an abortion and federally funded contraceptive services during his presidential campaign but now opposed all these in order to win the support of the conservative Moral Majority and Jerry Falwell, its evangelist leader. As Vice President, he had supported Reagan's efforts to pass amendments to the Constitution to allow states the right to require some form of religious observance following a Supreme Court decision to ban school prayer as a violation of the separation of church and state. He backed a pro-life amendment that would have overturned women's right to abortion (*Roe v Wade*) and as President in 1989 he tried to get Congress to pass an amendment outlawing the burning or desecration of the American flag (Lowi and Ginsberg, 1998).

Bush and the Republicans pursued the Southern Strategy. But the appeal to white racism was raw and no longer relied on the politics of euphemism. His campaign was shaped by Lee Atwater, a young conservative from South Carolina, who had earlier used negative campaign tactics, using Bush's earlier support for gun control legislation, to defeat Bush when he had sought the Republican nomination over Reagan. The same techniques ensured presidential success for the Vice President (Mark, 2007).

Willie Horton and the 1988 Campaign

Atwater used tactics familiar to southern Democratic Party demagogues which analysts had hoped were a thing of the past. The issue was race. The use of the race card was not new in Republican politics in the South where its most ardent players were Strom Thurmond of South Carolina, founder of the Dixiecrat Party in 1948 and later a Republican, and Jesse Helms of North Carolina (Furgurson, 1986). However, it was Atwater who used it in the national campaign to rescue George Bush from almost certain defeat. In the May Gallup poll, Bush at 38 per cent, was trailing his Democratic opponent, Michael Dukakis, Governor of Massachusetts. The liberal Democrat had a 16 per cent lead. 'Three Democratic losers, George McGovern, Jimmy Carter, and Walter Mondale, had negative ratings of 27, 28, and 29 per cent respectively in their unsuccessful campaigns of 1972, 1980 and 1984. Bush's negatives topped all of theirs' (Johnson, 1991). The Atwater campaign was designed to portray Michael Dukakis as an ultra-liberal and thereby to increase the Governor's negatives in the eyes of the electorate.

Thirty New Jersey voters who had supported Reagan in 1984 and who were thinking of returning to their traditional Democratic Party allegiance were selected by a marketing firm and were asked a series of questions by the Bush campaigners which emphasised the supposedly ultra-liberal stands of Dukakis. The group were unaware that they were participating in a survey organised by the Republican Party. It was stressed that, as Governor, Dukakis had vetoed a bill requiring the pledge of allegiance in schools but the survey did not indicate that this had happened in 1977. In addition, it was pointed out that the Democratic candidate was a member of the American Civil Liberties Union (ACLU) without explaining that the ACLU was a bi-partisan organisation which had defended not only radicals and civil rights workers, but also the KKK's right of free speech. They also told the group that it was Dukakis who had approved the furlough programme for Massachusetts prisoners when it had had the support of the previous governor – a Republican. In particular, they said Dukakis was responsible for giving a weekend furlough to a black prisoner named Willie Horton who had then raped and murdered a white woman in Maryland. They stated: 'As governor, Michael Dukakis vetoed mandatory sentences for drug dealers. He vetoed the death penalty. His revolving door prison policy gave weekend furloughs to first degree murderers not eligible for parole. While out, many committed other crimes, like kidnapping and rape, and many are still at large. Now Michael Dukakis says he wants to do for America what he's done for Massachusetts. America can't afford that risk' (www.pbs.org.frontline/atwater/script). The focus group was also told Dukakis was opposed to the death penalty. Half the selected group switched their allegiance to Bush.

Despite later denials, it was evident that the Bush campaign was shaped by Atwater. Bush continually contrasted his support for the pledge of allegiance with the veto that had been cast by his opponent. Dukakis was portrayed as an ultra-liberal and a 'card-carrying' member of the ACLU. Many of these assaults on his Democratic opponent were made on visits to factories that manufactured American flags or at American Legion meetings. Yet the most effective attack came with the linking of crime and race. Dukakis and the Democrats, according to Bush and the Republicans, were soft on crime. In America, where fear of crime was spreading as rapidly as racism, the linking of the two issues was ominous. The political maverick George Wallace had skilfully linked white working-class fears about job security and crime to the issue of race. 'For the age-old southern cry of "Nigger, Nigger", he substituted the political equivalents of apple pie and motherhood: the rights to private property, community control, neighborhood schools, union seniority' (Carter, 1995). But whereas Wall-ace, the third party candidate in previous elections in 1968 and 1972, might influence elections and popular opinion, he could not win the presidency.

It was the Republican Party and its leadership which exploited this, apparently gentler, demagoguery most effectively. The Vice President sim-ply followed the path laid down by George Wallace and also his Republican predecessors. Nixon had used 'bussing' as the code word for race and Rea-gan and Bush used 'affirmative action' and 'welfare' as well as 'violence.' Later President Clinton would use violence, especially teenage violence in the black community, to win the votes of the middle class and overcome the charge of being liberal. 'Richard Nixon initiated the use of thinly veiled racial code words that hinted at violence. Ronald Reagan imitated the prac-tice in 1980, and George Bush took it to a cynical level in 1988 with his Willie Horton advertisements' (Nightingale, 1993). The politics of crime linked young people, especially African Americans, to very violent crime. As Michael Males has argued: 'The higher rates of unwed childbearing or vio-lent crime among blacks and Hispanics relative to whites reflect the greater poverty of non-white populations. Where statistics on income are available, we find low-income whites also experience disproportionately high levels of these problems' (Males, 1996). Eric Alterman, a journalist and academic put it more succinctly: 'Race is poison, but it's poison that works for their side' (pbs. frontline).

The Willie Horton television commercial exploited the idea of the black male as peculiarly violent – a predator on the loose. It was shot in black and white, and depicted prisoners in a revolving door entering and leav-ing prison. Viewers were informed that hundreds of these men had been released and were still criminals. In another commercial by a Bush support group, the face of Willie Horton filled the screens as viewers were told of the rape and murder of a white Maryland woman. White fear of the black rapist has a long history. It was compounded in the 1960s by the re-issuing from 1966 onwards of Richard Wright's 1940 novel, *Native Son*, in which Bigger Thomas rapes and dismembers a white girl, and the work of Black Panther leader, Eldridge Cleaver, in his book published in 1968, entitled *Soul on Ice*, where he justifies raping black and especially, white women.

Ironically, national television's response to the Willie Horton advertise-ment was one of the few times that all three networks were critical of the Bush campaign, but by repeating the first commercial in their news bulletins and comment programmes, they were giving the Vice President free advertising. Political commentators who had argued that negative campaigning was counterproductive were proved wrong. 'In depicting Willie Horton as a symbol of Dukakis' alleged softness on crime, the Bush campaign fomented racial fears for political purposes and appealed to the worst elements of the American character' (Johnson, 1991). It also ensured George Bush his one term as president. The importance of the race card was not lost on his sons, George W. and Jeb, in the campaign of 2000.

George Bush Sr won the election in November by 53.4 per cent as opposed to 45.6 per cent for Dukakis. But the margin of victory was even greater in the South where Bush carried the 11 former Confederate states by 58.3 per cent compared with his opponent's 40.9 per cent. Apart from Washington DC, the ten states won by Dukakis were all in the north and this was despite the Democrats running their own southern strategy with the moderate Texan, Lloyd Bentsen, as vice presidential candidate. Although conceding racism was part of the Republican southern strategy, one analyst has asserted that it was not 'the factor.' He suggests that the regional disparity in white support for the Democratic Party 'would have been lessened significantly had the public's attention in the campaign been focused on economic issues and not on highly charged social issues' (Lamis, 1990). However, the aim of the southern strategy was to focus on these social issues. Incumbent US Senator Jesse Helms trailed his black Democratic opponent, Harvey Gantt, in the 1990 North Carolina election. Helms used an advertisement showing 'white hands crumpling a letter and a voice-over said, "You needed that job and you were best qualified, but they had to give it to a minority because of a racial quota"' (Klinkner and Smith, 1999). One commentator on negative advertising claims it did not affect the result (Mark, 2007).

It was no comfort to African American voters when Atwater, dying of a brain tumour in 1990, made a deathbed apology for the Willie Horton campaign and its exploitation of Americans' racial fears. Civil rights workers who had deserted the Democratic Party to campaign for Ronald Reagan returned to the fold. Ralph Abernathy supported the 1988 presidential bid of Jesse Jackson who adopted Martin Luther King Jr's major conviction that the issue was poverty. If the civil rights movement was to be successful and the gains were to be preserved, the movement had to be linked to the civil rights of poor whites, women and rights for the disabled. White Americans, according to Jackson, should join in a 'Rainbow Coalition' to protect civil rights gains by attacking the root cause of inequality – poverty (Abernathy, 1989).

Rodney King and the LA Police

Fifty-six per cent of whites in 1990 believed African Americans were prone to violence and Bush exploited this fear. However, only six per cent of murders and nine per cent of rapes in 1990 were the result of attacks by blacks on white victims. Although one-third of street muggings were committed by black men on white victims, it was the perception of the white community that 'mugging and black men were synonymous.' The use of violence by the police against black males has long been sanctioned by the white community – from the killing of 27 Black Panther Party members in 1969 alone, the use of live ammunition in riot control by police captain Frank Rizzo in Philadelphia in 1964, to the beating of Rodney King on a California motorway by members of the Los Angeles Police Department. 'The 1990 videotape of the beating of Rodney King in Los Angeles serves as another important reminder of the connection between racism and state repression in America' (Nightingale, 1993). The failure in the first trial to find the officers involved guilty of police brutality reminded African Americans that the judicial system benefited those who were white when the victim was black. The ensuing race riot in Los Angeles in 1992 was partly motivated by the belief that African Americans could not get justice. It was also a result of the 40 per cent cuts of the Reagan-Bush administrations in community funding and social service programmes, 63 per cent cuts in job training, and 82 per cent reduction in spending on subsidised housing in the years between 1981 and 1992. However, the riot 'was the catalyst forcing greater attention from President Bush and all Americans to the nation's widening economic and racial divisions' (Shull, 1993). It was tragic that it required a riot to make the President aware of such monumental problems and an even greater tragedy he did so little about them.

'A Kinder, Gentler America'

At his inauguration Bush called for 'a kinder, gentler America' which 'We must hope to give them [our children] a sense of what it means to be a loyal friend, a loving parent, a citizen who leaves his home, his neighborhood and town better than he found it.' In this society shaped by public generosity the community would care for 'the homeless, lost and roaming' (Shull, 1993). That so many Americans were in such a parlous state after eight years of the Reagan revolution was a sad commentary on years of economic mismanagement.

It was not the poor who benefited under Bush but the Savings and Loan Companies that took eight billion dollars. It was the homeless who had been the victims of the corruption in the Department of Housing and Urban Development. Central to the scandal that unfolded in the first days of the Bush administration were the Reagan political appointees who had funnelled tens of millions of dollars to those developers who had appointed influential Republicans as consultants. Presiding over this corruption was Samuel R. Pierce, a Wall Street lawyer who was Reagan's only black Cabinet appointment. The beneficiaries were Republicans such as disgraced former office-holder John Mitchell, Nixon's Attorney General. Mitchell made $75,000 for work on one project for the Department. Carla Hills, Bush's special trade representative, earned $138,000 for two projects (Johnson, 1991).

Bush Sr and Civil Rights

Bush not only faced the problems of mounting budget deficits but also a bitterly partisan Congress. Reagan had vetoed the 1988 CRRA designed to reverse the limitations the Supreme Court decisions had imposed on four recent civil rights laws making it very difficult for a complainant to prove job discrimination under the 1866 law and the 1964 Civil Rights Act. The CRRA was a major step to end federally funded discrimination as well as to extend civil rights legislation to women, the elderly and the disabled. Reagan and his conservative supporters did everything they could to kill it but eventually Democrats, with support from some Republicans, overrode the veto.

Democrats in Congress proposed further legislation in 1990. In *Wards Cove Packing Company v Antonia*, the Supreme Court ruled against Asian American women who had brought a case against the company for discrimination. The Court ruled that the plaintiffs had to prove they had suffered discrimination rather than that certain employment practices had different effects on different groups. The 1990 legislation provided for jury trials in cases where complainants brought charges of discrimination by employers and shifted the burden of proof from the employee to the employer, thus making it easier for those who had suffered discrimination to bring their actions to court. The legislation, The Civil Rights and Women's Equity Bill of 1991, co-sponsored by Senator Albert Gore Jr of Tennessee, would not just apply to African Americans but was extended to include gender, disability, religion and national origin and thus reduce the issues of race and quotas. However, Senator Dole, the minority leader, complained that the legislation went too far.

Republican Senator Orrin Hatch of Utah led the opposition to the Bill as proposed by Edward Kennedy. At first Bush was not involved, but as opposition mounted within the administration, led by Vice President Dan Quayle, the position of President Bush was crucial if the Bill was to succeed or fail. Bush vetoed the legislation. 'The veto represented the first defeat of a major civil rights bill in the last quarter century.' He exploited white fears that it gave advantages to African Americans that threatened whites when he defended his veto, '[He] used the word *quota* seven times in five paragraphs' (Klinkner and Smith, 1999). In the same year he vetoed a 'quota bill' designed to aid Native Americans claiming that it 'is so seriously flawed that it would create more problems than it solved.' Bush was attacked for caving in to the right wing of his party (Shull, 1993). Although Bush aides sought to limit the damage by claiming they supported some legislation for African Americans, such assurances were not accepted by the black community and the failure to extend the scope of the anti-discrimination legislation angered many women. In 1991 the Senate made compromises which limited the damages paid by an employer who had discriminated and defined legal defences employers might use. However, the Act extended civil rights protections to employees in the executive and legislative branches of the federal government. Although forced to sign the revised 1990 Bill, Bush complained it amounted to 'racial quotas,' and an administration directive was leaked which proposed the abolition of federal government affirmative action programmes which had existed since LBJ's 1965 executive order. It was denied that President Bush knew anything about the directive. As Shull has claimed, 'The controversial directive was to be appended to the bill, but the White House issued a new statement in the president's name eliminating the directive. Presumably President Bush tried to accomplish by administrative means what he had failed to do legislatively' (Shull, 1993). And southern Republicans were quick to follow his lead.

The veto of a civil rights bill and the controversy over the directive merely confirmed for most African Americans that the Bush administration was content to lead the resistance to black equality. The Civil Rights Division of the Justice Department had supported the struggle for justice under Kennedy and Johnson. With Reagan the Division had been headed by Bradford Reynolds who had consistently sought to narrow enforcement of civil rights laws. To replace Reynolds, George Bush nominated William Lucas, a leading conservative black Republican. Lucas has the dubious distinction of being 'the first black candidate for federal office rejected by the Senate after being formally nominated' (Shull, 1993).

Lucas had enthusiastic support from the right which is not surprising because he opposed racial quotas, supported racially segregated private schools that sought tax exemption and even argued that the recent Supreme Court decisions had not impeded those seeking equal opportunity. Faced with such staunchly conservative views, African American Representative John Conyers of Michigan withdrew his endorsement of Lucas. Jesse Jackson and the Mayor of Detroit, Coleman Young, also refused to continue their support. Most liberal groups backed away from Lucas and only the SCLC continued to support the nomination. Faced with this mounting opposition, Bush appointed Lucas to a post in the Justice Department which did not require Senate confirmation. The lack of interest in civil rights issues shown by President Bush is reflected in the collapse of the Civil Rights Commission in 1990 because only four out of the required eight were in post (Shull, 1993).

Appointing a Judge

Bush followed the example of Reagan. His nominations to the Supreme Court were judges who would actively support the conservative agenda. Thurgood Marshall, the NAACP lawyer who had led the battle in the *Brown* case and who was appointed to the federal judiciary by Kennedy, retired and George Bush in 1991 nominated a poorly qualified African American, Clarence Thomas, who has been described as 'the most controversial Supreme Court nomination in U.S. history' (Shull, 1993). For one African American political commentator: 'Thomas has emerged as the high court's most aggressive advocate of rolling back the gains Marshall fought so hard for' (*Time*, 2 June 1995).

Thomas was a devout believer in the conservative agenda. He opposed affirmative action although he himself had been a beneficiary by helping him enter Yale law school. Ironically, he also fills the quota of one black on the Supreme Court. Thomas also rejected class-action suits which enable large numbers of people to seek justice. Like Booker T. Washington at the turn of the twentieth century, he is a firm believer in black self-help. During his confirmation hearings in the Senate, Thomas was accused by Anita Hill, a fellow black conservative and law professor at Oklahoma, of sexual harassment (Mayer and Abramson, 1994). Having asserted he would never play

the race card, Thomas immediately accused liberals and women's groups
of a 'hi-tech lynching' and titled a chapter of his memoir, *An Invitation to
a Lynching* (Thomas, 2007). It was a cynical abuse of the horrors of lynching but very effective because Thomas' white, blonde wife sat conspicuously
behind her husband throughout the hearings. And Thomas was narrowly
confirmed because African Americans and liberal Democrats were deeply
divided over the issue. It may have been 'politically brilliant' for Bush to
appoint a black conservative but it cost him many votes from African Americans and especially women when he sought re-election in 1992 (Klinkner
and Smith, 1999).

Thomas followed the ultra-conservative views of Justice Antonin Scalia
who favoured extending the death penalty to children 15-years-old or
older (Males, 1996), and supported him in the first eight cases he heard.
The Court's 1992 attack on school desegregation in *Freeman v Pitts*,
weakening school desegregation orders, was later supported by Thomas.
Wade Henderson, Washington director of the NAACP, suggested that 'if
Thomas had been on the court at the time, he would have opposed
the decision in *Brown v The Board of Education.*' This assertion seems to
be borne out in Thomas's concurring opinion in *Missouri v Jenkins* in
June 1995 (see Chapter 8). Such was his conservatism that he even
opposed the Bush administration when it favoured 'broadly interpret-
ing the Voting Rights Act.' Clarence Thomas followed his white mentor Scalia and voted in support of the majority against Bush (Shull,
1993).

Bush not only appointed a black conservative judge to the Supreme Court
but continued Reagan's policy of appointing social conservatives to the federal courts. The appointments have had long-lasting effects. In addition, he
further weakened the gains made by the civil rights movement by dramatically reducing the financial support given by the government. Bush, like
Reagan, cut funding and staff to federal government civil rights agencies.
Government cases to enforce desegregation of schools, fight discrimination
in house sales and oppose employers who discriminated in employment,
all dropped dramatically. And although the Supreme Court had limited
affirmative action programmes, they had not ruled them unconstitutional
and, in *United States v Paradise* (1987), the decision required the Alabama
Department of Safety to hire African American state troopers 'to correct
the effects of past discrimination.' The courts increasingly required complainants to prove disparate treatment on the basis of discrimination as a
group by race, gender or disability rather than 'disparate impact' discrimination against an individual. Bush was content to leave it to individuals
to fight such harder cases in future. The triumph of conservatism made

possible by Bush and Reagan appointments was evident in a Supreme Court ruling in 1989. In *Richmond v Crosen*, the Court ruled that the 'set-aside' programme which required 30 per cent of the city of Richmond's construction contracts to go to minorities, including blacks, was unconstitutional because it violated equal protection guaranteed in the Fourteenth Amendment (Dye and Zeigler, 2000).

But Bush and the Republicans realised that without some gestures to win African American support, they would not win control of the House of Representatives or some state legislatures. Unlike Reagan, who had had only eight meetings with black leaders in eight years, George H. W. Bush had more than forty in his first two years. Whereas Reagan vetoed sanctions against South Africa Bush supported strengthening them and called for the release of Nelson Mandela. Although he increased the budget of the Equal Employment Opportunity Commission, the progress made was not good. However, he won wide support for the funding of 'historically Negro colleges'. These were all-black institutions and black academics praised his work for their universities. He won black support when he denounced the murder of a civil rights lawyer in Atlanta and a federal judge in Alabama. And he appointed a liberal Republican as head of the Civil Rights Commission. Manning Marable claims, 'The net impact of Bush's verbal and political overtures to black America reaped impressive political gains' (Marable, 1991).

African Americans in Mississippi

Although the civil rights movement suffered reversals at the federal level during the Bush administration, African Americans exercised increasing power at the state level. This was true even in the Deep South where resistance to civil rights for blacks had been the fiercest. Lyndon Baines Johnson knew when he signed the Voting Rights Act of 1965 that he was destroying the grand national coalition built by FDR which had meant the Democrats had been the majority party since 1932. And the Republican Party, the party of Emancipation, at a federal and state level was increasingly the white person's party, especially in the South. Rapidly losing traditional white segregationist supporters, the Democrats only reluctantly understood that if they were to have any influence at state level, they would have to compromise with the newly enfranchised black voters.

The first reaction of white southern Democrats, however, had been resistance, and after the 1965 Act, the Mississippi legislature redrew state districts to ensure only one black representative would be elected to the legislature out of 122 lower house members and 52 senators. Hinds County, for example, which included the state capital, Jackson, and had 40 per cent black population, did not have a single black representative out of the ten members from the district. But compliance with the Act was forced on reluctant whites after African Americans in the state sued 14 times and went to the Supreme Court nine times. As a result, it was enacted in 1979 that there would be only one member per district and 15 African Americans were elected to the house and two to the senate. In all the subsequent elections their representation increased dramatically.

By 1988 they had 21 representatives in the state house and four black senators. And in 1991 and the special elections of 1992, black representation jumped from 21 in the house to 31, and senators from 4 to 10. As Stephen Shaffer and Charles E. Menifield have pointed out, African Americans held significant power on state committees, especially in areas such as education, and they had built a biracial alliance with white Democrats which ensured the state's 1982 Education Reform Act. When the Bush administration in 1989 was cutting back on federal aid to programmes in education, such as the very successful Head Start programme, black and white Mississippi Democrats in the same year passed the School Equity Funding Act giving state funds to poorer school districts and requiring all districts to have a property tax that would support public elementary and high schools. This coalition would produce further successes in the 1990s and not just in education.

However, African Americans in Mississippi were no different from many white Mississippians and other people in the United States. They were deeply divided over the abortion issue. In 1986 all the black senators and 25 per cent of the representatives favoured legislation requiring parental consent for a minor before an abortion. When Governor Roy Mabus vetoed legislation on the abortion issue, even more black representatives joined their white colleagues, Democrat and Republican, to override his veto. It was an issue that would not go away and later a larger number of black representatives in the state opposed liberal abortion measures (Shaffer and Menifield, 2002).

As George Bush Sr and his opponent Bill Clinton exploited the law and order issues in the 1992 presidential campaign, black members of the Mississippi legislature were deserted by their white Democratic colleagues. As the pressures mounted for a crack down on juvenile crime, teenagers became synonymous with drugs, alcohol abuse, and single parenthood and African American lawmakers found themselves under the same pressure as white representatives not to be 'soft on crime.' Increasingly Americans were not viewing crime as a social and economic problem, but rather the wilful acts of vicious people many of whom, it was alleged, had been created by the permissive society of the 1960s and the civil rights movement's defiance of the law. There was only one victim, and that was the person assaulted by the degenerate criminal. The latter could not be helped. Prison was the only answer (Milligen, 2001).

The Black Caucus groups set up by African Americans in other states apart from Mississippi were very effective, but just as important was the ability of black persons to serve in state legislatures and gain experience which made it possible for them later to challenge for seats in the federal house. For example, black women were helped in this way. Corrine Brown was elected in the Florida First District in 1993 after serving 10 years in the state legislature, and in the same year Cynthia McKinney was elected in Georgia having been in the state legislature since 1988. And it was not only southern black women who were helped by the new black vote. Julia Carson was the first African American woman from Indianapolis, after serving 18 years in the Indiana legislature, to be elected to the House and in 1996 Barbara Lee in Oakland, California, succeeded Ron Dellums, a long-time leader in the Black Caucus when he retired in 1998. Lee had served in the state legislature from 1990 to 1996.

Women of Colour and the New Conservatism

Thomas, the sole black justice on the Supreme Court, not only opposed civil rights laws for African Americans but was also very hostile towards women and homosexuals. The great triumph of the feminist movement had been the court ruling in *Roe v Wade* (1973) legalising abortion throughout the United States. However, the 1980s and the new political conservatism meant that women of all races were forced to struggle to even hold onto what they had achieved. In his election George Bush's opposition to abortion and attacks on single mothers were always in the context of a campaign that stressed family values – supposedly confined to the white, middle class. It was the patriarchy supported by black men but bitterly opposed by increasing numbers of black women. They turned to the women's movement for alliances and as Angela Davis explained 'women of colour included' white women (Davis, 1988).

Although the Supreme Court had not overturned *Roe*, it limited the use of federal funds in such cases, a move which was particularly detrimental to poor women, black and white. In 1989 the Court ruled in *Webster* that states had the right to limit abortions. At his confirmation hearings in 1991, Thomas stated he supported the Court's decision. In this it is true that he reflected the views of many African Americans, male and female. Although Thomas did not say he agreed with them, many so-called militants such as the Black Muslims and the black fundamentalist and Catholic Christians, not only opposed abortion on moral grounds but also because they viewed it as genocide.

Although, as noted above, some black women, like the civil rights activist, Pauli Murray, joined NOW, most of them in the 1960s saw the movement as a race struggle not as a gender issue. The sexism of black nationalists, such as the Black Panther Party and Black Muslims, made some women re-think their attitudes. Even more did so following the nomination of Clarence Thomas and the accusations of sexual harassment made by Dr Anita Hill. Although the overwhelming majority of African Americans supported Thomas when the accusations were first made, this backing soon diminished (Dye and Zeigler, 2000). The conservative campaign to undermine Hill's credibility angered many black women, and 1603 of them put their names to a paid advertisement in the *New York Times* defending her. They denounced the 'malicious defamation' of Hill and that her experience only showed how throughout American history, 'Black women have been stereotyped as immoral, insatiable, perverse; the initiators in all sexual contacts – abusive or otherwise . . . [B]lack women who speak of these matters are not likely to be believed' (Giddings in Ruiz and DuBois, 1994). Giddings argues that sexual stereotyping of black women was 'the principle around which wholesale segregation and discrimination was organized with the ultimate objective of preventing intermarriage. The sexual revolution, however, separated sexuality from reproduction, and so diluted the ideas about purity – moral, racial, and physical.' She maintains integration and feminism made 'dissemblance and suppression in the name of racial solidarity anachronistic' (Giddings in Ruiz and DuBois, 1994). Despite charges of white racism by feminists, black women, in Giddings' opinion, should join forces with their white sisters to struggle against male oppression, black and white.

It was these wider rights that were threatened by the courts and the Bush administration. Equal opportunity laws for women in education and employment were weakened by the courts and by the attacks of Reagan and Bush. The Small Business Administration reduced its assistance to all women's enterprises; schemes for job evaluation, important for equal pay demands, were not carried out; day centres for working women had little funding, as did shelters for battered women and legal aid centres (Kerber and Sherron De Hart, 1991). The only concession offered by George Bush to working women was a campaign promise of a small tax concession to the poorest families to help pay for day care. Women of colour, who were often the sole providers for their families or were forced to work in low paid jobs because their partners were so badly paid, were disproportionately affected by the failure of state and federal government to provide child support.

In 1984 George Bush proudly boasted that he had 'kicked a little ass.' The 'ass' involved was that of Geraldine Ferraro, the vice presidential nominee for the Democratic Party. Ferraro recalled, 'There are rumours about me being involved in lesbianism, about my having affairs, about me having an abortion' (Faludi, 1992). One of the short-term effects of this negative campaigning was a dramatic decline in the number of women seeking public office. This was reversed in 1992 when the number of black and white women candidates for office, overwhelmingly Democrats, increased again and several were successful in their election campaigns, including the Senate race in Illinois which saw the election of the first black woman senator in American history, Carol Moseley-Braun. Dubbed 'the year of the woman' by the popular press, there was much talk of the Political Action Committee to increase the number of Democratic pro-choice women elected to Congress, the so-called EMILY's LIST. Some Republican women were sensitive to the possibility of losing votes and set up a Political Action Committee to fund pro-choice Republican women candidates – the Women in the Senate and House (WISH List). However, Bush's vetoing of civil rights legislation, because it would ensure gender equality, and his boast of 'kicking a little ass' go a long way to explain why he failed in his re-election bid in 1992. American women voters switched their votes to the Democratic Party. The role of Hillary Clinton, a successful career woman and pro-choice, also played an important part in Clinton's success.

George H. Bush and the Gay Community

If the issue of interracial sex between heterosexual men and women disturbed many conservatives, the majority of African Americans who had fought to overcome state laws against interracial marriage were just as conservative as their opponents when it came to matters of same sex relationships, whether intraracial or interracial. White Americans have had a long history of fear of interracial relations as can be seen in the gruesome evidence of the lynching of black men accused of raping or having sexual relationships with white women (James Allen *et al.*, 2000). This traditional loathing of interracial sex was even greater when explicit images of black men and white men were displayed in the National Endowment of the Arts exhibition of Mapplethorpe's photographs in Cincinnati, Ohio. Opponents of homosexuality were just as vociferous in their condemnation of white and black lesbian relationships.

During the Bush administration gays and lesbians of all races demonstrated against discrimination in the American armed services. However, General Colin Powell, the first African American head of the Joint Chiefs of Staff, was strongly opposed to the idea of gays and lesbians serving in the military, even though his stand was openly opposed by the conservative Barry Goldwater, and lesbians and gays had fought in all America's wars. For example, General Eisenhower in the Second World War issued an order that all homosexuals should be dismissed from the military but when his assistant offered her resignation and revealed she was a lesbian, he rescinded the order (Faderman, 1992). And so long as gays and lesbians denied their sexual orientation the issue was ignored and Eisenhower accepted a 'don't ask and don't tell' approach to gays in the services.

Encouraged by the backlash against homosexuality in both the black and the white public, Bush chose not merely to neglect gay rights but to attack them. The Bush administration's attitude towards African Americans and women was one of verbal re-assurance if not action, but this was not true for the homosexual community who were singled out by most Republicans as the group that was destroying America. Homosexuals and lesbians, according to George Bush, were not 'normal' and throughout his administration, and especially at the Republican National Convention in 1992, they were subjected to fierce assaults in the name of family values. Despite his bitter battle with the conservative journalist, Pat Buchanan, for the presidential nomination, Bush supported his former opponent who declared a 'religious war' against gays. Bush also worked closely with anti-gay extremists such as the Reverend Donald Wilmot of Tupelo, Mississippi, and the Californian Reverend Louis Sheldon (Signorile, 1993).

After the GOP convention, the conservative *Time* magazine wondered, 'After Willie Horton Are Gays Next?' (Miller, 1995), but 'gay bashing' did not become a major theme of Bush's campaign partly because opinion polls showed that the convention rhetoric had not been well received by most Americans. Although Bush and Vice President Dan Quayle stepped back from an all-out attack, their example was not followed by others whose vehemence encouraged anti-gay groups to initiate action.

In Oregon the state voters were asked to vote on Ballot Measure 9, which intended to insert into the state constitution that homosexuality was 'abnormal, wrong, unnatural and perverse' and on a par with bestiality.

The measure was proposed by the Oregon Citizens Alliance, a fundamentalist group supported by prominent Republican, Pat Robertson, and his Christian Coalition. The campaign was marked by neo-Nazi attacks and some murders of homosexuals. Although the proposal was defeated, 42 per cent of Oregon voters favoured positive discrimination against the homosexual community. A similar measure which encouraged discrimination against gays was passed by a narrow majority in Colorado and immediately violence against that community rose by 300 per cent (Signorile, 1993). Eventually on 20 May 1996, in *Romer v Evans*, a US Supreme Court majority ruled that the Colorado amendment violated the Unites States Constitution.

The failure to meet the needs of the homosexual community, especially the AIDS crisis, made black and white homosexuals more militant (Miller, 1995). The witch-hunt against them in the military, which resulted in the dismissal of over 13,000 from 1982 to 1992, particularly angered gay activists.

Civil Rights for the Disabled

However, the Bush administration was not always opposed to civil rights legislation for African Americans, whether gay, lesbian or straight, and there was one notable exception when he did help members of these groups. To awaken the administration and the public to their demands, the disabled had been forced to use the same methods as the civil rights movement such as legal action, sit-ins, demonstrations and boycotts.

Testimony to Senate hearings also had a major impact. Judy Heumann, a polio victim confined to a wheelchair since childhood, had 'reenacted dramas that the civil rights movement for blacks had charged with symbolism' (Berkowitz, in Graham ed., 1984). Like the schoolchildren in Little Rock, she had been excluded from her high school on the grounds she was a fire hazard. Like James Meredith she had been denied a dormitory place at university and like Rosa Parks on the Montgomery bus she was refused travel on an aeroplane because she did not have an attendant. Such testimony, combined with the demonstrations and protests, succeeded when in 1990 the Americans with Disabilities Act was signed by the President at a ceremony on the White House lawn. This legislation 'brought civil rights protections for people with disabilities to a level of parity with civil rights protections already enjoyed by racial minorities and women.' Why did Bush support such a proposal when he was prepared to veto legislation that benefited African Americans?

This legislation was designed to help rehabilitate the disabled and make them self-sufficient tax payers, a proposal that no conservative could oppose and also because so many disabled were Vietnam veterans. The legislation stressed employment rather than affirmative action or quotas, which Republicans had been attacking throughout the 1980s. Many disabled people, moreover, voted Republican, unlike African Americans, for example, who overwhelming voted for the Democratic Party. 'The political strategy of playing upon racial resentments did not have to affect civil rights for people with disabilities who,' according to Edward Berkowitz, 'in many people's minds, personified the deserving poor, lived in the suburbs and not just the cities, and were the antithesis of the stereotypical, menacing members of the underclass' (Graham ed., 1994). An estimated 50 million disabled were the largest minority group in America. The resulting legislation linked disability with civil rights.

However, although they did not resist the struggle by the disabled, the Republicans neglected the new-found political activism of minorities and women at state and city level. It was this neglect, combined with an over-confidence based on the opinion poll ratings following the invasion of Iraq, which contributed to Bush's errors in his campaign for re-election.

The 1992 Campaign

George Bush's support for disability civil rights laws may have been influenced by the fact that he was a Second World War veteran. Certainly, throughout his presidency he had stressed his war record and he did so again when he sought re-election in 1992. This strategy was dictated partly because his opponent, Bill Clinton, the Governor of Arkansas, had opposed the war in Vietnam and when at Oxford University, participated in anti-war demonstrations in London. Bush's personalised attacks on Clinton as a coward, draft dodger, liar and a 'Slick Willie' reduced Clinton's lead but also reminded voters of the racist Willie Horton campaign that had brought Bush to the White House. Although most Americans saw him as an effective leader in foreign affairs, as during the Gulf War, his domestic policy was a failure. 'He came to office with no clear policy agenda, publicly referring to the "vision thing" as a public relations gimmick rather than as a guide for the nation.' Americans wanted a presidential candidate who showed he cared about their problems. As Clinton strategists were aware – 'it's the economy, stupid.' Americans 'want a president who will personalize government, simplify political issues, and symbolize the "compassionate" and protective role of the state. They want someone who seems concerned with them' (Dye and Zeigler, 2000). And Bill Clinton had these skills in abundance.

For many liberals, Clinton demonstrated that the sixties generation could achieve power and help shape the world. And his wife, Hillary, was a brilliant woman, who had strong political views and had also opposed the Vietnam War. Her determination to actively shape policy attracted many women voters who supported the Democrats and with Perot's third party campaign, Clinton's election was ensured.

8

A THIRD WAY FROM HOPE?
BILL CLINTON

George H. W. Bush, most of the media and many in both parties, underestimated the campaigning skills of the Governor of Arkansas, William Clinton. After Yale Law School, he spent a short time teaching law at the University of Arkansas and in 1974, as a young man, challenged the incumbent, conservative Republican congressman. Despite his anti-Vietnam War background, he almost won and the recognition he gained helped his election as state Attorney General. He quickly established himself as a populist and defender of consumers against giant utility companies. In 1978, aged 32, he became the youngest governor in the country. And it was the failure of his liberal programme and his defeat in 1980 that made him reconsider his liberal views.

In 1982 he was re-elected Governor advocating a 'third way.' This meant abandoning many welfare programmes and adopting the conservative view that the poor and unemployed should work for help – so-called 'workfare.' Much of the populist criticism of private enterprise was toned down, if not abandoned; harsh treatment of criminals and unswerving support for capital punishment were part of his New Democrat policy. In addition he did not hesitate to sideline some traditional Democratic supporters such as minorities and trade unions. This centrism was advocated in his 1992 presidential campaign when he claimed, 'We can be pro-growth and pro-environment, we can be pro-business and pro-labor, we can make government work again by making it more aggressive and leaner and more effective at the same time, and we can be pro-family and pro-choice' (*Time*, 2 November 1992).

160

Coming from a minuscule town called Hope, from a broken family and an alcoholic stepfather, Clinton's background for many Americans made him a candidate who would understand their problems – including the hardship of single mothers in a society where many marriages ended in failure and 'divorces, many initiated by women, soared' (Rowbotham, 1997). And after his nomination he did not balance the ticket in the conventional way by picking a northern liberal, but rather he chose a fellow border state southerner as his running mate, the senator from Tennessee, Albert Gore Jr.

The vice presidential aspirant came from a very different background. Unlike Clinton, he had had a stable, loving family whose father had been an outstanding senator and whose prescription for a southerner seeking the presidency (see Chapter 6) would later be adopted by his son when he ran for the White House in 2000. Gore Jr also had the advantage of having served in Vietnam and this would deflect criticism from Clinton's anti-war activities. Therefore, it seemed to many that the nomination of Clinton and the selection of Gore was a triumph of the new liberal South, and a re-assertion of the liberal agenda first established by FDR and his successors. But during the campaign there were signs that the candidates had a different agenda from many liberals. Gore, who had unsuccessfully sought the Democratic nomination in 1984, was an intelligent, ardent and internationally admired environmentalist, but he was better known for his wife's attacks on popular music, especially black rap music. Tipper Gore, shocked by Prince's 'Darling Nikki,' was instrumental in setting up the bipartisan group, Parents' Music Resource Center, designed to warn parents of the dangers of 'porn rock.' Her husband also took part in a Senate investigation of the music industry. Certainly the popularity of rap artists such as Tupac Shakur with raps in favour of the Black Panther Party and Black Power made middleclass whites uneasy (Werner, 2002). Gore disassociated himself from her crusade during the election. However, the main appeal of Gore to the Clinton campaign staff was his ability to attract younger, wealthier, middle-class, white voters. In 1984, Gore defeated his Republican opponent for the Senate by a crushing margin despite Reagan's landslide victory and the Republican candidate's unswerving loyalty to Reagan. Gore's victory (by over 60 per cent of the vote) was achieved in spite of efforts to portray him as a liberal with close ties to Edward Kennedy and Walter Mondale. Gore's response was: 'The old labels – liberal and conservative – have far less relevance to today's problems than the efforts to find solutions to these problems. There's no need to rely on outdated ideology as a crutch' (Lamis, 1990).

Clinton and Gore stressed their view that it was the end of liberal ideology. In 1991, as chair of the Democratic Leadership Council, Clinton
persuaded Democrats to reject 'quotas' and when challenged, said the party
still supported affirmative action and civil rights (Klinkner and Smith, 1999).
In the election campaign in 1992, Clinton promised to 'end welfare as we
know it' and told the poor, 'We will do with you. We will not do for you.'
However, Gore and Clinton had to keep the support of those traditional
groups such as African Americans, blue-collar workers and women who had
made the Democrats the majority party. The Bush Administration's hostility
to some of these groups had made him vulnerable.

This was particularly true of the new politically active and influential
group – homosexuals. Conservative commentators ascribed Clinton's election to gay power, but their significance in the election is difficult to judge.
CNN exit polls estimated Clinton won 72 per cent of their votes while others
put the figure closer to 90 per cent. But the major factor was the quixotic
campaign of Texas billionaire Ross Perot. Running on a populist campaign,
Perot claimed to speak for working people who could not get their opinions
heard by Washington bureaucrats. This was George Wallace's argument
when he had campaigned for the presidency (Carter, 1995). Perot won the
support of many blue-collar Republican voters and helped to ensure Bush's
defeat. It was these, the very voters whom Bill Clinton and Albert Gore had
hoped would return to the Democrats, who preferred the independent candidate. Clinton won with only 43 per cent of the votes cast, but he had a
massive Electoral College landslide.

Although President Clinton can be criticised for some of his policies and
their effect on the black community, as a southerner he knew only too well
that white racism was still a major force in the land. Most of his bitter critics
in his home state of Arkansas not only despised him for not fighting in the
Vietnam War but also, if not mainly, because Clinton admired JFK and supported the integration of public schools such as Central High School, Little
Rock. When he was state governor he invited the nine black students who
had led the integration of the school to the state mansion and honoured
them again as President on the 40th anniversary in 1997 (Wickham, 2002).
Clinton's sympathy for African Americans and his evident pleasure when
he attended their church services only increased his opponents' anger. As
Governor, his appointment of African Americans to the Arkansas Departments of Health, Human Services, Finance and Administration and the
Development Finance Authority meant that blacks held important offices
in Arkansas for the first time.

The assaults on Clinton throughout his eight years in the White House were also fuelled by his and Hillary Clinton's support for the pro-choice campaign and women's rights. As with African Americans, Clinton had promoted women and the disabled in state government and opposed a California popular ballot initiative opposing affirmative action in college admissions. The important changes in 1996 which benefited women were merely, according to his critics, designed to ensure he would win the women's vote (Dye and Zeigler, 2000). He did by a 16 per cent margin over his Republican rival, Senator Robert Dole. This may have been short-term ambition, as suggested, but he had long advocated the changes he succeeded in getting.

African Americans and Clinton's Campaign

During the campaign, Clinton stressed his support for black communities, the civil rights movement and financial assistance to minority businesses. He opposed 'racial quotas' but promised sweeping legislation to advance the black community. And he summed up his 'Third Way' in his campaign literature: 'Fight for civil rights, not just by protecting individual liberties, but by providing equal economic opportunity; support new anti-poverty initiatives that *move beyond the outdated answers of both major parties* and instead reflect the values most Americans share: work, family, individual responsibility, community' (Emphasis added). And the Clinton–Gore manifesto claimed they would, 'Empower people to make their own choices and regain control of their destinies.'

From the 1988 campaign and his knowledge of Arkansas Clinton understood the potency of race as an issue that swung votes. As Governor he allowed the execution of Rickey Ray Rector, an African American prisoner, on 24 January 1992, even though he was severely brain damaged from a failed suicide attempt and was totally unaware of his crime. (Clinton does not mention this in his 957-page autobiography.) The legacy of the Willie Horton advertisements linking race and crime hung over the election of 1992 and Clinton was not going to be seen as soft on crime. He knew Nixon, Reagan and Bush had successfully made law and order a race question. He sidelined the leading African American politician, Jesse Jackson, by associating Jackson with the alleged call by the rap singer Sister Souljah for blacks to kill whites (Klinkner and Smith, 1999). After mounting criticism from civil rights activists, Clinton campaigned for an African American woman as senator for Illinois. In this he achieved not only endorsements from African Americans but underlined his support for women's issues.

The First Black Woman Senator

Clinton and Gore not only campaigned for a black woman candidate, Carol Moseley-Braun, for the Illinois Senate seat but also for candidates from the Hispanic and Native American minorities as well. There is no doubt that the Clinton–Gore campaign was responsible for the election of the first African American woman to the United States Senate, one of six women that year to be elected to that body. Moseley-Braun, from Chicago's South Side, graduated in law from the University of Chicago and served in the Illinois legislature. Her determination to run for the Senate was fuelled by her outrage at the Democrat incumbent, Allan Dixon, who voted in favour of Clarence Thomas for the Supreme Court. In addition, she believed that an all-male, white Senate committee's treatment of Anita Hill, who had accused Thomas of sexual harassment, was disgraceful. She defeated Dixon and her Republican opponent despite a liberal agenda to ban discrimination against gays in the military, to improve family leave, to make voter registration easier and supporting programmes for the inner cities similar to LBJ's Great Society. Her only major political achievement, however, was to amend legislation so that absent fathers who failed to provide for their children would not get grants from the Small Business Administration (Lowi and Ginsberg, 1998). She was defeated for re-election in 1998 and President Clinton appointed her ambassador to New Zealand, a post she held until the election of George W. Bush. She was one of 17 African Americans appointed to ambassadorships during Clinton's two terms (Wickham, 2002). Moseley-Braun's success in 1992 was part of the wider drive to ensure greater representation of women at all levels of the federal government and Clinton and Gore supported the so-called EMILY's LIST of Democratic women seeking election to the House of Representatives and the Senate.

African American Appointments

African American women, like black men, voted overwhelmingly for Clinton. He persuaded Colin Powell, despite the latter's reservations, to stay on as the head of the Joint Chiefs of Staff and many African Americans were given high-level posts in the Administration, including Ron Brown as Secretary of Commerce. Later a Republican House of Representatives would start investigations accusing Brown of many things but he did not have to answer them because he was killed in an air crash. Other African American Cabinet officers appointed by Clinton were Jesse Brown, Secretary of Veteran Affairs; Mike Espy, Secretary of Commerce, Hazel O'Leary, Secretary of Energy, Togo West, Secretary of Army and Veteran Affairs, Alexis Herman, Secretary of Labor, Rodney Slater, Secretary of Transportation and Lee P. Brown, Director, Office of National Drug Control Policy. This was the highest number of black Cabinet officers in the history of the United States.

Moreover he appointed 36 black men and women to high posts in all departments. Nineteen senior White House staff included Terry Edmonds, the first African American speech writer, Thurgood Marshall Jr, assistant to the President and director of presidential personnel and Maggie Williams, the First Lady's chief of staff. Another 32 served on the White House staff. And 180 black men and women were executive branch political appointees. Joseph Lowery, an Atlanta civil rights worker, maintained: 'Clinton made some very significant appointments. I think his appointment record will probably exceed the level of all presidents before him, maybe combined' (Wickham, 2002). Clinton was enthusiastically supported by the Congressional Black Caucus because of these appointments.

Losing Battles? Jocelyn Elders, Henry Foster and Lani Guinier

In 1993, he appointed Jocelyn Elders as the first black woman Surgeon General of the United States. She was the eldest of eight children and her parents were sharecroppers with a three-room cabin in Arkansas. Following army service, she attended the state university medical school, gained a master's degree and joined the faculty. When he was Governor of Arkansas, Clinton appointed her state public health director. As Surgeon General, she angered the Catholic Church and many conservatives when she defended abortion, distribution of contraceptives in schools and legalisation of some drugs. In 1994 she infuriated them and many moderate Democrats when, at a United Nations conference on AIDS, she answered the question of a psychologist about the promotion of masturbation by saying, '. . . I think that is something that is part of human sexuality, and it's a part of something that perhaps should be taught. But we've not even taught our children the basics' (*New York Times*, 2 December 1994). This stand might be seen as sensible – the spirit of Clinton's 'Third Way' that claimed social problems, such as teenage motherhood, was to be solved primarily by personal responsibility. This stance allowed her to argue that young girls especially could end the 'crisis of single-parenthood' and young men and women could help reduce AIDS cases. She contended that 'the children of unwed teenage mothers account for nearly all crime,' a statement based on an unscientific survey of a central area of New York City that was virtually all black or Hispanic. Elders underestimated, and others ignored, the influence of poverty, and the sexual and physical abuse of young women who fled their homes and later became pregnant (Males, 1996). Her remarks at the United Nations might have been consistent but they were reported in the *New York Times*. She should have known that the decades-long arguments over basic sex education in schools would have forced Clinton to repudiate her statement. He went further and fired her.

Clinton's reputation for avoiding tough battles resulted in charges by some liberal and civil rights leaders that he was unwilling to stick by the decisions of the staff he appointed and that he betrayed his black supporters. Wishing to retain African American support, Clinton nominated Henry Foster for the post, a leading obstetrician who had been praised by George Bush Sr. The nomination linked the issues of race and abortion. The right-wing Christian Coalition immediately swung into action in their assault on Foster, who was charged with carrying out abortions – a legal operation. Foster did not help the President by underestimating the number of abortions he had done. Conservative Republicans, especially Phil Gramm of Texas, wanted the support of the Christian Coalition movement and its new leader Ralph Reed, in his bid for the Republican nomination in 1996. Moderate Republicans were concerned that a strong anti-abortion stance would alienate many pro-choice voters. Republican Bill Frist of Tennessee supported Foster's appointment and as he told *Time* reporters: 'I know he must have seen botched abortions, women coming in the hospital bleeding.' In addition, he knew about the segregation black doctors had suffered. 'I'm the only person on that panel who knows what it was like in the South in the 1960s' (*Time*, 15 May 1995). Despite the efforts of the Administration and support of moderate Republicans, conservatives prevented the nomination coming to a vote and Foster was not appointed. However, another African American, David Satcher, was.

But the greatest betrayal for most African Americans was his failure to defend Lani Guinier. It has been noted, 'When the Clinton Administration has found itself linked with persons identified with strong civil rights activism, such as Lani Guinier, it has quickly severed those links' (Klinkner and Smith, 1999). And African Americans were quick to respond to his failure. Clinton's support among black voters, regularly over 90 per cent, was dramatically affected by his unwillingness to stand by his long-time friend and fellow Yale Law School classmate. His popularity rating dropped among blacks to just 53 per cent, down by 34 per cent (Wickham, 2002).

He had nominated her to be Assistant Attorney General in charge of civil rights in 1993. Although she did not favour strict racial quotas, she was a staunch defender of affirmative action programmes. In addition, she argued that the districts, as drawn up for the House, were undemocratic because they resulted in over-representation of white people. African Americans, Hispanic and Asian Americans were trapped as a permanent minority (Guinier, 1994). Conservatives not only accused her of favouring quotas but also of refusing to believe that whites were willing to vote and work for black interests and that she considered black men, such as David Dinkins elected mayor of New York in 1989 with white votes, as not truly black (D'Souza, 1995). She staunchly defended redistricting to ensure a fairer representation of minorities. The civil rights movement had changed the voting habits of many whites but her critics failed to acknowledge that for years not only were districts in the North and West deliberately drawn to disenfranchise black Americans, but virtually all had been denied by law the right to vote in any district in the South. Ironically, her views were similar to those of the nineteenth century reactionary and pro-slavery defender, John C. Calhoun, who criticised the tyranny of the majority and proposed a system of 'concurrent majorities' – majorities in the North and the South. Guinier was not strident in her criticism but pointed to the federal court ruling against the city of Mobile, Alabama. The council of seven had a permanent majority of four whites to three blacks and because the whites refused to consider the views of the black councillors, the court ordered that there had to be a majority of five – one black vote had to count. As John Safford argues, although Calhoun had used the idea of a concurrent majority to ensure slavery's survival, 'that alone, however, does not invalidate the minority veto as a democratic means of dealing with extreme or otherwise irreconcilable cases of majority tyranny' (Safford, 1995). And it was the tyranny of the majority, as imposed on black people in Mobile, Alabama, that she opposed.

Although she used the arguments of Calhoun to demand fair representation for African Americans when confronted by intransigent white opposition, it was her persistent support for affirmative action polices, in line with Clinton's promises at the election, that enabled the conservatives in Congress to dub her 'the quota queen' and block her appointment. He did not struggle against the bitter resistance put up by conservatives and demonstrated that, 'the Democratic record on civil rights in the 1980s and 1990s has been characterized more by fairly passive resistance to conservative efforts than by any strong positive program' (Klinkner and Smith, 1999). However, his betrayal still angered many blacks who otherwise supported him. The leading New York City lawyer Johnnie Cochran, who worked on O. J. Simpson's defence team, claimed, 'We differed with him over Lani Guinier. I thought he ran away from her much too soon. He should have stood up for her' (Wickham, 2002). A harsher assessment by two white students of American government is: 'Clinton's actual choices were a careful blend of women, minorities, and white men, few of whom (especially those in important cabinet positions) had the inclination or the political stature to call for a strong agenda in support of racial equality' (Klinkner and Davis, 1999).

The Million Man March

For the millions of African Americans excluded from state and federal government or the offices of business, there remained the Black Power preached by the Nation of Islam. The popularity of the sect grew in the ghettos in the 1980s and 1990s in the era of not so benign neglect. The head of the Nation, Louis Farrakan, sought to demonstrate this with the Million Man March on Washington DC, on 16 October 1995. According to some estimates, there were only 400,000 black men listening to him 'indulge himself in lunatic numerology that went on for a mind-numbing two hours' (Thernstorm and Thernstorm, 1997). Jesse Jackson was attacked in the white press for attending the March but they failed to point out that many in the crowd represented Christian churches. And Jackson knew he could not be seen joining the attacks on Farrakan because 'it would have branded Jackson as a leader under the control of the white "they". Whatever the mainstream doubts about Jackson, he was one of the few political figures able to communicate at all across racial lines' (Werner, 2000). Another sign of the growing re-segregation of America was the adoption of Ron Karenga's substitute for 'the white man's Christmas.' A 1960s cultural nationalist, Karenga invented the December holiday, Kwanzaa, and although an increasing number of African Americans in cities like Washington DC celebrate Kwanzaa Day, just how many do and whether they no longer celebrate Christmas is not known (Thernstrom and Thernstrom, 1997). Radical rap music which praises black nationalism or the Black Panthers is popular, but the most successful 'gangsta rap' with its violent and homophobic language is equally popular with young whites and marketed by white-owned companies such as the Disney Corporation (*Independent*, 12 June 1995).

Clinton and the Supreme Court

Clinton agreed with arguments of the Black Caucus that the balance of the Supreme Court should be changed. Reagan's appointment of right-wing judges, vigorous opponents of the civil rights movement, such as William Rehnquist and Antonin Scalia and Bush's battle for Clarence Thomas, meant that the Court restricted the interpretation of the 14th Amendment to the Constitution and had started the process of limiting the nationalisation of the Bill of Rights begun by the Court in 1925 and accelerated by the Earl Warren court during the 1950s and 1960s. In order to achieve this goal, previous courts had been activist, seeking out breaches of the Bill of Rights and the 14th Amendment. Rehnquist reversed this trend dramatically. When he took over as Chief Justice in 1986 the Court heard an average of 150 cases and this declined steadily to 107 in 1992–93. By the term of 1995–96 this collapsed to a mere 75 (Lowi and Ginsberg, 1998). And this swing from being proactive also seriously eroded a woman's right to choose an abortion in rulings such as *Webster v Reproductive Health Services* (1989) and *Planned Parenthood of South-eastern Pennsylvania v Casey* (Riches, 2002).

The difficulties Clinton faced with the Court in trying to implement his civil rights policy must not be underestimated as can be seen in the 5 to 4 ruling in *Missouri v Jenkins* (1995) – a ruling enthusiastically supported by the black Justice Clarence Thomas. A lower federal court had ruled that the state of Missouri was wrong to fund Kansas City's predominantly white, suburban 'magnet schools' established for the benefit of children considered outstanding students because tests were culturally biased and instead the money should go to the predominantly black inner-city schools where scores were below the national average. Thomas attacked this ruling and argued that Supreme Court decisions had been misconstrued, including *Brown*, and consequently the lower court judge had supported 'the theory that black students suffer from an unspecified psychological harm from segregation that retards their mental and educational development. This approach not only relies upon questionable social-science research rather than constitutional principle, but it also rests on the assumption of black inferiority.' Thurgood Marshall, the lawyer who had impressed the young African Americans seeking to integrate Little Rock Central High School, would have been astounded and angered at the suggestion that he had supported the belief in black inferiority or that he had used 'questionable social-science research' in his great triumph in the *Brown* case. It is not surprising that Thomas has been described as 'Uncle Tom Justice' (*Time*, 26 June 1995).

In the same year in *Adarand v Pena*, the Court over-ruled affirmative action policies which required companies working on state contracts to use minority sub-contractors. Clinton undertook a review of the affirmation action programmes in his Administration and concluded that he would continue to support affirmative action but reform it so that there was no support for unqualified companies or people and 'no reverse discrimination against whites, and no continuation of programs after their equal opportunity purpose had been achieved. In a phrase, my policy was, "Mend it, but don't end it"' (Clinton, 2004). Certainly it was a better response than the efforts of many Republicans who wanted abolition of affirmative action but Clinton did not explain what the criteria that had to be met to prove that affirmative action goals had been achieved, and did not explain how he would mend it or when it was time to end it.

In his first term, Clinton appointed two justices. His first appointment in 1993 was the first Jewess to serve on the Supreme Court and increased the number of women from one to two. Ruth Bader Ginsburg, an ACLU member, consistently voted with the moderate judges, unlike Sandra Day O'Connor, appointed by Reagan, who is 'very conservative on blacks' if not women's issues' (Shull, 1993). The second was typical of the majority of previous appointments in that it was of a white man but Stephen Beyer moderated the Court's rulings. Unfortunately for those who supported the rights of African Americans and other ethnic groups, women and the disabled, Clinton did not have the chance to appoint another justice. Rehnquist's refusal to retire, despite serious health problems, ensured a five to four conservative majority and this proved vital to the election of George W. Bush in 2000. Consequently, civil rights groups and pressure groups were increasingly reluctant to take issues to the Supreme Court because they believed they would not succeed. Those who had struggled for civil rights had looked to the Court as the best way to achieve justice and it was a view held by many since the founding of the NAACP at the beginning of the twentieth century. The Court, perceived to be a partner in the struggle in the 1950s and 1960s, was now seen as part of the resistance and would reverse gains already made. In fact the Court made 12 rulings in 1995, 1996 and 1997 which 'placed limits on affirmative action, school desegregation, voting rights, the separation of church and state, and the power of the national government vis-à-vis the states' (Lowi and Ginsberg, 1998). Moreover, a Court which approved of the incarceration and execution of juveniles was not one to sympathise with liberals. And it was not until 2002 that the court decided that execution of the learning disabled (the majority on death row being black) was unconstitutional.

Clinton attempted to redress the balance of lower federal courts. He appointed six African Americans as federal appeal court judges, including two women, Ann Claire Williams and Judith Rogers. In the federal district courts he appointed 47 black men and women. No other president in the history of the United States had given so many black people power and influence at all levels of the federal government.

Lower courts followed the Supreme Court in opposing affirmative action programmes. A University of Texas Law School programme was declared unconstitutional in *Hopwood v Texas* after a white woman claimed she had suffered discrimination because she had not been admitted despite her higher scores than black students. The Fifth Circuit Court of Appeals ignored the fact that many *white* students with lower scores had been accepted as part of the University's policy of social diversity. And California and Washington state initiatives abolished affirmative action in their universities, with disastrous results for African Americans, Latinos and Asians. Clinton attacked the California decision only after his re-election in 1996. Critics have argued that he encouraged the backlash against affirmative action because he claimed he would end every programme that 'creates a quota, creates preferences for unqualified individuals, creates reverse discrimination or continues even after its equal opportunity purposes have been achieved' (Klinkner and Smith, 1999). Clinton, however, argued that affirmative action policies to achieve equal opportunity were right and although it is charged he only mentioned women, all the programmes he defended also protected minorities and the disabled. As for the action of the Appeals Court and the refusal of the Supreme Court to even consider the *Hopwood* case, no amount of rhetoric on the part of a president could have influenced the courts. Clinton would have ended up looking like an American King Canute. It can be argued he went as far as it was possible with his 'mend it don't end it' defence of affirmative action (Wadden, 2002). African American author, Blair Walker, and Mary Lane Berry, historian and law professor, considered Clinton's defence of affirmative action as a positive feature of his time in office (Wickham, 2002).

The War on Crime

Although Clinton sought to moderate federal courts, he had approved Rickey Ray Rector's execution in 1992 to demonstrate he was not soft on crime. And Stephan and Abigail Thernstrom maintain that the judicial system is not biased against African Americans and they point to the higher number of whites than blacks who are executed, even in a Deep South state like Georgia. They fail to explain why the number of black men executed is disproportionate to the number of blacks in the state. If the explanation lies within the pathology of the black community, then why are so few African Americans executed for murdering African Americans and why, in the sample years of 1996 and 1998, were there only three executions of whites where the victim was black?

In 1996, according to the Death Penalty Information Center statistics for the US, 45 men were executed. Only three were black-on-black murders. Apparently no black men had been killed by a white man. (In 1998 two white men were executed for killing a black man and a third for murdering two whites and one black. Even though predominantly white jurors were now finding the white killers of civil rights workers such as Medgar Evers guilty, they were not sentenced to death.) The only woman to die was Judy Buenano, identified as white, who was electrocuted in Florida. Following Clinton's re-election, the law-and-order rhetoric of both Democrats and Republicans became almost hysterical. The fact that George W. Bush, Governor of Texas, had approved more executions than any other governor in the United States probably was a significant advantage in his bid for the Republican nomination in 2000. It is ironic that a black community that has suffered the highest proportion of judicial executions should still favour the death penalty.

Clinton knew strict law measures against crime were popular and even if he had proposed the abolition of the death penalty for federal crimes, Congress would not have approved. Following Timothy McVeigh's bombing of the Oklahoma City Murray Federal Building on 19 April 1995 which resulted in the death of 129 whites, 32 blacks and 2 Native Americans, men, women and children, abolition of the federal death penalty was unthinkable. The American terrorist, Timothy McVeigh, was the first of two federal executions in 2001.

If the death penalty reflects the society and its wider attitudes, race clearly plays a part in the numbers of black men who have been executed and the many who are held on death row. The Supreme Court suspended executions in the 1970s when it was clear that states were discriminating against African Americans in the application of the law. But it is not only in cases of murder where African Americans suffer discrimination under the law. For example, Florida legislators made rape a capital offence but out of the 66 electrocuted, 65 were black, all 'guilty' of raping white women. The only white man executed had also raped a white boy. Apparently no black woman had been raped either by a white or a black man in the history of the state! Although Americans condemned the lynching in Jasper, is it too harsh to suggest there is judicial lynching in America? One thing is certain, many civil rights lawyers who work for the Southern Poverty Law Center (SPLC) see the application of the death penalty in this way.

The states are responsible for incarcerating most prisoners and the penal system was one of the growth areas of the 1980s and 1990s, attracting considerable investment from private enterprise in building and running prisons. In the years between 1994 and 1997, 1.4 million Americans were confined at the cost of $70 billion a year. Although this dramatic increase was primarily due to state laws and actions, the Clinton Administration supported longer sentences and prison building. State and city governments, under the Violent Crime Control Law Enforcement Act of 1994, were given $30 billion for more police, prison warders, prisons and crime prevention schemes. The rhetoric of linking race and crime meant that African Americans were disproportionately affected by the law-and-order policies. 'In total, between 1980 and 1999, the incarceration rate for African Americans more than tripled from 1156 per 100,000, to 3620 per 100,000 per year' (Center on Juvenile and Criminal Justice [hereafter CJCJ], 2002).

President Clinton could not directly affect crime legislation at the state level, but he and Congress controlled the federal prison system. Although the numbers of federal prisoners increased dramatically under Reagan and Bush, the greatest increase occurred during Clinton's presidency when 'the number of prisoners under federal jurisdiction doubled, and grew more than it did the previous 12-years of Republican rule, combined (to 147,126 by February 2001).' And as the author of the CJCJ report points out, spending on the Justice Department rose by 75 per cent while funding of the Environmental Protection Agency (EPA) declined by 15 per cent and by 28 per cent for the Energy Department (CJCJ, 2002). However, the report fails to acknowledge that Congress was controlled by conservative Republicans such as Newt Gingrich with their right-wing agenda called 'A Contract for America' and which liberals dubbed 'The Contract ON America.'

Drugs and Racism: The Coke Issue

And the law was seen as discriminatory in other ways – especially in the penalties for drug offences. It must be stressed that although many African Americans were unhappy with Clinton's unwillingness to fight against racially biased law enforcement, they knew that most black men and women

were imprisoned because of legislation passed during the Reagan Administration. Many African Americans point to the discrepancies in the penalties
for possession of the same narcotic. Cocaine laws meant that a person guilty
of trading in five grams of crack received a mandatory sentence of five years
in a federal penitentiary but it did not apply to powdered cocaine unless
it was 500 grams or more. Although crack is used by whites and blacks,
'84.5% of defendants convicted of crack possession in federal court in 1994
were African American, 10.3% were white, 5.2% were Hispanic. Trafficking
offenders were 4.1% white, 88.3% black, and 7.1% Hispanic.' Sentencing
reflects the popular view that crack is a black person's drug and confined to
the ghetto. Powder cocaine sentencing reflects a more even base but given
the percentage of blacks to the population still seems out of line. 'Defendants
convicted of simple possession of cocaine powder were 58% white, 26.7%
black, and 15% Hispanic.' However, prosecutions for trafficking were 32
per cent white, 27.4 black and 39.3 Hispanic (Jamison, 2002).

The laws passed under a Republican president were enthusiastically
enforced by the Clinton Administration and his African American 'Drug
Czar', Lee P. Brown. Some legislators who supported the draconian drugs
laws were motivated by racial attitudes, but as Michael Males has argued
passionately, the laws did not discriminate between black and white, but
more between young and old. And it was not just the cocaine laws. In 1995
Brown was reported by the Associated Press as wanting to change the image
of marijuana 'to that of an addictive killer.' Brown claimed that over 4000
emergency admissions of children aged between 12 and 17 were directly due
to the drug, but according to Department of Health and Human Services
statistics for 1994, only four in every 100,000 (4293) involved teenagers and
marijuana/hashish and most involved the use of more than one drug. And
97 per cent of the emergency admissions due to illegal drugs were white
and black adults (Males, 1996).

However, it was not the adults who were targeted. Some critics, such
as Males, go so far as to suggest, 'Drug laws and their selective enforcement represent the new Jim Crow laws.' At first President Clinton and
Brown approved a report which demonstrated racial discrimination in drug
arrests – that although African Americans were only 13 per cent of the
monthly drug users, 'they represent 35 per cent of arrests for drug possession, 55 per cent of convictions, and 74 per cent of prison sentences' and
the conclusion was: 'Public policies ostensibly designed to control crime and
drug abuse have in many respects contributed to the growing racial disparity
in the criminal justice system, while having little impact on the problems they were aimed to address.' Clinton and Brown deplored the racial

discrimination revealed in the study. But they did not change the policy or make powder cocaine as punishable as crack. It was the reverse. Following the continued success of conservatives in the elections and growing rumours of impeachment, Clinton supported Republican initiated legislation that made discrimination worse. The proposed Bill stipulated that the sale of $225 of crack would carry the same sentence as someone who trafficked $50,000 of powdered cocaine. As Males points out: 'Most arrested for powdered cocaine are older white and more affluent; 96 per cent of those arrested for crack are blacks or Latinos, primarily in young age groups' (Males, 1996).

Many deny, as did the Supreme Court, that the difference between crack and powdered cocaine sentencing is racist and others say that the Congressional Black Caucus supported the measures. They assert, 'They knew that crack was much more common in black neighborhoods than in white ones, and that more blacks than whites were likely to be incarcerated as a result of the change. And in fact, that was precisely their reason for supporting the legislative change: a conviction that it might reduce the havoc on the streets where their constituents lived' (Thernstorm and Thernstorm, 1997). They do not understand the widespread belief in urban ghettos that the CIA collaborated with the underworld to import the drug, not only to help shore up friendly regimes in Italy and Colombia, but also as an experiment in mind control over the black community. These fears were not allayed with government reports and the revelation that black men had been allowed to die of syphilis in the Tuskeegee Institute 'Bad Blood' experiment that continued into the 1970s even though a cure had been discovered in the 1940s (Jones, 1993).

Whatever the reason, it is important to acknowledge the increasing risks for blacks and whites, especially adults, who use illegal narcotics. The events in Tulia, Texas, in 1999 should be enough to give serious re-consideration of the effect of these laws. Tulia's population of 4500 included approximately 10 per cent African Americans. On the 23 July 1999, 43 people, 40 black, were arrested and later sentenced for selling small quantities of cocaine. This was about 12 per cent of the residents of the town. The three white people had close ties with the black community. Cash Love, for example, had many black friends and a mixed-race child. Perhaps this partially explain why he was sentenced to more than three hundred years, or as the *New York Times* reporter, Jim Yardley, suggests, 'prosecutors did not want the operation to be seen as racist.' Tom Coleman, a white undercover agent who provided the evidence, had been described by Pecos police as 'a compulsive liar.' The Cochrane County sheriff in 1996 stated he 'should not be in law enforcement.' Despite this, Coleman, who received training from the Drug Enforcement Agency, had no audio or videotape evidence and no witnesses to corroborate his testimony. Following protests and legal action from the NAACP and the ACLU, 30 cases were dismissed (*The New York Times*, 7 October 2000). The state governor pardoned those arrested and they settled for $6 million in damages. Coleman was prosecuted for perjury and put on probation for 10 years (CBS Sixty Minutes, 4 July 2004).

The town of Tulia was not the only town in Texas which used cocaine laws in a racially discriminatory manner and undercover agents to intimidate white men like Cash Love who were too friendly with black folks. The Texas legislature tried to sort the mess out but this did not solve the problem of falsified police reports. In Dallas authorities found it was not only a problem of unsubstantiated evidence. Investigations found 'many cases that not only lacked such corroboration but were based on fake drugs. Much of what police had seized as cocaine or amphetamines turned out to be baggies of finely ground Sheetrock.' The report continues, 'In fact, a couple of cocaine seizures that Dallas officials boasted set records were actually only powdered wallboard' (*Houston Chronicle*, 18 October 2002). George W. Bush was Governor of Texas when this happened but they did not feature in the 2000 campaign.

Illegal drug abuse was used to discriminate against pregnant women, especially women of colour. Pro-life activists, especially in South Carolina, have punished mothers for endangering the children they carry. These cases are overwhelmingly brought against minority women such as Margaret Valesquez Reyes who was addicted to heroin and accused of endangering her twins when they suffered withdrawal symptoms after birth. And in a similar case Selena Dunn was charged with second degree criminal mistreatment of her child because of her cocaine habit (Riches, 2002).

Health Care Proposal

Despite bitter battles, defeats and sometimes neglect of civil rights issues for the sake of expediency, Clinton tried to push through major reforms that would benefit African Americans. Like LBJ's Great Society programme, they were designed to benefit others as well and to tackle some of the basic and most serious problems affecting Americans regardless of their race, gender or religion. And one area that needed sweeping reform was health care.

Although the United States spends more per person on health care than any advanced country in the world, seven out of every ten dollars are swallowed up in administration costs. Defenders of the system argue that 85 per cent of Americans have some form of health care but critics point out that that means 40 million Americans have none and another 30 million have inadequate coverage. These figures would be worse if it were not for LBJ's Great Society reforms of Medicare and Medicaid for the elderly and acutely disabled helping almost 58 million in 2001 (us.gov/hhs). These groups are also eligible for Medicaid. This programme helps women with children on welfare and those with huge medical bills and absolutely no assets, a total of 36.3 million in 1997 (US Bureau of the Census). The federal government pays 57 per cent and the states 43 per cent.

In the 1992 campaign, Clinton promised to reform the inadequate health care provision by increasing its accessibility and yet ensuring it was affordable. After his election, he established a commission in 1993 headed by his wife, Hillary Rodham Clinton. It was an action which pleased many women and demonstrated that First Ladies did not have to confine themselves to the usual female support role. Although a formidable advocate, her appointment gave his opponents ammunition – he was accused of nepotism and she was attacked because she was formulating government policy. Others did not forget she had been one of the lawyers who brought impeachment charges against Nixon.

It was not these factors that defeated the plan. Business opposed it because they were required to provide a health care plan for their workers and dependants; benefits would also have included provision for prescription drugs, immunisation, eye and dental care for children. But in the era which saw individuals rather than society responsible for many of their problems, it was not popular to include cover for drug users and, even more controversially, the costs for some abortions.

Despite some compromises, the plan would have been especially helpful to black and white workers just above poverty by providing a comprehensive scheme that improved on Medicare and Medicaid. The progressive tax system had been reversed by Reagan so that the 70 per cent top rate of tax had fallen to 28 per cent by the time he left office in 1988. Although George Bush had made a minimal increase in taxes on the rich, and Clinton continued this trend, those who had benefited from tax cuts were frightened by the perceived cost of the plan. The insurance industry spent huge sums on television advertising opposing the scheme. And it was not only the usual vested interests who fought it; the Republican Party was well aware that if it passed, it might build a Democratic majority along the lines developed by FDR. Senator Robert Dole, leader of the Republicans, was initially very impressed with the plan and with Hillary Clinton's presentation to the Senate. But colleagues in the party reminded him that if he wanted to win the presidency he had to oppose it. He did. In this he was supported by the 85 per cent of Americans who had some health insurance and did not see why they should help the 15 per cent who did not.

Clinton is attacked by many for being too ambitious in his health reform efforts. But he faced a partisan Congress after the mid-term elections and the Republicans, with their 'Contract for America', were not going to let the Democrats pass a bill that might prove an attractive vote winner. In Clinton's second term, in 1996, Democrats and moderate Republicans passed limited reforms. However, the battles over Clinton's impeachment meant that his proposal to extend Medicare to all people of 55 and over failed. The modest aim that children whose parents had no medical insurance but were not below the poverty line should get Medicaid was not even discussed seriously (Dye and Zeigler, 2000).

Despite this failure at national level, small gains were made by the Black Caucus at state level. In Mississippi, for example, the Caucus, in a bi-racial, alliance established 'a state Children's Health Insurance Plan designed to provide health care insurance for children in families without health insurance or with inadequate health insurance' (Shaffer and Menifield, 2002). There is a great deal of evidence that African Americans have had a significant and positive influence at the state level, even in a state that still clings to the Confederate flag.

Welfare Reform

Meanwhile politicians asserted that the Social Security system was facing bankruptcy and health care reform would make things worse. Halfway through Clinton's second term, 13.7 per cent of the total population lived in poverty. And it was the dramatic rise in poverty in female households, especially in households headed by black women, that was emphasised by conservative critics. In 1998, 28.4 per cent of black families without a resident father lived below the poverty line and 29.4 per cent of Hispanics. More white children lived in similar circumstances but only made up 11.2 per cent of families living with the mother only. But, it was argued, social security was no longer sustainable because for every 10 retirees there were only two workers and the majority of those benefiting from social security were wealthy because social security was not means tested. One commentator, who seeks to defend Clinton's record, maintains he was 'consistent' about welfare reform because 'he believed it was fundamentally unfair to pay some people not to work while members of the "forgotten middle class" were struggling so hard to make ends meet' (Klein, 2002).

But Clinton blamed Congress, and Republicans especially, for the draconian welfare reforms which hurt the poor, black and white, so much. Speaking to the Trotter Group, an organisation of African American journalists, on 1 November 1995, Clinton assured them he would oppose the House Bill but added:

> My belief is that we ought to have a welfare reform bill that is both pro-family and pro-work, that promotes work, that has the possibility of ending welfare after a certain length of time if people have a job they can take, that gives the states more flexibility in the way they run their welfare programs, but that protects little children. That's what I believe we should be doing. (Wickham, 2002)

It sounded reasonable. However, he knew, since Nixon's complaints about 'welfare crap' (Ambrose, 1989) and Reagan's lies about the black Chicago 'welfare queen' who defrauded the system (Cannon, 1991), that people on welfare were portrayed by many politicians as indigent black people. It was obvious that Newt Gingrich, the Georgia Republican, was referring to black people when he said, 'It's impossible to maintain civilization with 12-year-olds having babies, 15-year-olds killing each other, 17-year-olds dying of AIDS, and 18-year-olds getting diplomas they can't even read' (Klinkner and Smith, 1999). He and many rich white Americans totally ignored the evidence that masses of white people were dependent on welfare. Many of these white and black poor were working but they were paid so little they were forced onto the welfare system (Ehrenreich, 2001). The word 'welfare' was part of the politics of euphemism. As Neubeck and Cazenave point out, 'Today, whenever politicians want to exploit white racist animus for political gain they need not say the words *Niggers* or *Nigras*, as did the white southern segregationists. They now need only mention the word welfare' (Neubeck and Cazenave, 2001).

The argument that welfare did not benefit white people as well as minorities was a lie but Clinton, the man from Hope, unlike LBJ who pushed through the Voting Rights Act against strong opposition from his own party, deprived some of the poorest families in America of any hope. In the process he claimed the draconian welfare 'reforms' as his own work and tore up decades of commitment by the Democratic Party to the most needy.

Before the welfare 'reform,' Clinton went to Memphis in 1993 and lectured a group of black ministers, telling them what he thought Martin Luther King Jr would have said: 'I fought for freedom . . . but not for the freedom of children to have children, and the fathers of the children to walk away and abandon them to anything. . . . That is not what I lived and died for' (Klein, 2002). He spoke to, and was cheered by, his middle class black audience, and Clinton was peddling the stereotypes about welfare mothers and fathers a year before the Republicans won Congress. The billionaire Texan, Ross Perot, described what he believed was a typical black man. 'I define what a man is from the rap music I hear. . . . A man is defined in that culture as a breeder who gets the woman pregnant and she gets welfare' (Neubeck and Cazenave, 2001). Perot's comment was made on television in support of the welfare reform as it was being debated in Congress in 1996. Clinton, like the conservatives, issued no ringing denunciations of the billions of dollars handed to farmers in subsidies, or the billions wasted or stolen in the defence industries.

To many critics on the left, welfare is class-based allowing the capitalist elite to buy off the poor and ensure a passive, low-paid work force; or it is a way of ensuring the survival of a patriarchal society in which women, especially women of colour, are made dependent on the handouts of a white male elite. But the essential point is that a well-funded welfare programme is vital in the absence of a guaranteed minimum income for poor families regardless of race or marital status. It is true, as Neubeck and Cazanave contend, that welfare has often been a means of aiding the white and denying people of colour. But as they point out programmes such as the Aid to Families with Dependent Children (AFDC) were vital to the poor regardless of race. The proposal passed by the House of Representatives in 1995 emphasised high pregnancy rates, especially among unmarried young black women, and claimed that young boys born in these circumstances were twice as likely to be criminals. The Bill sought to restrict welfare to the first child only, and to fund state programmes for birth control. Women between 18 and 20 years old could be denied all benefits by the states. Women who had no money were to have their children taken from them and put up for adoption. African American congressman, William Clay of Missouri, denounced the Bill seeking to limit cash aid to mothers. He demanded, 'If that doesn't work, what's next? Castration? Sterilization?' (Neubeck and Cazenave, 2001). Clay should have known that sterilisation, especially of black women, had been practised in the United States for years and young black schoolgirls were forcibly operated on to implant the Norplant contraceptive. These measures prevented births but did not stop the spread of sexually transmitted diseases or AIDS (Davis, 1994). However, disparate interest groups combined to defeat these new proposals explicitly designed to curtail black female fertility.

In addition, Clinton said he would veto the proposed legislation passed by the House of Representatives. He did sign the Personal Responsibility and Work Opportunity Reconciliation Act in 1996 that wiped out the 31-year-old AFDC programme and replaced it with his 'work-fare' agenda. AFDC was seen, erroneously, to be a 'black' programme benefiting mainly inner-city teenage women who preferred welfare to work. The new Act emphasised mandatory work but states could, if they wanted to, deny benefits to teenage mothers and stop additional payments for children born to mothers on welfare. Clinton and Congress did this knowing the historic discriminatory use of welfare programmes by the states, benefits frequently denied to the poorest minority families. And the linking of welfare and race was underlined when Clinton was photographed signing the new law surrounded by overwhelmingly African American single parents (Neubeck and Cazenave, 2001). In a White House press release in May 2000, the emphasis was on the economic achievements of the Administration, claiming that 'unemployment rates for African Americans and Hispanic Americans are both at historic lows, while the unemployment rate for women is the lowest since 1953.' No specific figures are given about the number of minorities unemployed or the sort of low-paid jobs many of them filled. They were more precise in their boasts about welfare cuts. 'Welfare rolls are down by 7.2 million (or 51 per cent) since 1993, after increasing by 22 per cent from 1981–92' [i.e. the years of Republicans Reagan and Bush]. They were proud to announce that this was the lowest number on welfare since 1969 (White House Press Release, May 2000).

Voter Registration: 'The Motor Voter Act'

No matter how displeased they were with Clinton's workfare programme, African Americans were delighted with the new southern President when he extended the Voting Rights Act by pushing through the National Voter Registration Act of May 1993. Despite the 1965 Voting Rights Act, some state registrars of voters had been reluctant to register African Americans, and the Justice Department under Reagan and Bush had done little to ensure its enforcement. Indeed, their administrations had tried to weaken the Act. Clinton avoided these state and federal complications by ensuring that registration to vote could be completed easily especially with the renewal of a

car licence in the motor vehicle department or when renewing non-driver
identification. In addition, groups, such as ROCK the VOTE, set up booths
and registered people on the streets.

Initially, states were reluctant to introduce the new procedures but most
states had implemented the Act by 2000. In 1995, after the first full year
of implementation, over 11 million voters had used the Act to register or
to notify change of address. Nine million of these were new voters and
the League of Women Voters and the NAACP believed another six million would register in time for the 2000 election. The press release of May
2000 stressed that the Act was 'helping to eliminate historic disparities by
registering citizens who have traditionally been left out – people with disabilities, minorities, young people, anyone who has recently moved, and
people with lower incomes.' What Clinton and most Americans did not
realise at the time was just how easy it was to get around this law. Jeb Bush
worked on that and his success was demonstrated in the presidential election
of 2000.

Clinton and Women of Colour

In 1992 Clinton won the support of the majority of American women.
His backing for the pro-choice campaign meant that he continued to hold
their allegiance despite Elders' resignation and his failure to support Lani
Guinier. The conservative response was a coded attack on black and poor
women which emphasised 'family values' and women's role as homemak-
ers. And this campaign found many adherents among the black community,
especially in Christian churches, and with Jesse Jackson and Louis Farrakan,
the leader of the Nation of Islam. Many black men asserted their role
as patriarchal leaders and attacked ambitious black women whose actions
allowed white men to consider black families matriarchal. As Cathy Cohen
and Tamara Jones point out, 'Black women – straight or gay – are particularly subject to surveillance and control in a black heterosexist system.' They
are 'punished' and 'chastised' for behaviour that is not considered wrong in
men. 'Even more unbelievably, black women's very survival has also been
used against us. For example, single-headed households are regarded as a
triumph of personal will and commitment' if headed by a man but in the
case of lone mothers it is 'seen as a pathology and a mark of the community's weakness' (Cohen and Jones, in Eric Brandt ed., 1999). Ironically, this
'warrior' message became more strident after the massive success of the conservative Republicans in the midterm elections of 1994, and the attack on

women, teenage mothers and especially on a woman's right to choose an abortion became one of the major issues.

Clinton continued to support the pro-choice movement and moderate Republicans, such as Arlen Specter of Pennsylvania, appealed in 1995 to Democrats to vote in the Republican primaries to stop the 'antiabortion crazies' from taking over the party. Specter's fears were not unfounded when it was clear that some right-wing Republicans refused to condemn pro-life people who harassed women as they went to abortion clinics, and even those who bombed these clinics and murdered the doctors who worked in them.

The majority of Republican hopefuls ran on a pro-life platform. The Governor of California, Pete Wilson, was accused of having a 'multiple choice' abortion record. According to Roger Stone of Planned Parenthood and the National Abortion Rights Action League, 'He used to favor government funding for abortions for poor women, but doesn't any longer, and twice when he was Senator he cast the deciding vote restricting federal health-insurance plans from providing abortion coverage' (*Time*, 5 June 1995). Ironically, these pro-life conservatives saw white women as vessels and encouraged multiple births because of artificial reproductive techniques (ART), ignoring the 'increased risks for women, foetuses and children.' A recent study shows that, 'women who expose themselves and their future offspring to such risks are not considered negligent, selfish or malicious, though the harms they impose on their offspring may be as great or greater than the harms in the cases of mothers who use drugs.' Bobbi McCaughey, white and working class, who already had a child, became pregnant by ART, and ignored warnings that bringing multiple foetuses to term was dangerous. She gave birth to septuplets two of whom had to be artificially fed, one was blind and all suffered delayed development. A grateful nation rewarded her with a free house, two minivans, congratulations from the Governor of Iowa and an invitation from Bill Clinton to the White House. An African American gave birth to septuplets without the use of ART and she was ignored. As Linda Bugg, the head of the small Washington DC group, Sisters in Touch, noted, 'the President didn't even lean out of the window and holler, "Hello, Mrs Thompson"' (Riches, 2002).

But women received attention during Clinton's two terms, and he appointed more women to the cabinet than any previous president. The most prominent positions went to white women, Madeleine Albright as Secretary of State and Janet Reno, Attorney General. When Reno was attacked for her handling of the siege of the David Koresh cult compound in Waco Texas, Clinton stood by her and constantly defended her. This was in marked contrast to his treatment of Lani Guinier. The sordid affair with the intern, Monica Lewinsky, only temporarily harmed him in the opinion of women. Ironically, the publication on the Internet of the pornographic 'Starr Commission Report' where it could be accessed by children, infuriated many who were disgusted by the President's behaviour. To others, it was simply one more attempt at the cost of millions of dollars to destroy Clinton. It started with Gennifer Flowers, moved to alleged crimes by Hillary and Bill Clinton in the Whitewater land scandal, allegations about illegal fund raising (especially cynical considering the enormous abuses by Nixon), and the ultimate vote for impeachment. African Americans knew that the people who were seeking to remove Clinton were conspicuous in their opposition to minority rights. Moreover, they noted that Clinton turned to two African Americans in his time of crisis – Vernon Jordan, a businessman and long-time friend, and Jesse Jackson, whose help he had spurned in 1992. Both men did exactly what the vast majority of African Americans did – they stood by their man. Although Clinton may have been found not guilty, he had damaged himself, his party and the people he had lied to about his sexual relationship with Monica Lewinsky.

Clinton, Powell and Gays in the Military

Faced with fierce opposition from the first African American general who was head of the Joint Chiefs of Staff, Colin Powell, Clinton backed away from his commitment to revise regulations permitting gays to serve in the military. Just as Clinton had not stood by his friend Lani Guinier in 1993, he failed to stand by gays and lesbians, black and white, who had supported him overwhelmingly in 1992. As early as 1991, he promised that if elected president he would end the discrimination against homosexuals in the military, regardless of race.

When he was in the White House, Clinton wanted to follow Harry Truman's example. Truman as Commander in Chief ended racial discrimination in the military by executive order and Clinton said he would do the same for homosexuals. Clinton thought it would be just a stroke of the pen, but instead it became the main issue during his first days in office and his hesitant response lost him support with liberal and gay groups. Colin Powell warned that homosexuals in the military would destroy military effectiveness and group morale. Ironically, this was exactly the same advice that General Eisenhower had given to President Truman about racial integration of the armed forces. Powell also had the support of the head of the Senate

Armed Services Committee, Democrat Sam Nunn of Georgia. Robert Dole, a perennial presidential aspirant, also opposed the President.

Faced with mounting criticism, Clinton sought a way out to allow him to concentrate on other issues. He announced that the ban on homosexuals would remain for six months. The dismissal of gays from the armed services would stop and new recruits were not to be asked about their sexual orientation. Meanwhile the military were told to produce a code of sexual practice. William Schneider of the *New York Times* commented: 'I thought all along that the Willie Horton issue of the campaign would be gays and Clinton's support for gay rights. Well instead of happening in the campaign, it has come true now' (Miller, 1995).

The resulting compromise drawn up by Senator Nunn and General Powell was the 'Don't Ask, Don't Tell' proposal following Eisenhower's policy as Commander in Chief during the Second World War. Homosexuals could serve in the forces so long as their sexual preferences were kept private. Clinton was eager to get a settlement. Senator Nunn, however, pushed through an amendment to a defence appropriation bill that 'persons who demonstrate a propensity or intent to engage in homosexual acts' were 'unacceptable risks' and new recruits could be questioned about their sexual orientation. Clinton's proposal to end witch-hunts was not included in the amendment. Eager to be rid of the problem, Clinton signed the measure into law.

Ironically, the conservative Republican Barry Goldwater, the party's candidate for president in 1964, wrote in the Washington *National Post Weekly* in 1993, 'After 50 years in the military and politics, I am still amazed to see how upset people can get over nothing. Lifting the ban on gays in the military isn't exactly nothing, but it's pretty damned close.' The former senator from Arizona, who had a distinguished Second World War record, stated, 'I think it's high time to pull the curtain on this charade of policy' (Miller, 1995). For Clinton, the issue had been 'a political disaster' (Wadden, 2002).

Homophobia in the Unites States was reflected in increased attacks on gay men and lesbians. Despite the formation of the National Coalition of Black Lesbians and Gays and the Combahee River Collective, hatred for homosexuals is widespread in the black community. As Clinton's civil rights policy disillusioned some African Americans, they held a meeting in Chicago in June 1998 and set up a Black Radical Congress. They realised that if they were to protect the gains made by the movement and ensure more, a broader alliance of issues had to be addressed. But one of the most divisive topics was homosexuality. The problem was: 'Overcoming homophobia in black communities requires that we also commit ourselves to the broader struggle against heterosexism in black communities.' According to the black lesbians, Cohen and Jones, 'Because dominant gender norms define our common oppressions, the fate of black lesbian, gay, bisexual, and transgender people is inextricably joined to the fate of heterosexual black men and women. Our joint social freedom will signal the freedom of all black people' (Brandt ed., 1999).

His Popularity with African Americans

Clinton's many critics have a problem. If Clinton was merely smoke and mirrors when it came to civil rights issues, why was it that he was the most popular president ever as far as most African Americans are concerned? Toni Morrison, the Nobel winning African American writer, said in 1998: 'Years ago, in the middle of the Whitewater investigation, one heard the first murmurs: white skin notwithstanding, this is our first black President. Blacker than any actual black person who could ever be elected in our children's lifetime. After all, Clinton displays almost every trope of blackness: single-parent household, born poor, working-class, saxophone-playing, McDonalds-and-junk-food-loving boy from Arkansas' (*New Yorker*, 5 October 1998). Black businesswoman, Gwen McKinney, claimed Morrison's comment was partly 'tongue-in-cheek' but added that Clinton 'understands the psyche of oppressed people – black people – people who are on the outside looking in.' However, Washington DC African American political columnist, George Curry, said, 'I never bought the garbage about Bill Clinton being a black president. He is not black but he was better than George Bush.' A black-owned polling company found in August 1998, during his impeachment difficulties, that Clinton had an approval rating of 93 per cent from African Americans. This was four points higher than the most popular black person, Jesse Jackson. Even after the vote to impeach him, 91 per cent of African Americans supported him as did 71 per cent of white voters. Joe Klein of *The New Yorker* points out that even in the dying days of his presidency in 1998 and 1999, Clinton fought for programmes that benefited many people. Despite opposition, the Headstart programme, part of LBJ's Great Society reforms, had its budget increased from $2.8 billion in 1993 to $6.3 billion in 2000; child care assistance increased from $4.5 to $12.6 billion in the same period and the programme that Clinton set up as a domestic Peace Corps, Americorps, had an additional $100 million to $473 million despite bitter opposition from his Republican opponents (Klein, 2002). And following a spate of racist bombings of black churches, reminiscent of the 1960s, Clinton in 1993 signed the Church Arson Prevention Act. The terrorism, however, continued (CNN Report, 1996).

Clinton may have ignored his grand Civil Rights Commission headed by the eminent black historian, John Hope Franklin, and he did not deliver on many of his promises, but African Americans blamed the ultra-conservatism of the Republicans who controlled Congress and who sought to impeach their man. The majority believed, as did Ben Johnson, head of the Initiative for One America, that Clinton got 'a bad rap on welfare reform' and Clinton was 'forced to settle' for the reform passed by Republicans (Wickham, 2002).

And although many critics dismissed Clinton's acts as symbolism, for many who struggled for the civil rights movement and had met so much resistance, they were more than mere gestures. For example, he awarded the Presidential Medal of Freedom, the highest award that can be given to any civilian, to Mrs Rosa Parks whose courage had ignited the movement. In 1998 another five people who had fought for African Americans and other minorities were honoured. These included long-time associate of Dr Martin Luther King Jr, Arnold Aronson, who set up the Leadership Conference on Civil Rights and James Farmer, former director of CORE and Freedom Rides organiser. Their communities did not see the awards as mere symbolism but an important recognition by the President for what they had achieved. And for Clinton at every testing time for the nation: '[W]e have chosen union over division . . . and in the sixties and seventies, by advancing civil rights and women's rights. In each instance, while we were engaged in the struggle to define, defend, and expand our union, powerful conservative forces resisted, and as long as the outcome was in doubt, the political and personal conflicts were intense' (Clinton, 2004).

Home to Harlem

Clinton moved to Harlem after leaving the White House still fond of quoting Toni Morrison that he was the 'first black president.' His Vice President, Al Gore distanced himself from Clinton but started his campaign for the White House endorsing the so-called 'Third Way.' Republicans, concerned about their harsh image during Senator Robert Dole's campaign against Clinton in 1996, chose the slogan 'caring conservatism,' and to the surprise of many, including many in their own party, the eldest son, George W. the Governor of Texas, rather than the younger Jeb, Governor of Florida, was chosen from the Bush clan to fight the former Senator from Tennessee. It was a campaign that shook the world, if not America. For historians of the African American experience, it had disturbing memories.

9

1876 AND ALL THAT: GEORGE W. BUSH

Why 1876? Because the twentieth century ended in much the same way as the latter part of the nineteenth century. The November 2000 election resulted in a furore over corruption similar to that of the 1876 election when the nation had faced a crisis. Democrat Samuel Tilden needed one Electoral College vote to win the presidency over his Republican opponent Rutherford Hayes. Both parties claimed victory in four states, especially in Florida, South Carolina and Louisiana, where there had been massive fraud and vote-rigging by both parties. Terrorist groups in South Carolina intimidated Republican voters, black and white. The threats were largely aimed at the newly enfranchised African American voters – the backbone of the Republican Party in the South – and most were prevented from voting. In the twentieth century, Florida was crucial to the outcome of the 2000 election. And corruption in elections by both parties was not new as shown by Mayor Richard Daley of Chicago on behalf of John Kennedy. This author was told in 1968 by the son of a successful East Tennessee politician that his father gave his best speeches in graveyards – the audience never walked away and they always voted early and often.

In the Compromise of 1877, Hayes was pronounced the winner and he agreed to remove the last federal troops from the South. Hayes and the Republican Party abandoned African Americans in the South and the long march of the Republican Party away from the black community and their civil rights had begun. By 2000, the South, which had supported every Democrat since the Civil War, aligned itself with a Republican party that was virtually all-white and even attracted ex-Nazis such as David Duke.

188

The Gore Campaign of 2000

It became a familiar refrain, especially by Clinton admirers, that Gore lost the election. Most Americans want to forget that Gore *won* the election. However, his critics argue that during the campaign, Gore showed 'almost [a] pathological need to prove that he could stand on his own, outside of the shadow of the political master [Clinton] – and perhaps outside his father's shadow, as well; his pride and discomfort paralyzed his campaign, compounding his natural awkwardness.' According to Joe Klein, Clinton was 'frustrated' by Gore's 'mortal clunkiness as a campaigner' (Klein, 2002). He admits that the Lewinsky affair was 'a mess' but fails to say that Clinton lied to Gore about it. Klein ignores Gore's role as a valuable and effective vice president, loyally supporting Clinton's 'Third Way' (Lowi and Ginsberg, 1998).

Gore did not want Clinton's help but his loyalty to the 'Third Way' explains his early difficulties. Klein is wrong when he argues that Gore wanted to get away from 'his father's shadow.' Far from trying to escape from his father, Gore dropped Clinton's shift to the right and espoused his father's view that a southerner running for president must follow radical populist positions. When his son did, his campaign was far from 'clunky' and he won support from most African Americans and women, and won back many traditional Democrats who had deserted the party for Reagan, Bush and Perot. Clinton sought to deny liberal criticisms that he had failed the poor, the disabled, ethnics and African Americans or to help gay rights (Michael Paterniti, *Esquire*, December 2000). Gore promised to do what Clinton failed to do. Gore reminded the NAACP convention that he was a member. He used George Bush Sr's phrase, 'I'm not asking you to *read my lips*. I am asking you to read my heart' (emphasis added). He would defend public schools, affirmative action, pass a national hate-crimes law, and appoint Supreme Court Justices who would defend civil rights. In the old civil rights movement fashion, Gore quoted the Bible: 'Show me the faith without the works and I will show thee my faith BY my works. That is MY text for today.' Bush, angered by Gore's attack, promised he would follow his father's example and he had 'talked from my heart' (*North County Times*, 13 July 2000).

The Republican Nomination Battle

Colin Powell ruled himself out because his wife worried he might be assassinated by white extremists. Many political commentators had believed that the Republican challenger would be Arizona Senator John McCain, a Vietnam War hero and former prisoner in the notorious North Vietnamese Hanoi Hilton. A conservative, he chose a populist campaign to appeal to many independent voters. Or it would be Bush's son, Jeb, a fluent Spanish speaker, married to a Mexican-American, and governor of one of the most important states in presidential elections – Florida. However, it was not Jeb but his older brother, Texas Governor, George W. Bush, who was chosen by main figures and funders of the Republican Party to challenge Senator John McCain in the primaries.

George Walker Bush was known for his friendship with oil men, his part-ownership of a baseball team, and that he approved the execution of more prisoners than any other governor in the United States (*The Observer*, 12 January 2003). Despite big business support, especially from the oil companies and 35 Republican senators, his nomination was not assured. Unlike McCain the war hero, or Gore Jr, Bush had not served in Vietnam. McCain was very popular with independents and he campaigned against Bush's record as governor, his inexperience and ignorance of foreign affairs.

Bush lost the first primary in New Hampshire. A high turnout of independents ensured McCain's victory. The shock was all the greater because, although Bush and his family claimed to be Texans, they were New Englanders. According to the *Washington Post*, 'Bush's lacklustre performance represented the worst defeat suffered by a front-runner of either party in the modern history of the New Hampshire primary.' In response, Bush dropped 'compassionate conservatism' and appealed to hard-line right-wing party members – those who opposed the civil rights gains made by minorities and women. The nomination battle became very ugly. Bush appealed to religious fundamentalists and the anti-civil rights wing of the party and even questioned McCain's patriotism. Ironically, McCain used this tactic in 2008.

During the South Carolina primary, Bush went to Bob Jones University, a university that had refused to admit African Americans or Catholic students. In 2000 it still banned inter-racial dating on the grounds that God had reasons for separating races and nations. Bush sought the endorsement of Bob Jones III. On CNN's 'Crossfire,' Bill Press asked the lone black Republican Congressman, J. C. Watts of Oklahoma and co-chair of the campaign, why Bush had spoken at the university. Watts denied Bush supported the university's racist policies. When questioned why Bush had apologised to Catholics (Bush to Cardinal O'Connor, 25 February 2000) but not to African Americans, Watts argued Democrats who had spoken there had never apologised. Co-anchor, Mary Matalin, pointed out that Bush told the NAACP convention he wanted to 'increase racial harmony.' Press said he had attended every Republican convention since 1984 and they were 'a sea of white faces.' In 1996, out of 1990 delegates, only 54 were African American and only 47 were Latinos. Watts said Bush's proposals were the issue not the race of delegates (Cable News Network, 10 July 2000).

Charges of racism dogged the Bush campaign. He was accused of having backed an alleged racist for governor of Georgia and in 1999, he had promoted Charles Williams to head the committee responsible for training Texas law enforcement officers – a man who had testified in 1998 that the expression 'porch monkey' was not racist (www.bushwatch.com, 12 January 2003). Democratic Congressman Robert Menendez attacked him for supporting Republican welfare reform that removed rights from legal permanent residents and for 'Voting Rights Act infringements that they created with ballot security fraud' (Cable News Network, 10 July 2000). Bush's campaign website assured voters he opposed racial preferences and quotas but favoured an undefined scheme of 'affirmative access.' Affirmative action programmes were 'soft bigotry' (*Time*, 1 August 2000). He proposed to encourage small businesses to bid for federal contracts but after the *Adarand* decision, which declared racial preference in sub-contracting unconstitutional, it was uncertain how black business would benefit. He also promised economic programmes to benefit the poor.

The Strange Election of 2000

The media saw Gore as the loser but on election night Gore did better than his critics expected. When it was declared that Gore had won the key state of Florida, it seemed the presidency was his. His popular vote mounted and he retained over 500,000 lead in the popular vote even though he lost most southern states, including his own of Tennessee. But the Bush camp was not downhearted and a Republican supporter outside the State House in Austin, Texas, carried a prophetic sign which read, 'Don't Worry Jeb Will Deliver Florida.' The public and Democrats did not realise that officials appointed by George and Jeb Bush had delivered the state before the election. At first Gore conceded. When it was apparent there were problems in Florida, he and the Democratic Party sought a hand recount in some counties. Hendrick Hertzberg concluded, 'the votes of some citizens ... are more equal than the votes of others, and that the votes of the citizens of Florida are worth everything or nothing, depending on who, if anyone, is doing the counting' (*New Yorker*, 18 December 2000).

Bush claimed he had African American support but only 8 per cent voted for him (BBC News Online, 15 December 2000), less than for Bob Dole in 1996 who had won 12 per cent (*The New York Times*, 20 December 2002). In Florida, 93 per cent of African Americans, who were allowed to, voted for Gore. It would have been higher but thousands of them had had their names removed from the voting register in 1999. Following fraud in a 1998 Miami mayoral election, the state hired 'a private firm with tight Republican ties' to prevent duplicate registrations, dead voters or ex-felons from voting. Mostly black people were removed from the 67 counties' lists.

Many alleged ex-felons had moved to Florida from Texas and the company was given the names by people appointed by George W. Bush and the list was passed to Florida officials appointed by Jeb Bush. Sixty-four-year-old African American Wallace McDonald was denied his vote because in 1959 he was found guilty in Texas of the misdemeanour (not a felony) of 'sleeping on a bus-stop bench' (*Harper's Magazine*, 1 March 2002). Thirty one per cent of black voters were listed as felons and denied the vote but some registrars knew the reports from the company, DBT, were wrong and ignored them. DBT had warned that the guidelines set by Katherine Harris, Florida Secretary of State appointed by Jeb Bush, would result in many 'false positives' and it later admitted that addresses they used for Orange County were 20 years out of date. The Texas list should never even have been sent to Florida because ex-felons are permitted to vote in Texas and no state can deny them the vote. A spokesman confessed it was 'a little bit embarrassing in the light of the election' but said it was a 'minor glitch – less than one-tenth of one per cent of the electorate.' This 'glitch' was 15 times the majority claimed by the Republican's 'win' in Florida of a mere 537 votes. In 2001, Florida Republican House Speaker, Tom Feeney, opposed ex-felons voting because an election should not mean that everyone 'with two arms and two legs' had the right to vote. 'It's less important to me that I have the right to vote than the people that do are upholding the integrity and legitimacy of the society and culture.' The Florida felony law dated from 1868 and was one of many measures to undo the gains made by former slaves after the Civil War. Historically 'felony disenfranchisement laws have their roots in Jim Crow in the South' (Green, 2007).

Some of the actions of DBT and the Florida Secretary of State, Katherine Harris, almost defy belief. For example, African American Linda Howell, elections supervisor for Madison County, was told she could not vote because she was a felon. She was not. A black woman was disenfranchised because she shared the last name of a male criminal. Other supervisors did not question the names issued by Harris. Over 3000 in Hillsborough City were given prior notice and 551 appealed, 245 successfully. This was a 15 per cent error rate. As Geoffrey Palast reported for BBC, 'If that ratio held state-wide, no fewer than 7000 voters were incorrectly targeted for removal from voting rosters' (BBC Newsnight report on www.Salon.com, accessed 3 January 2003). Errors included a man listed as a felon in Texas who had never been there. The same investigation found that African Americans were guilty of felonies in the future! Thomas Alvin Cooper would be convicted of a felony in 2007. According to Florida computer files, Mr Cooper planned to move to Ohio, add a middle name and change his race. Over 300 people were listed in June 2000 as having 'Future Conviction Dates' (*Harper's Magazine*, 1 March 2000). Harris and elections chief, Clay Roberts, said county supervisors were responsible for checking alleged felons' lists. This was untrue. The company contract stated it had that duty.

In addition, the *New York Times* reported that 'precincts with more black, Hispanic and elderly voters had substantially more spoiled ballots.' Some blamed poorly educated voters but as Ford Fessendon says lack of education does not explain why 9–10 per cent of black votes were discarded and only 2 per cent were of whites. In 17 counties with two column ballots rather than the usual one, as well as the 'infamous butterfly ballot of Palm Beach,' there was a high percentage of rejected ballots. 'But again, blacks fared worse than whites – 18.2 per cent of ballots in mostly black precincts where two-column or butterfly ballots were used were rejected, three times higher than in white areas' (*New York Times*, 12 November 2001). An ultra right-wing candidate, Pat Buchanan, was surprised by his many supporters in Miami County, an overwhelming Jewish precinct, and he believed that the butterfly ballot, which put his name next to Gore's, was responsible. There was no name opposite Bush and no confusion for the voter. Old or faulty voting machines that did not punch out the voting cards properly were located in areas with high percentage of minority and elderly voters. These 'hanging chads' were not counted. But those who questioned the result were dismissed as 'conspiracy theorists' and Ari Fleischer, White House press secretary, maintained, 'Anybody who invests time and money in this is wasting their time and money. The president is paying no attention to this – and neither is the country' (*New York Times*, 12 November 2001). Lani Guinier summed it up: 'This was not a robbery of the African American community. This was a robbery of democracy. It was not just black votes that weren't counted, there were also white people' (*American World*, February 2000). Bush stole the election but he needed yet more help.

The Supreme Court Decides

The Florida Supreme Court ordered a hand recount but Bush and the Republicans went to the US Supreme Court and argued that under the equal protection clause of the 14th Amendment, a hand recount in some counties was unfair and discriminated against voters in other counties. According to Justice Antonin Scalia, a recount 'threatened irreparable harm to [George Bush], and to the country, by casting a cloud over the legitimacy of the election.' Radical journalist, Michael Moore, argues that Justice Clarence Thomas and Antonin Scalia should have disqualified themselves from the case on the grounds of conflict of interest because Thomas' wife was working for Bush and Scalia's son was a member of the law firm bringing Bush's action (Michael Moore, 2001). Neither did and both voted to deny a recount.

Compounding the confusion surrounding the election was the way in which the Supreme Court issued its decision. A unanimous ruling is unsigned and published as '*per curiam*,' that is 'by the court,' but this one was not. Most of the newspapers and TV reporters, realised that two justices were opposed and quoted the unsigned conclusion as saying, 'Seven justices of this Court agree that there are constitutional problems with the recount ordered by the Florida Supreme Court. The only disagreement is as to remedy.' The opinion stated, 'The press of time does not diminish the constitutional concern. A desire for speed is not a general excuse for ignoring equal protection guarantees.... Having once granted the right to vote on equal terms, the State may not, by later arbitrary and disparate treatment, value one person's vote over another' (*Bush v Gore*, 12 December 2000).

However, it was not a 7-2 ruling, but 5-4. As Hendrick Herzberg reported, the Court's unsigned ruling 'suggested that the opinion, or part of it, had been agreed to by all the justices. This was false. But it was only a drop in the rancid bucket of the majority's bad faith.' The Court should have upheld the Florida court's decision to recount because the state voting process had unconstitutional aspects. Hertzberg concludes that even if Gore had won the electoral and popular vote, 'the election of 2000 was not stolen. Stealing, after all, is illegal, and, by definition, nothing the Justices of the Supreme Court do can be outside the law. They are the law. The election was not stolen. It was expropriated' (*New Yorker*, 25 December 2000, 1 January 2001). However, it was claimed that 'a comprehensive review of the uncounted Florida ballots proved that even if the Supreme Court had not ruled, Bush had won the state. Later the same report says 'a state-wide recount could have produced enough votes to tilt the election his [Gore's] way, no matter what standard was chosen to judge voter intent' (*New York Times*, 12 November 2001). Some admired 'Gore's determination' and saw it as more like 'grit' (*New Yorker*, 11 December 2000), but on 13 December, Gore conceded and congratulated Bush as President. He met with Bush 'so that we can start to heal the divisions of the campaign.' He said, 'Now the US Supreme Court has spoken. Let there be no doubt, while I strongly disagree with the court's decision, I accept it.' And he told the nation, 'Some have asked whether I have any regrets and I do have one regret: that I didn't get the chance to stay and fight for the American people over the next four years, especially for those who feel their voices have not been heard. I heard you and I will not forget.' He would 'honor the new president elect,' but made pointed reference to earlier elections, perhaps of 1876. He said, 'this belatedly broken impasse can point us to a common ground, for its very closeness can serve to remind us that we are one people with a shared history and a shared destiny' (CNN Web Services, 13 December 2001).

Questions About the Election of 2004

In 2004 similar questions were raised about election fraud. The campaign against a Vietnam War hero, John Kerry, was difficult for Bush who had used his father's political influence to join the Air National Guard and thus avoid combat. He had spent most of that time campaigning in Alabama for a conservative Republican. Right wing Texans supported the so-called Swift Boat Campaign in which veterans accused Kerry of lying about his service in Vietnam (Mark, 2007). It was a repeat of the campaign against McCain in 2000.

Following the election of 2000, many states abandoned paper ballots in favour of Direct Recording Electronic voting machines. Unlike ones used in Brazil, most used in the United States provided no paper record of voting which made recounts impossible. Many votes could be switched automatically from one candidate to another and any hacker could easily break into the machines. Confidence was further undermined when Willy O'Dell, the head of the Ohio based company Diebold, that manufactured the voting machines, said that 'he would do everything possible to deliver' the state in 2004 for Bush.

Some of the tactics employed in the 2000 election were used in Ohio and Florida. Democratic areas, especially African American districts, had insufficient or broken voting machines, and places to vote. In some Democratic areas people waited nine hours to cast their vote and in some precincts barely 75 per cent were able to vote. In Lake County, Ohio, a flyer was sent to minority and Democratic precincts saying voter registration by groups such as the NAACP might have been done illegally and the result would be 'you will not able to vote until the next election.' These attempts to reduce the vote were aided by the African American Secretary of State for Ohio, Kenneth Blackwell. A member of the Congressional Black Caucus, John Conyers, reported Blackwell's activities. Voter fraud that had seriously affected the poor, urban and ethnic minority districts did not affect the suburban, Republican districts (Green, 2007).

Bush in Office

In 2000, George W. Bush seemed aware of the bitterness of many African Americans his election had caused because the denial of their voting rights had ensured him the White House. He spoke to Jesse Jackson after the Supreme Court ruling and assured Jackson he understood there was a 'need to heal the nation.' And the difficulty of Bush's task was obvious when Kweisi Mfume, president of the NAACP, maintained many African Americans believed the election was 'stolen' and without a condemnation of what had happened and positive policies from the Administration it 'would foster a deeper belief in the minds of a lot of people that the nation did not care about them' (BBC News Online, 15 December 2000).

Mfume had good cause for concern. A senior Bush aide told *USA Today* that Bush would close the offices on civil rights and AIDS set up by Clinton. A spokesman denied it but admitted the staff in the AIDS office would be cut and no senior member of the White House would liaise with the Task Force for Uniting America (*Washington Post*, 8 February 2001). In his Inaugural Address, Bush appeared to want to begin the 'healing process' and he repeated his earlier plea to the NAACP convention 'to give me a chance to tell you what's in my heart.' He continued: 'In the quiet of American conscience, we know that deep, persistent poverty is unworthy of our nation's promise. And whatever our views of its cause, we can agree that children at risk are not at fault. Abandonment and abuse are not Acts of God, they are failures of love' (*New Yorker*, 5 February 2001). Despite the conciliatory tone, for Bush and the New Right 'abandonment and abuse' were parental failures, not government indifference.

His first act appeased pro-life supporters by cutting federal support to organisations, such as International Planned Parenthood, because taxpayers should not 'pay for abortions or advocate or actively promote abortion' abroad. His critics maintained he did this because he did not have the constitutional power to impose similar restrictions in the United States. This act particularly damaged the lives of women in the Third World, especially Africa, where HIV/AIDS had reached pandemic proportions. In addition, Bush supported US drug companies who fought to charge the full price for patented drugs that prevented the disease spreading from pregnant women to their children.

A Disciple of Reagan and Clinton?

After many African Americans, Hispanics, the poor of all races and many elderly had been denied their vote, and despite the mounting homophobia, many commentators hoped that George W. Bush would moderate his right-wing views and understand the alienation of the popular majority who had voted against him in two elections. Sadly they were disillusioned. Some argued the terrorist attacks on New York City and Washington DC, explained the hardening of his fundamentalist beliefs in Reagan's policies benefiting the privileged, his deafness to the needs of the underprivileged and to those derisively labelled 'the underclass.' Despite reassuring words in his Inaugural Address and other speeches, he consistently opposed the rights and needs of those who made up the civil rights movement. And there were no kind words for others, such as gay couples who wanted to adopt even when his lesbian sister and her partner adopted a young child (*Newsweek*, 24 April 2000).

George Bush understood Clinton's view that politics was symbolism, an ability to show concern, and play the Oprah Winfrey. The big difference was that, although Clinton might have been motivated by many psychological reasons (Renshon, 1998; Draper, 2007), he was genuinely interested in people and had had a shared experience of deprivation. Critics said that with the 'disgrace' of Jesse Jackson's 'love child' and the demagogic politics of the Reverend Alan Sharpton, the civil rights movement had lost its way (*New Yorker*, 22 October 2001; 18–25 February 2002). Sharpton and Carol Moseley-Braun, one-term senator from Illinois, were the only African Americans who declared an interest in the 2004 Democratic presidential nomination simply to remind politicians that civil rights issues had not been resolved (*Washington Post*, 17 January 2003).

Appointments

The men and women appointed by the President in both terms reflected his business interests. The Vice President, Richard Cheney, was former CEO of Halliburton Industries, an oil services company. He had worked with Donald Rumsfeld in the Nixon Administration where they virtually dismantled many of LBJ's Great Society programmes (*New Yorker*, 7 May 2002). As a Wyoming congressman, Cheney voted against the ERA, federal funding for all abortions (even victims of rape or incest), funding the Head Start Program and a resolution by the House of Representatives which sought the release of Nelson Mandela. He refused to hand over documents or testify when it was alleged he knew of suspected illegal dealings by Enron or of his former company, Halliburton, in Iraq. Other appointments included Donald Evans, former head of a giant oil and gas company, as Secretary of Commerce, and Secretary of Health Tommy Thompson, a large investor in Philip Morris tobacco company. Spencer Abraham, a former conservative senator from Michigan, who had opposed environmental laws and had a zero rating from the League of Conservation Voters, became Secretary of Energy. The only gesture to inclusiveness was retaining Clinton's Secretary of Transport – Norman Minata.

The African American, Colin Powell, was to be the only moderate voice in the administration. He was heard in silence at the Republican Party convention when he defended abortion in some circumstances, argued that the Republican Party should be inclusive and that some form of affirmative action was necessary. Although he failed to win African American voters for Bush, he was only accepted because he was very popular with the general public, a popularity that exceeded that of Bush. This may partly explain why he was given one of the highest offices – Secretary of State (Draper, 2007). However, Powell was continually out-manoeuvred in the struggles between the State Department and the Pentagon, headed by Secretary of Defence, Donald Rumsfeld, who had worked in every Republican administration since Richard Nixon. Powell's position was weakened by subtle attacks from Republican conservatives such as Newt Gingrich (*New Yorker*, 26 November 2001). Powell's greatest moment was his speech to the United Nations defending the invasion of Iraq, a policy he had opposed, and his career was ruined when the misinformation he had been fed was exposed. He was not re-appointed after the 2004 election.

Condoleezza Rice, the only African American woman in the Administration in the first term, was National Security Advisor. She had served on the national security panel under Bush's father as senior director on Russian and East Asian affairs. In 2004 she told the black academic, Henry Gates, of her childhood in Birmingham, Alabama, in the 1960s when the city was known as "Bombingham." She was silent about the civil rights abuses and argued that the Republican's faith-based politics and 'ownership society' would produce 'the pillars of the black community. . . . In my community Birmingham, Alabama, in the 50s and 60s, there were black-owned businesses everywhere and everybody owned their own homes. They made our community strong. We've got to get that back again' (*New York Times*, 19 September 2004). She failed to say that these 'advantages' existed only because of vicious segregation enforced by the city and state. When necessary, however, she readily exploited the violence in Birmingham, especially at her confirmation hearing for Secretary of State in 2005. She did the same on overseas visits. Ms Rice, unlike her critics, believed her appointments had nothing to do with being black or a woman and never associated herself with any aspect of the feminist movement. She opposed all affirmative action programmes.

In 2003, the Executive Director, Kweisi Mfume, awarded her a NAACP 'Image Award', an act defended by Julian Bond. But not all African Americans were so impressed. Yolanda White, academic, poet, and composer, under the headline 'Condoleezza: Brown Rice As Bleached As White' criticised Rice for doing nothing to help African Americans and maintained that the award proved the black leadership still relied on white men's opinions on who was important in the African American community (*Baltimore Chronicle and Sentinel*, 7 August 2002).

In his first term, Bush chose Rod Paige, an African American from Texas, as his Secretary of Education. Although Bush claimed that black students in Texas high schools got better results than other states, one critic pointed out Texas had the 'highest drop-out rate for young black students and not including them in the results scewed the data' (CNN, Web Sites/Crossfire, 10 July 2000). A NAACP member, Paige graduated from Jackson State University, Mississippi, and earned his doctorate at Indiana University. A press release stated, 'he first distinguished himself coaching college-level athletics (Department of Education, 28 March 2001).' Later dean of education at Texas Southern University, he was popular with many African Americans because he won more federal money for all-black colleges. This was popular with white conservatives who favoured segregation. He backed the policy to assist faith-based schools, opposed affirmative action and social diversity programmes set up by state universities. He resigned in November 2004.

George W. Bush made a recess appointment of African American, Gerald Reynolds, as Assistant Secretary for Education, in charge of civil rights rather than face the battles that had occurred when Clarence Thomas was nominated. Originally recess appointments, which do not need Congressional approval if they are essential, were allowed if Congress was not in session. All presidents have used and abused this device to place controversial people. Reynolds' role was to supervise federal funding to ensure schools, colleges and universities complied with civil rights laws protecting minorities, women and gays. In 2005, Reynolds, a vocal opponent of affirmative action and especially the Americans With Disabilities Act, was appointed head of the Civil Rights Commission (*Washington Post*, 17 January 2005).

Other appointments were harmful for minorities, women, gays and the disabled. The new head of the Office of Personnel Management, Kay Cole James, did not support any form of affirmative action and Terence Boyle, who openly opposed civil rights, was nominated to be federal judge.

The End of History and the Movement?

In the years dominated by neo-conservatism, supported by several African Americans, when the dogma was that an unfettered free market was vital for American prosperity, Republicans and Democrats saw the collapse of the Soviet Union as the triumph of the free market and 'the end of history.' Poverty, family breakdown, and violent crime were the responsibility of individuals – not society. Most Americans agreed with Clinton's assertion, 'The era of big government is over.' And Dinesh D'Souza, of the right-wing American Enterprise Institute, insisted there was a 'destructive stance that seems deeply ingrained in African Americans, especially those in the middle class, who are too dependent on government' (D'Souza, 1995).

Others admitted the 'racial divide' persisted, but 'the status of blacks had improved enormously' because of the civil rights movement but media reports of persistent racism lacked 'analytic rigor.' Affirmative action, overwhelmingly supported by the black community, disregarded the growth of interracial marriages which had increased from 0.7 per cent in 1963 to 12.1 per cent in 1993. The children of these marriages, until 1989, were counted as black and 'simply expanded the size of the black population. As did the offspring of those offspring, even if they all married whites.' People in 1995 who wanted to call themselves multiracial, 1.7 per cent of the population or over 4 million people, could not because the Census Bureau racial categories were exclusive and mixed-race children were counted as black for affirmative action. This perpetuated the 'once-pervasive caste system.' It ignored the role of neo-conservative economics for the poverty of many black families and claimed it was 'a consequence of the huge rise in female-headed households among African Americans.' America needed a colour blind society as demanded by Justice Harlan in 1896, Thurgood Marshall in 1954 and Martin Luther King Jr in 1963 (Thernstrom and Thernstrom, 1997). As Peggy Pascoe points out: '[C]olorblindness' was reconstituted from an oppositional weapon in the fight for racial justice to a conservative statement of American values .... The battle against inter-racial marriage came to be regarded as a mere ghost of America's troubled racial past' (Pascoe, 2009). Sadly, Americans are not colour blind. Racism made three white men in Jasper, Texas on 18 June 1998 drag James Byrd Jr to his death chained behind their pick-up (*Houston Chronicle*, 19 June 1998). The *Minnesota Daily* condemned the murder but the editorial linked blacks and the KKK to violence, with the emphasis on African Americans. 'With black militants and the Ku Klux Klan standing in the shadows, any further killing will result in a classic Hatfield-McCoy dispute, with each side trading murder for murder' (*Minnesota Daily*, 27 June 1998). When lynching produced only mild condemnation it was not surprising that the old civil rights organisations lost influence. Demands from the National Urban League for a domestic Marshall Plan, backed by civil disobedience, failed because, as Stephen Tuck points out, 'this typified the early efforts that were often based on traditional community institutions such as the church, the campuses, labor groups, and women's groups' (Hudson and Davies, 2008).

Malcolm X and Black Conservatism

Neo-conservatism, advocated by Milton Friedman, the Thernstroms and D'Souza, had African American believers. Thomas Sowell and Clarence Thomas, early admirers of Malcolm X and Black Power, vehemently opposed integration and affirmative action. Malcolm had attacked the NAACP because its 'agenda reflects the priorities of the elite: equal access to white institutions and white neighbourhoods allowing them to escape the black masses.' Affirmative action meant the poor were neglected. But Malcolm X believed blacks should turn to their own community for help while Sowell followed his white mentor, Friedman, and argued that everyone must depend on themselves (Mayer and Abramson, 1994). Thomas believes affirmative action has 'stigmatizing effects [that] perpetuate racism, averting what would otherwise be its natural death' (Tate and Randolph, 2002). But he was a beneficiary of it. Clarence Thomas claims racist seminarians and Yale law students brought him to Malcolm X, Black Power and Thomas Sowell. Reading his Supreme Court rulings, it is difficult to square them with his assertion: 'What I cared about more than anything else ... was the condition of blacks in Savannah and across America'

(Thomas, 2007). Neo-conservatives claimed that he had triumphed over the poverty of the hamlet of Pin Point. Bush Sr even bussed folks of Pin Point to DC, to support Thomas. Thomas lied to the confirmation hearing. He claimed his sister stayed home and waited for welfare checks when she was employed (Mayer and Abramson, 1994). Thomas repaid his white benefactors handsomely.

Another black neo-conservative was Alan Lee Keyes, a Harvard graduate. A perennial political office seeker, he was appointed by Reagan to the UN and State Department. Keyes opposed sanctions against South Africa and aid to family planning groups who supported abortion. A homophobic, he attacked his daughter for being a lesbian. His three attempts for the presidency (1988, 1992 and 2004) were disastrous and in the Illinois federal Senate election against Barack Obama he won only 26 per cent of the vote (Obama, 2007). He left the Republican Party in 2008 because they were not true conservatives (BBC News, January 2008).

James Carville, Clinton's campaign manager and native of Louisiana, points out, 'It is one thing to propose self-reliance, and quite another to propose that the government had no responsibility for the poor, no responsibility for the victims of discrimination. Republicans want to get rid of affirmative action and return America to a meritocracy, but America has never been a meritocracy' (Carville, 1996).

Bush Triumphs with Supreme Court

During his term in office, neo-conservatives hoped Bush would appoint a right wing majority to the court. After his re-election in 2004, he had two appointments and hoped to ensure a conservative control for years to come. His nomination of John G. Roberts and Samuel Alito dramatically altered the balance of the Court (www.naacp.org, 2006). Roberts was initially proposed after the surprise resignation of Sandra Day O'Connor but his nomination was withdrawn after the Chief Justice died and the 50-year-old Roberts was nominated to head the Court. Liberals did not expose his opposition to women's rights or his close connections with ultra-right wing evangelicals. To replace O'Connor, Bush nominated Antonin Alito who, like Roberts, agreed he would be bound by historic decisions of the Court. Alito's nomination was given the full White House preparation and Alito emphasised his poor background and contrasted the worst of what he saw at Princeton 'with the good sense and decency of the people back in my community' (Greenburg, 2008). It was a repeat of the Clarence

Thomas Pin Point strategy. The Legal Defense Fund of the NAACP were proven right when they warned his appointment would 'shift significantly the Supreme Court's jurisprudence relating to affirmative action, voting rights, employment and criminal justice issues' (www.naacp.org, accessed 30 January 2009).

The triumph of ultras is seen in two major rulings on school desegregation and voting rights. In 2007, the Court in a 5-4 decision rejected the constitutionality of school district plans that used race as a factor in student assignment to ensure racial desegregation in schools. The ACLU press release stated, 'The Supreme Court of the United States has issued an opinion in two cases that will affect school integration programs throughout the country. Parents in Louisville, Kentucky and Seattle, Washington argued that those districts' school integration programs – each of which was voluntarily adopted by local school boards to promote racial integration – violated the Equal Protection Clause of the Fourteenth Amendment.' Programmes that used race to assign pupils for public schools were unconstitutional, even if based on voluntarily agreements to provide children with more diverse education. According to Roberts, Scalia, Thomas and Alito, 'to achieve a system of determining admission to the public schools on a nonracial basis [as per *Brown*] is to stop assigning student on a racial basis. The way to stop discrimination on the basis of race is to stop discriminating on the basis of race' (*Washington Post*, 29 June 2007).

The Court not only effectively overturned *Brown*; they also upheld Indiana legislation that restricted the right to vote which is protected by both the 15th Amendment and the Voting Rights Act of 1965. On 28 April 2008, the Court ruled on an Indiana law of 2005 that required voters to present identification prior to casting a ballot. It included some exemptions and those without identification could submit provisional ballots. These were to be counted only if the voter presented identification within ten days of the election. The Democratic Party and the ACLU, challenged the Act, arguing it violated the First and Fourteenth Amendments because many voters could not meet the arbitrary requirements and were disenfranchised due to the costs of fulfilling identification requirements. They were essentially a poll tax. But the Court ruled against them and its ruling virtually overturned the 1966 case of *Harper v. Virginia Bd. of Elections*. The fees were not labelled as a poll tax but the Indiana requirements did disenfranchise voters. Bush later claimed at a meeting honouring African American History Month that, 'We will continue to enforce laws against racial discrimination in education and housing and public accommodations. We believe every child can learn and we expect every school to teach. And we measure. And guess what's happening? Test scores are going up. There's an achievement gap for minority children that is closing in America' (*AfricanAmericans.com*, accessed 1 February 2009).

The Nomination of Judge Pickering

If Bush had wanted to heal the wounds and speak to the African American community in his first term, he would not have nominated Pickering to the Fifth Circuit Court of Appeals, a choice that angered many – black and white. It was reminiscent of Nixon's nominations of Haynesworth and Carswell for the Supreme Court. The *Houston Chronicle* urged Pickering's rejection because as a district judge, appointed by Bush's father, he had urged federal prosecutors in a 1994 case to be lenient on a man convicted of burning a cross on an interracial couple's lawn and shooting into their house. Pickering had complained to Justice Department officials about the guidelines for a five-year sentence and threatened a new trial if they were followed.

In 1959, he advised the Mississippi legislature on how to strengthen state law against interracial marriage. He left the Democratic Party in 1964 because it insisted future state delegations had to be integrated. Moreover, he had criticised one-person-one-vote as required by the Supreme Court. However, some civil rights leaders defended him because he had testified against a KKK defendant in the 1960s and in 1994 he had protected the Mississippi lesbian commune, Camp Sister Spirit (Log Cabin Republicans, 17 January 2003). Others argued this was not significant because the Klan had become an embarrassment to southern political leaders (*Houston Chronicle*, 5 March 2002). The *Detroit Free Press* was equally hostile charging the judge as someone who opposed civil rights and that the opposition of the NAACP and the black lawyers' association in Mississippi should not be ignored (*Detroit Free Press*, 6 March 2002). Republicans on the Judiciary Committee ignored the criticism. But Democrats, with a one vote majority in the Senate (following a Republican defection), rejected Pickering 10-9. At a Texas rally, Bush said he admired Justices Antonin Scalia and Clarence Thomas and defended his nomination using the old southern view of 'strict construction' of the Constitution.

Bush insisted on re-nominating Pickering when Republicans regained the Senate after the 2002 mid-term elections. It was a defiant act but he was exploiting his newly acquired 'legitimacy' following the terrorist attacks on 11 September 2001. Pickering's re-nomination came even though some

Administration officials believed his chances were nil after the furore caused by Senator Trent Lott (*New York Times*, 19 December 2002). Pickering was appointed in Bush's second term.

The Resignation of Trent Lott

Pickering's first nomination was enthusiastically supported by the Republican leader in the Senate, Trent Lott of Mississippi. Although many southerners accepted the need for civil rights legislation, Senator Lott disagreed. On 5 December 2002 at the 100th birthday celebration for Dixiecrat turned Republican, Strom Thurmond of South Carolina, Lott proclaimed: 'I want to say this about my state. When Strom Thurmond ran for president, we voted for him. We're proud of it. And if the rest of the country had followed our lead, we wouldn't have had all these problems over all these years either.' This praised Thurmond's 1948 boast that there would not be enough troops to end racial segregation in the South. (After Thurmond's death it was revealed that when he was 21 he raped the 15-year-old daughter of a servant in his house. Having a black daughter did not stop him from denouncing the perils of miscegenation.)

Following a storm of criticism, Lott regretted that he had 'spoken from the heart rather than the head' about the 'discarded policies' of segregation. Was Lott swept along by the emotional celebration? No. He had a history. African American columnist, Stanley Crouch, complained that apart from the *New York Times*, no one had supported his calls for Lott's resignation from the Council of Conservative Citizens. He wrote that the Council's journal, the *Citizen Informer*, 'advocated separation of the races and discouraged interracial marriage.' Lott had written for the magazine and had had his picture on a 1992 cover. Crouch recalled that the Senator had addressed a Mississippi rally of the Sons of Confederate Veterans in 1984:'The spirit of Jefferson Davis lives in the 1984 Republican platform' (*New York Daily Post*, 12 December 2002). Three years earlier Lott had filed a brief to the Fifth Circuit Court of Appeals defending Bob Jones University's tax exempt status even though he knew of the racist policies of the university (*Bob Jones v The United States*, 27 November 1981).

Under pressure, Lott admitted his remarks were 'terrible' but did not resign as Republican leader. At first Republicans defended Lott. Representative J. C. Watts, the black Republican Congressman, did and Bush's spokesman, Ari Fliescher, thought that Lott's remarks did not affect his leadership of the Senate. And Lott was determined to stay but Republicans were vulnerable on race issues. He had said what many white Americans believed but he was not helped by a white North Carolina Republican who admitted that a dispute with black Congresswoman, Cynthia McKinney, gave him 'segregationist feelings' (*New York Times*, 20 December 2002). Some worried the party was seen as a haven for white extremists and had to change to attract African Americans (GOPOutreach, 2 February 2002). Colin Powell opposed Lott and his defenders. He said he was 'disappointed... There was nothing about the 1948 election or the Dixiecrat agenda that should have been acceptable in any way to any American at that time or any American now' (*New York Times*, 19 December 2002).

Appearing on Black Entertainment Television, Lott asked for forgiveness and declared he had changed his views on civil rights. He regretted voting against King's birthday as a federal holiday, and now backed affirmative action and claimed he would help all minorities, especially African Americans. The black representative from Georgia, John Lewis, a Selma-to-Montgomery March leader, believed Lott was sincere. African Americans liked Lott's conversion but the remarkable promises ensured Lott's defeat for Senate leadership. Some believe that Bush masterminded Lott's removal to erase the taint of racism from the Republicans and win black votes in 2004. It was maintained that Bush was fighting the racially exclusive policy of the party and he was genuinely committed to a multiracial America (*New York Times*, 12 and 20 December 2002). Lott believed unnamed people in Washington conspired against him because of his conservatism (AP report, 21 December 2002). And with challenges to affirmative action coming to the Supreme Court which Bush wanted to support and with virtually every Republican extremely hostile to affirmative action, Lott's efforts to appease African Americans doomed his chances of remaining Senate leader. A Bush ally challenged Lott and defeated him. Bush's continued support for Lott was impossible but he described Lott as 'a valued friend, and a man I respect. I am pleased he will continue to serve our nation in the Senate' (*New York Times*, 29 December 2002). Lott had not offended Mississippi white voters who returned him to the Senate.

Bush and Affirmative Action

The President and his party opposed affirmative action to aid minorities and the underprivileged and welcomed its abolition in California despite the disastrous consequences on black enrolments in the state universities. When the Court in *Hopwood* struck down the University of Texas programme that

benefited poor people regardless of race, gender, disability or sexual orientation, the party supported the decision. A new challenge to affirmative action
came against the University of Michigan. Although accused of introducing
a quota system designed to give preferential treatment to black students, the
university countered that their policy was based on income not race and
their contention, supported by General Motors, was that if students were
to be properly educated they should be drawn from the widest social background possible. The Court was evenly divided with the swing vote being
Sandra Day O'Connor.

Bush rejected the university's contention that their policy did not favour
blacks and asserted they were operating an unconstitutional 'quota system
that unfairly rewards or penalizes prospective students based solely on their
race.' He singled out California and Texas as states which had 'affirmative
access' policies that benefited young people regardless of race. He ignored
the collapse in admissions of black students in California, Florida and Texas
universities and claimed: 'Race neutral policies have resulted in levels of
minority attendance ... that are close to, and in some instances surpass,
those under the old race-based approach.' His attempt to make a distinction
between 'affirmative action' and 'affirmative access' was greeted with scep-
ticism by civil rights supporters. They pointed out that Bush would never
have been accepted by Yale University because his entrance examination
scores were too low and he was admitted because the university had a quota
scheme which allowed children of former alumni privileged access. Almost
30 per cent of university funding in the United States comes from grateful
alumni. These quotas have never been challenged by liberals or conservatives. The leader in the Senate, Tom Daschle, commented, 'They have
to decide whether they're for civil rights and diversity or not' (*USA Today*,
16 January 2003). Democratic Party women leaders and women activists
defended affirmative action which benefited women more than minorities.
Representative Nancy Pelosi attacked the Administration's intervention in
the case. 'If the Supreme Court agrees with President Bush and prohibits
affirmative action in our colleges and universities, the dreams of countless
eager young people will be crushed.' African Americans, and others, doubts
about the ruling were proved wrong when O'Connor joined the liberal justices and in *Grutter et al v Bollinger* (23 June 2003) upheld the *Bakke* decision by
5 to 4. However, three of the majority argued for a 25-year limit on diversity
programmes.

During Bush's first term his Attorney General, John Ashcroft, in 2001,
disbanded several committees made up of veteran civil rights lawyers and
changed the rules for appointments. They became political appointees and

the main criterion was applicants with 'strong conservative credentials' and not experience with civil rights cases. In 2001, 77 per cent of lawyers in the Civil Rights Division of the Justice Department had civil rights experience but by 2003 only 42 per cent of new appointees had done any work for civil rights. During the years 2003–2006, after Bush's re-election, only 19 out of 45 had fought civil rights cases. Eleven of the nineteen were members of the very conservative Republican group called the Federalist Society. Some of them had taken civil rights cases against blacks. As the investigative journalist wrote, '[T]he kinds of cases the Civil Rights Division is bringing has undergone a shift. The division is bringing fewer voting rights and employment cases involving systematic discrimination against African Americans, and more alleging reverse discrimination against whites and religious discrimination against Christians' (Charlie Savage, *Boston Globe*, 23 July 2006). When Roberto Gonzales took over, the politicisation of the Justice Department continued. Eight federal prosecutors were dismissed and the ensuing storm forced his resignation and investigation by a special prosecutor (*New York Times*, 29 September 2008).

Hurricane Katrina

Even a sympathetic biographer of George W. Bush realised that, 'Katrina had blown a hole through his presidency' (Draper, 2007). Robert Draper says Bush's apparent indifference to the hurricane of 28 August 2005 was the fault of the black mayor of New Orleans, Ray Nagin, the governor of Louisiana and other staff members. But Bush knew well in advance that a terrible storm was heading towards the Gulf Coast. Unlike his response to previous hurricanes in Florida, Bush kept to his normal schedule before returning to Texas.

During his absence television showed dead bodies floating in the streets of the city, families desperately clinging to rooftops, the flight of rich white city dwellers while the poor residents in the 9th Ward, black and white, struggled to stay above the waters of the broken levees. When he did visit Biloxi, Mississippi, he praised the head of the Federal Emergency Management Committee for doing a great job. His first sight of the devastation was from the comfort of Air Force One. When he went to New Orleans he avoided the 9th ward and the demonstrators and went to the virtually undamaged lower Garden District where he told community leaders that the city was 'a heck of a place to bring your family. It's a great place to find the greatest food in the world and some wonderful fun. And I'm glad you got your infrastructure back on its feet' (Draper, 2007). At the time he was speaking, the football stadium was crowded with flood victims who could not escape the city. Many had had their families divided and scattered to numerous states as children and the elderly were evacuated. The Administration's incompetence and lack of concern appalled the international and national media. To make matters worse white residents were described as 'finding' food and African Americans were described as 'looters.' The white town of Algiers Point had not been damaged because the levees had not broken there. But the residents did not help the people trying to leave New Orleans and instead blocked the roads with felled trees. 'They stockpiled handguns, assault rifles, shotguns and at least one Uzi and began patrolling the streets in pickup trucks and SUVs. The newly formed militia, a loose band of about fifteen to thirty residents, most of them men, all of them white, was looking for thieves, outlaws or, as one member put it, anyone who simply "didn't belong" ' (*The Nation*, 17 December 2008).

Over a year after the hurricane, a CNN investigation found that in the small community of Pearlington in Hancock County, Mississippi, there was no main street, no grocery, the water was foul smelling and contaminated with coliform bacteria. One family had rebuilt their home and others were still living in FEMA supplied trailers which had dangerous levels of formaldehyde (CNN Report, 30 August 2006). A Census Bureau study after Katrina found that New Orleans was 64 per cent smaller, with an estimated 278,833 residents, many white and middle class (*New York Times*, 7 June 2006). And as late as August 2008, Bush told a sympathetic crowd at the Louisiana National Guard that 'hope is coming back' to New Orleans. At his final press conference as president, Bush described his performance during Katrina as a 'disappointment.' 'He reflected on whether or not he should have landed Air Force One in Louisiana after Hurricane Katrina, and argued passionately that in retrospect, he made the right decision in not burdening local officials with his presence.' The conservative journal accused him of 'paralytic incompetence' (*Time*, 12 January 2009).

'Gagging on the Donkey'

In July 2005, at a meeting with the National Urban League, Bush quoted a Republican Illinois legislator, '[B]lacks are gagging on the donkey but not yet ready to swallow the elephant.' The President asked, 'How is it possible (for Republicans) to gain political leverage if the (Democratic) party is never forced to compete?' (*New York Times*, 10 September 2005). But Bush had never competed for the black vote. During his first term he never accepted the invitations to speak to the NAACP and never disguised his intense dislike of the organisation. At the height of the tensions, he said his relationship with the NAACP was 'basically nonexistent.' Until the meeting in 2006, he had been the first president since Herbert Hoover to refuse to speak with the organisation. In 2005 the National Republican chair admitted at the NAACP convention that some of the party 'were trying to benefit from racial polarization' (Green, 2007). Bush addressed them after six years in office and promised, 'We'll work together, and as we do so, you must understand I understand that racism still lingers in America.' He considered it 'a tragedy' that the party had not fought hard enough for their votes. But it was a tragedy of his making. And it did not help that the IRS was threatening the NAACP's tax-exempt status because they had often criticised Bush's policies (*USA Today*, 10 March 2004; Green, 2007). Most NAACP members 'gave him credit for simply showing up', others were sceptical. Kathy Sykes from Mississippi said, 'He waited until the 11th hour of his presidency to come to us with all of his great plans of working together.' She considered it mere rhetoric (*New York Times*, 21 July 2006). A day later, the Senate approved a 25-year extension of the Voting Rights Act by a vote of 98 to 0.

The Rich Get Richer

Democrat Nancy Pelosi vigorously opposed the President's economic policies which she claimed only favoured the rich. However, the three women in Bush's cabinet did not support such views. Condoleezza Rice did not and neither did Gale Norton, Secretary of the Interior, nor Elaine Chao, Secretary of Labor. Norton had defended paint companies when families brought actions for damages because of the lead content, and Chao was a board member of a company fined for producing faulty heart catheters and another which had opposed health insurance reform (Moore, 2001).

But 9/11 exposed the flaws of Bush's policies. Congress mandated that the head of the federal Victim Compensation Fund, Kenneth Feinberg, follow rules which seemed to help those with the least need. A 25-year-old, childless widow whose husband had earned $125,000 a year would get $4.5 million whereas a 40-year-old widow with two dependent children, mainly African American, whose husband had made $20,000 would get just over $900,000. And even then some of the richest were not satisfied (*New Yorker*, 25 November 2002). It was Reagonomics with a vengeance.

Although $10 billion went to education, $30 billion in tax cuts went to the richest 1 per cent of the population who gained another $30 billion with the abolition of estate tax. Rich heiresses and heirs benefited by $6.2 million on average. As one commentator noted, 'a reward not for effort, enterprise or work but simply for having been, like Bush himself, born rich' (*New Yorker*, 5 February 2002). He reduced a public housing programme by $60 million and slashed $200 million off the federal Childcare and Development grant – a programme set up to provide transitional help to families, partners and single parents who were forced to find work and lose their welfare benefit. Bush, during the campaign, said he supported the Americans with Disabilities Act and was proud that his father had signed the legislation. But his budget cut support for the disabled and even natural supporters, such as the Disabled American Veterans, Paralyzed Veterans of America, and the Veterans of Foreign Wars, demanded full funding of disability programmes (AMVETS letter to Bush, 25 January 2003). It was eight years of gross neglect of wounded veterans that hurt Republicans in 2008.

As the recession in America deepened, Bush announced another budget proposal which he claimed would revitalise the economy but it did nothing for poor blacks, other minorities or poor whites. He claimed, 'Ninety-two million Americans will keep an average of $1083 more of their own money.' The claim was dismissed as 'bogus' by the *Financial Times*. And Hendrick Hertzberg wrote that 'a typical tax-payer – one right smack in the middle of the income range – will get a couple of hundred dollars. And a worker in the bottom twenty per cent will get next to nothing – at most, a dime or a quarter a week.' However, Bush would get $44,500 and Vice President Cheney as much as $327,000 (*New Yorker*, 20 January 2003). It was as Michael Douglas declared in Oliver Stone's movie *Wall Street* – 'Greed is good.' It was good for bankers and hedge fund managers until 2008 when, having ignored Enron and World Com scandals, Bush was forced to virtually nationalise the home loan and banking sector while the companies involved in the scandals left people homeless. The catastrophic collapse of the economy created Katrina victims on a national scale. The bankers were rescued but the middle and working class, regardless of race, lost their homes and their jobs.

The Law and Discrimination

In 2002 when the Supreme Court ruled that execution of the 'mentally defective' was unconstitutional, the death penalty was seriously debated because of the extraordinary events in Illinois. George Ryan, a conservative

Republican, had campaigned for the death penalty when he ran for governor. It was later discovered by a group of young journalism students at Northwestern University that 13 men had been wrongfully condemned to death since 1977. He ordered a moratorium on executions. On 19 December 2002 he pardoned three men including one who had spent ten years on death row until DNA proved he did not murder a young woman. Before leaving office, Ryan commuted the sentences of 167 prisoners on death row to life imprisonment (AP, 11 January 2003). He said the process was 'arbitrary and capricious, and therefore immoral' and 'My concern is not just with the death penalty. . . . It's with the entire criminal justice system. If innocent people are sentenced to death – cases that get all the scrutiny – what does that say about invisible low-level cases – drugs cases and so on?' (*The Guardian*, 10 January 2003). It was not a popular decision. The governor of Maryland refused to reconsider capital punishment despite a detailed study that proved massive racial discrimination in death penalty cases in the state. The Justice Department did not comment when a mentally disabled African American woman was sentenced to death for murdering her sister's child when it was born. Although reduced to 15 years for manslaughter, she was released without compensation after one year because it was discovered her sister could never have had a baby because she had been sterilised after the birth of her sixth child (*North County Times*, 18 July 2002).

Racial discrimination not only influenced capital crime cases. The ACLU continued its campaign to reform the cocaine laws but the US Sentencing Commission's suggestions on sale were very modest. They argued crack was much more dangerous than powdered cocaine and the only change should be that after the first arrest for possession, the five-year sentence would apply at 25 grams rather than five. The only other change was increasing the amount from 50 to 250 grams to trigger a mandatory ten-year sentence (*ACLU*, 20 May 2002). The right-wing group, Children Requiring a Caring Kommunity (CRACK), expanded its programme to pay $200 to women with drug or alcohol problems if they agreed to long-term contraception or sterilisation. Almost 50 per cent of the women sterilised were African Americans (*Washington Post*, 8 January 2003).

Where Have All the (Male) Leaders Gone?

The reaction of black men and sects such as Nation of Islam to black women choosing to ally with their 'sisters,' women-of colour, rather than black men, was an attempt to reassert their leadership, especially over black women.

The two Million Man Marches were not a sign of strength but desperate acts by men increasingly aware of their weakening hold on civil rights issues. It was the old assertion of male dominance that set the conservative tone; black men had abandoned the dream of a coalition of the poor. King's last years showed an analytic awareness of the issues of poverty that afflicted millions of Americans. The Vietnam War was not only immoral because it upheld a corrupt regime in South Vietnam; it was immoral because the poor died to enrich the few. To fight the war, programmes to help the poor were as starved as the people they were supposed to support. In his last address as SCLC president, King said Jesus demanded that the 'whole structure must be changed.' A country that enslaved people for 244 years made them into things. 'Therefore they will exploit them, and poor people generally, economically. And a nation that will exploit them economically will have to have foreign investments and everything else, and will have to use the military to protect them. All of these problems are tied together.' The nation needed to be 'born again' (Jackson, 2007).

The man who claimed King's mantle, Jesse Jackson, followed King's battle with Richard Daley, Mayor of Chicago. Jackson's move to Chicago gave him an urban power-base. Jackson ran Operation Breadbasket and People United to Save Humanity (PUSH). This organisation with the NAACP, the Urban League and a black millionaire's backing, ensured the election of the African American Harold Washington as mayor. Jackson's two bids for the presidency under the banner of a Rainbow Coalition attracted many new voters, not just because he was articulate and black, but because his message was conservative, an endorsement of black capitalism. He proved that a black candidate could be viable and paved the way for Obama in 2008. Unlike King, it was not that the pie had been badly made but rather African Americans wanted a bigger slice.

Although Jackson had battled for better education and extending integration, the 1980s saw a rapid re-segregation of schools. White flight to suburbia, private schools, church schools and other devices meant that by the 1980s the number of integrated schools had fallen from 70 per cent in the 1970s to below 50 per cent. In the North the situation was worse with 90 per cent of black children attending all-black schools. 'As the nineties began, the combination of massive white opposition to bussing for racial balance and increasing residential segregation had quieted talk of integrated education. It no longer seemed an attainable, however distant goal' (Sitkoff, 1993). With the exception of Little Rock, Arkansas! A federal appeals court in 2009 upheld a judge's ruling that the Little Rock School District had met the terms of a long-standing desegregation order. A three judge panel of

the Eighth Circuit Appeal Court ruled unanimously that there was insufficient evidence to overturn the 2007 ruling that the education district had
complied with a 1998 desegregation plan (*New York Times*, 2 April 2009).
According to the education authorities, over 50 per cent of pupils at Central
High were black and over 40 per cent were white.

But Jackson concentrated on strictly economic issues. The Wall Street
Project operates through PUSH in four major cities and the Silicon Valley
and raised $17million in 2000. Critics claim Jackson's methods are 'some-
what tenuous morally, mainly because his dealings with business look so
much like shakedowns' because he threatens to boycott big corporations
unless they have diversity and tolerance programmes and help black business. It is said he abuses his power to benefit his sons who were awarded
a valuable distributorship by the beer company. Even his $7.8 billion deal
with Toyota for minority training programmes, black dealerships, and contracts for minority-owned business has been described as virtual blackmail
(*New Yorker*, 22 October 2001). Apart from these claims in the liberal white
journal, former associates, the Reverend Wyatt Tee Walker in Harlem and
a former Jackson aide, Al Sharpton, challenged him.

When the news of Jackson's 'love child' was leaked to the *National Enquirer*,
perhaps by Bush aides, Jackson did not apologise. But he needed Walker's
support. Walker agreed to a church service conducted by Sharpton. Jackson could speak but only apologise and ask for forgiveness. Jackson did not.
Walker's letter to Jackson was also published in the *Village Voice*: 'Your addic-
tion to the need for media attention seems to be fatal and you have fallen
into the practice of *using* people for your advantage and personal aggran-
dizement' (*New Yorker*, 22 October 2001). Obama's criticisms of irresponsible
black men might explain Jackson's attacks on him.

The man who saw himself as Jackson's successor was the flamboyant minister from New York City – Al (Alfred) Sharpton. He dismissed the black Ivy
League-educated middle class. There were no fancy universities in Selma
but 'we always had our self-esteem and self-respect. Columbia can't give
that to you.' Despite his claims, Sharpton was born in New York in 1954,
the son of a prosperous building contractor and he did not take part in the
civil rights struggles (*New Yorker*, 18 and 25 February 2002).

There are similarities. Jackson was Sharpton's mentor and he worked for
Operation Breadbasket and PUSH. Sharpton moved to New York and his
Madison Avenue Initiative and his National Action Network compete with
PUSH. He was damaged by making false charges of white racism. He sup-
ported a young black girl, Tawana Brawley, who lied that she had been
raped by white men. But, despite this setback, Sharpton waged successful

campaigns against NYC police brutality. His presidential bid in 2004 was to show he had replaced Jesse Jackson as the undisputed leader of the African American community. He repeatedly told Jackson. 'If you want to be comfortable, you should do what Muhammad Ali did. You should get a ringside seat and watch the fight' (*New Yorker*, 18 and 25 February 2002). Jackson responded: 'All this talk about trying to determine who the leader is, and all this campaigning, is so trivial' (New *Yorker*, 22 October 2001). And Sharpton's other white critics were blunter. 'If Sharpton were a white skinhead, he would be a political leper . . .' (Boston *Globe*, 16 January 2003). These feuds damaged the civil rights movement at the national level and made it easier for conservatives to dismantle earlier gains.

Old and New Alliances

The dreams of King, Rustin, Randolph, Hamer and Pauli Young had turned into a nightmare for many minorities. But nonviolence had not died as was demonstrated by the FSAM. African American women and men kept alive alliances with unions, women's groups, lesbians, gays, bisexuals and transsexuals (LGBT) and the environmental movement. It was, after all, the poor and minorities who suffered most from environmental pollution. The Bush Administration's neglect of social problems was anything but benign. For many observers of the civil rights movement the battle had been won or lost depending on one's sympathies. But old politics and new allies meant that at no time had people given up on the struggle to overcome. Among these effective older leaders was John Lewis, a speaker at the 1963 March on Washington, who was elected to Congress. And in 1972, Barbara Jordan a Congresswoman from Texas became a national figure during Nixon's impeachment hearings.

Congressional Black Caucus

Despite the efforts of George Bush and Republican politicians, such as Tom DeLay of Texas, redistricting and the Voting Rights Act had ensured better representation of African Americans in government. The newly elected representatives formed a powerful Congressional Black Caucus (CBC) to enhance their influence in the Democratic Party and co-operated with the Congressional Caucus for Women's Issues and the Hispanic Caucus. They

worked with state governments and professional organisations. Reagan discovered CBC's power when it backed the FSAM and overrode his veto
to impose sanctions on South Africa. The FSAM, launched by Randall
Robinson and others in 1984, resulted in sit-ins at the South African
embassy, nonviolent demonstrations and arrests that galvanised national
opinion against apartheid. Others took direct action against Reagan's support of the terrorist groups in Central America. In 1991 the CBC was vital in
overriding George H. W. Bush's veto of the 1990 Civil Rights Act. Although
they could not prevent compromises, the Act reversed many judgements
of the Supreme Court which severely restricted civil rights. For 40 years the
CBC has wielded power and John Conyers chairs the House Judiciary Committee. One paper editorialised that, 'The Black Caucus is going through an
identity crisis.' It was claimed they had to question 'the need for their existence and are in the midst of an uneasy generational shift, as the old lions of
the civil rights era begin to give way to a younger generation of black politicians who do not want to be pigeonholed by race' (*International Herald Tribune*,
7 January 2009). This underestimates the CBC and Democrats know it. It
is too early to bring in the coffin.

Black Power in the States

The Voting Rights Act of 1965 had always been renewed and led to
important changes that ensured the election of many sate representatives,
mayors and even governors. To protect the gains of the civil rights movement, representatives at state level formed back caucuses to coordinate
campaigns with the CBC and local community and pressure groups. The
National Black Caucus of State Legislatures monitors domestic policy at
state and federal level. It has over 600 representatives from 42 states and
Washington, DC, and represents over 50 million Americans of all races. In
South Carolina the minority party Democrats had 40 black legislators in
its Caucus and they ensured the election of a black woman, Gilda Cobb-
Hooper, as leader. Contrary to expectations, the white Democrats accepted
the result. But there were hazards such as how far to push their agenda and
keep white Democrats' party loyalty. In 2009 the Black Caucus in the state
General Assembly was made up of 38 members of the House of Representatives and nine senators (South Carolina Black Caucus website, 11 February
2009).

    Law-and-order issues presented problems for African American repre-
sentatives at state level. Under pressure from their own voters, one-third of

the Mississippi Black Caucus supported the Street Gang Act in 1996, allowing confiscation of gang members' property. Although they persuaded only
two white legislators to oppose the Truth in Sentencing Act (1995) it passed
and all felons, including those who were nonviolent, had to complete 85 per
cent of their sentence. But the Caucus stressed the costs to the tax payer and
the Act was amended and limited to violent criminals.

Governors

No African American had been a governor; the highest state post held had
been a lieutenant governor in Louisiana after the Civil War. Virginia, the
home of Confederate hero Robert E. Lee, was the first state to elect an
African American as lieutenant governor in 1986. In 1989, L. Douglas
Wilder became the first black governor in the history of the United
States, defeating a conservative Republican in a campaign in which Wilder
defended women's right to an abortion. Although Wilder won white support, the election allegedly demonstrated polarisation along racial and
party lines; a danger predicted by LBJ when he signed the Voting Rights
Act, that the South's 'recently acquired two-party politics may become
one party for blacks and one party for whites, a disquieting reminder of
the past' (Cooper and Terrill, 1991). This is true in many southern states
for presidential and Senate elections, but in Virginia Wilder kept white
votes and the Democratic presidential candidate in 2008 would do the
same. And David Paterson, first African American and blind lieutenant
governor of New York State, won handsomely. When his colleague and
white governor resigned amid sex scandals, Paterson replaced him. Deval
Patrick in 2006 became the first black governor of Massachusetts in a
state where African Americans are only 7 per cent of the population (Ifill,
2009).

Mayors

Carl Stokes' parents fled to Cleveland to escape the segregated South. Their
son was the first African American mayor elected in any major city in 1967.
Thanks to the GI bill, he escaped poverty, graduated from the University of
Minnesota and returned to Cleveland as city prosecutor. Later he served in
the Ohio state house and on his second attempt to be mayor he narrowly
won but did not seek re-election after black riots. President Clinton made
him ambassador to the Seychelles in 1994.

Stokes demonstrated that African Americans could win large cities. Harold Washington defeated the powerful Daley machine in Chicago twice and David Dinkins won in New York City. Byron Brown in Buffalo, New York, and Cory Booker of Newark, New Jersey, became mayors. Perhaps the best known was Tom Bradley of Los Angeles who held office from 1973 to 1993. A sharecropper's son, Bradley won although African Americans made up only 15 per cent of the population (*Christian Science Monitor*, 30 September 1998). Ironically, he is not remembered as much for his accomplishments as mayor as for the so-called 'Bradley Effect.' He ran for governorship and had a massive lead in the polls but was defeated by the Republican. Many said he lost because white voters deserted him at the last moment. Others claimed it was not race but he was too liberal. The important thing was African Americans believed in the 2008 campaign that they would suffer the 'Bradley Effect.'

African Americans are represented in city government and state police forces. The white state troopers who had happily resisted violently against civil rights are now integrated and many counties have black sheriffs and deputies. In Meridian, Mississippi, where civil rights workers were murdered, the police chief Benny DuBose's election was celebrated at an all-white church (*Christian Science Monitor*, 18 March 2002). On inauguration day in 2009, Congressman John Lewis met the young police chief of Rock Hill, South Carolina. Lewis said, 'Imagine that, I was beaten near to death at the Rock Hill Greyhound bus terminal during the Freedom Rides in 1961. Now the police chief is black' (*New Yorker*, 2 February 2009). And Joseph Lowery boasted that black elected officials in 2009 numbered around 10,000 (*Hartford Courant*, 19 January 2009). But when black law sheriffs tried to make the 'extra income' of white sheriffs they replaced they found the law was strictly enforced! (Greene, 1992). The movement needed to work with 'the new social justice organizations' such as the environmental movement (Hudson and Davies, 2008).

Environmental Coalition

A 1987 study, sponsored by the United Church of Christ (UCC), proved there were more hazardous waste sites in minority neighbourhoods than in mainly white neighbourhoods. In 1998, Dr. Snead, President of the National Missionary Baptist Convention of America, toured toxic sites in Louisiana and visited the predominantly African American area of Convent, where a multi-racial residents' group sought to block the Shintech Corporation from building a $700 million PVC plant in their already heavily polluted community. 'Black, white, young, old are dying before their time,' Patricia Melancon of Convent told Snead and the visitors. 'There are other ways to develop economies than to ask people to give up the lives of their children' (National Council of Churches News Archive 1998). With opposition from the Louisiana Environmental Action Network and Greenpeace USA (Corpwatch, accessed 13 February, 2009), Carol Brown of the EPA overruled state approval for the plant. Corleta Smothers, who lived in a house built on a landfill with 150 toxic chemicals, said 'the dream turned into a nightmare for us.' The EPA cleaned up the site while residents remained in their homes.

The 'Chemical Corridor' – known as 'Cancer Alley' – stretches some 85 miles between New Orleans and Baton Rouge. Residents of Oakville fought to close and clean up a private toxic dump and others wanted compensation for their homes to escape the fumes, explosions and fires from the parish's 27 oil refineries. The accusation of environmental racism led to the setting up of an environmental justice movement that pressed for legislation to protect people of all races, ethnicities and incomes. Racism and toxic waste is thoroughly documented in a Council of Churches in Christ & Witness USA report (National Council of Churches, 1998).

Church leaders, civil rights and environmental groups united to fight all forms of pollution, a new generation, especially women, led these movements. Over 9 million people live within a two mile radius of the country's 413 toxic waste sites and 56 per cent of these are from minority communities. Many campaign with environmental groups. Genevieve Brooks moved to the Bronx from South Carolina. White flight and landlord neglect turned the area into a ghetto. Reagan cited the Bronx as proof that, 'The government fought a war on poverty, and poverty won.' Brooks and her coalition, the Desperadoes, restored thousands of apartments for low-income families (Tuck in Hudson and Davies, 2008). Also in the Bronx, Majora Carter battled for clean air (*New York Times*, 14 December 2008). But the political climate for the environmental movement was poor during the Bush years. Neo-conservatives argued that the environmentalists would reduce the United States to Third World status. Local community projects were threatened by corporations who used sponsorship to dictate grassroots action (Buell, 2004). The role of minorities in the environmental movement resulted in major federal appointments in 2009.

Labour

The civil rights movement had always sought union collaboration and King gained support from union leaders such as Walter Reuther of the Auto

Workers. Michael Honey demonstrates how Memphis sanitation workers educated northern white union leaders and showed them how to organise and the best tactics to use (Honey, 2007). But the anti-union attitudes of the Bush administration and Supreme Court threatened the gains made over years when more African Americans were unionised.

Lilly Ledbetter, a white supervisor at the Goodyear tire plant in Gadsden Ala., got raises during her 19-year career, but they were considerably lower than the men she worked with. The effect of the discrimination grew until she was being paid 15–25 per cent less than her male colleagues, even those with much less experience. The Supreme Court in *Ledbetter v. Goodyear Tire & Rubber Co, 2007,* by 5-4, ruled that a Title VII complaint must be filed within 180 days of the specific action that sets discriminatory pay, regardless of its impact on the employee. Alito was supported by the other conservatives on the Court, Roberts, Scalia, Thomas and Kennedy. They ignored the facts that pay discrimination is often not detected, difficult to prove and employers, like Goodyear, keep salary and pay information confidential. Their interpretation of Title VII narrowed the scope of pay discrimination precedents and made litigation virtually impossible. *Ledbetter* overturned 20 years of federal court cases and Equal Employment Opportunity Commission rulings (NOW press release, 30 May 2007).

A coalition of African Americans, women's rights organisations, Latinos and unions lobbied Congress. The House of Representatives legislated on 9 January 2009 to greatly strengthen the right to challenge pay discrimination. Congress wanted a sharp break with the civil rights policies of the Bush Administration. A second bill, supported by three Republicans, gave workers more time to file lawsuits and overturned the 180-day deadline. Another made it easier to prove violations of the 1963 Equal Pay Act, which generally required equal pay for equal work and allowed women to obtain compensatory and punitive damages from employers who violated the law. Defences that superior education or market forces or a man's previous salary permitted pay discrimination were greatly curtailed. Although President Bush threatened to veto the bills, Congress did not give him the opportunity (*New York Times*, 10 January 2009).

Abortion and Gay Rights

Just as affirmative action, so-called 'forced bussing', law and order, poverty and the war on drugs were linked to the African American community, so pro-choice demands by women and the gay community's fight for equality were used by conservatives in the Administration and the Republican Party to launch an attack on the civil rights of African Americans – even though a large number in the black community opposed abortion and homosexuality. Except for a minority of Republican women, Bush and the party supported the anti-abortion movement. And the same was true of the judges he chose for the federal courts. For example, Judge Pickering, a Bush favourite, testified to the Senate Judiciary Committee that he would abide by the civil rights rulings of the Supreme Court but he had actively supported an anti-abortion resolution at the Republican Convention in 1976 (*Houston Chronicle*, 6 March 2002). His critics highlighted the fact that as president of the Mississippi Baptist Convention in 1994, he had supported the group's determination to ban virtually all abortions, even in cases of incest and rape.

Bush supported Priscilla Owens and other anti-abortion candidates for the judiciary. Owens was a Texas Supreme Court justice and Bush wanted her on the Fifth Circuit Court of Appeals. Texas law followed the abortion guidelines established by the Supreme Court but Owens ruled they were not strict enough. Bush defended her saying, 'judges should interpret the law, not try to make it from the bench.' Opponents said Owens was 'a dedicated conservative judicial activist . . . intent on rewriting Texas' statutes on the right to choose in an effort to impede access' (NARAL Online Newsroom, 16 January 2003). Bush's anti-abortion stance encouraged opponents of *Roe*, including Catholics, to march on the Supreme Court and the President told another rally in St Louis that he supported 'compassionate alternatives' to abortion and said, 'I admire your perseverance and your devotion to the cause of life' (*Washington Post*, 23 January 2003). Feminists complained about black opposition to abortion. And some suggested that African Americans found it difficult to work with other civil rights groups.

Many, including gays, believed black homophobia ensured the success of Proposition 8 in California which overturned a State Supreme Court ruling legalising gay marriage. Some African Americans voted for it but they did not ensure its success (*San Francisco Chronicle*, 7 January 2009). Critics have ignored the support for lesbians and gays from prominent African Americans who saw the civil rights movement as inclusive. Julian Bond of the NAACP pointed out that Hispanic, Native American and lesbian and gays movements all 'took their cues from the African American civil rights movement.' AIDS threatened everyone regardless of race or sexual orientation. He admitted that some blacks were homophobic, especially some preachers, and said this was 'disgraceful.' Asked if more black gays should come out, he answered that if more did, 'this situation would be immeasurably eased. At the same time those who are out need to take a more active role . . . .' One NAACP board member had AIDS. 'I don't doubt that others are gay or lesbian. Their situation would be immeasurably helped if those folks said, "Here I am" ' (*The Advocate*, 12 October 2009). Newspapers did not report Coretta Scott King's campaign with gay activists or her keynote address on 18 October 1999 at the AIDS memorial quilt initiative in Atlanta. She spoke about her 'dear friend' who had died of AIDS and said the disease thrived 'on ignorance, bigotry and fear.' She was saddened 'when I hear black people, including some in leadership positions, making homophobic comments and attacking the human rights of gay and lesbian people.' She insisted, 'African Americans have suffered for too long because of prejudice and bigotry to be parroting the rhetoric of the Ku Klux Klan and other hate groups who bash people because of their sexual orientation' (www.GiftsofSpeech.org).

The Patriot Act and its Consequences

Bush had helped reawaken the unity of civil rights activists with the abuses that resulted from the Patriot Act of 2001. After the terrorist attacks the Act had widespread support from both parties and the general public. Dissenting voices were ignored. Throughout his years in office he used powers of arrest, search and seizure, wiretapping, searching emails and library checkouts and even deportation of American Muslim citizens – powers that even Richard Nixon had only wished for. The FBI, without court orders, issued 'national security letters' to an unknown number of people. For example, in late 2003 they issued an orange alert for Las Vegas which has 300,000 visitors a day. Using the letters, FBI men led by Gurvais Griggs collected data on all cars and trucks hired, storage leased, every airport and hotel check-in and cross-matched this information with the addresses, utility bills and telephone numbers of assumed terrorists. Nothing was found and the programme was abandoned in 2004 (*Washington Post*, 6 November 2005). It was claimed that people could appeal for information but because the letters were classified neither those targeted nor their representatives could do anything. Marie Mason, a 47-year-old environmentalist was sentenced on 6 February 2009 to almost 22 years in prison for an arson attack on Michigan State University's Agriculture Hall. Baltimore Black Panther leader, Marshall 'Eddie' Conway spoke to the leftwing *People's Weekly World* and compared his sentence for murder of two policemen to the arrests under the Patriot Act. Conway had spent 35 years in prison, a victim, he claimed, of the COLINTELRO abuses under Nixon (30 October 2004). Faculty Senate at Berkeley, home of the 1960s Free Speech Movement, condemned the Act and ordered the university authorities to prevent violations of civil rights and civil liberties (UC Berkeley News, 10 May 2004). Stanford University also condemned the Act, and especially racial profiling. Marion Bray, of the Muslim American Society of Freedom, recalled that the KKK had firebombed and shot up his grandparents' house when he was staying with them. 'That was my first experience with terrorism. Not September 11. And I was only 5 years old' (*Cardinal Enquirer*, www.Stanford.edu, 16 February 2005). Bray and others would have agreed with the conservative news magazine's assessment of Bush's last days in office: 'He is less than a President and that is appropriate. He was never very much of one' (*Time*, 12 January 2009).

Despite neo-conservatives assertions, nonviolence did not end during the years of their ascendancy. African American women and men kept alive alliances with the poor and minorities who suffered most from years of neglect. The grassroots' movements helped elect representatives and together they continued the civil rights struggle. As they retained old allies and brought in new ones, they no longer needed a single leader. And it was a community organiser and member of the NAACP who became not a leader of African Americans but of all Americans. For millions of people the election of 2008 saw a dream they had struggled for come true. For others it was what they had resisted for so long; the nightmare they had dreaded.

10

'Post-Racial' America? Barack Obama

Liberals, independents, women, unions and even some Republicans were convinced that 2008 would be the Democrat's year. For his loyalists, Bush had saved the United States from further terrorist attacks, overthrown Saddam Hussein and saved Iraq by sending troop reinforcements. Although Osama Bin Laden was free, a Republican candidate might be elected. But Bill Clinton said in 1992, 'It's the economy stupid.' George H. W. Bush never understood the economic crisis and neither did his son whose response to the hurricane that hit the banks and Wall Street was more decisive than his reaction to the devastation wrought by Katrina. As his approval rating hovered around 30 per cent, there seemed no hope for Republicans.

In 2006 many believed the two major contenders were the ex-POW Republican Senator from Arizona, John McCain, and former First Lady and NY Senator, Hillary Clinton. Commentators saw a historic battle. McCain was the oldest candidate to seek the presidency and Clinton was the first serious female candidate. But both had problems. In his 2000 campaign, McCain had attacked evangelical preachers Pat Robertson and Jerry Falwell (Welch, 2008). And he told the press that he would fight both men who were 'an evil influence ... over the Republican party.... I can't steer the Republican Party if these two individuals have the influence that they have on the party today' (Alexander, 2003). But evangelicals were the core of the party and they did not want him.

Religion and Race

Religion and race played crucial roles in the 2008 primaries. McCain's desire to placate the religious right led to several mistakes during his campaign. But he was not the only one with religious problems. Mitt Romney, a former governor of Massachusetts, was a Mormon and a significant number of voters were suspicious of Mormons. Rudy Giuliani, mayor of New York, exploited his alleged heroism during 9/11 but was twice divorced. Making life difficult for them was the fundamentalist Mike Huckabee, Governor of Arkansas, who combined easy charm with denunciations of abortion, homosexuality and evolution (Leslie, 2008). Huckabee easily won the first contest in Iowa. McCain stressed his conservative credentials and sought to win over fundamentalist preachers like Rod Parsley of Ohio. Parsley operates a school, a Bible college and makes TV programmes shown on 1400 stations around the world (Thomas, 2009). McCain abandoned moderation and aligned himself with Parsley who denounced all Muslims as terrorists and maintained Mahomet's revelations came from demons. McCain belatedly rejected the endorsement of Texas evangelist, John Hagee, who described the Roman Catholic church as 'the great whore' and Catholics as followers of 'a false cult' (*New York Times*, 12 March 2008). Diatribes by Parsley had racist overtones shared by many Americans – Muslims equalled Arabs and Arabs were racially inferior. Hagee's denunciations of Catholicism were no different from the Klan's and believers in the Apocalypse (Boyer, 1992).

At first Hillary Clinton seemed to have few problems. Women voters had swung decisively to the Democrats and the vast majority were devoted Hillary supporters. In addition, she had the party machine, her husband – the enormously popular former President, unions, and most Hispanic voters. Most pundits were positive it was the year of the woman. But she did have problems. Many liberals distrusted her record as a senator; others did not want 'two-for-one' with Bill Clinton as *de facto* President; the Democratic Governor of New Mexico, Bill Richardson, was Hispanic and Hispanic votes were crucial in many key states. John Edwards, the party's vice presidential candidate in 2004, ran as a southern populist. Senator Joe Biden would take many union and blue-collar voters. But Clinton was certain this was her time, and the majority expected her to win the party's nomination easily (Ellis, 2009; Thomas, 2009).

The Audacity of Barack Obama

Few expected the newly elected Senator from Illinois, the self-described 'skinny kid, with a funny name,' would be a candidate and those who did feared 2008 was too early. His keynote address to the 2004 Democratic

Convention had made him a celebrity – a Bill Clinton. Like the former President, Barack Hussein Obama asserted that 'people do not expect government to solve all their problems' and picked up Clinton's 1992 theme of hope. Denying categorisations of liberals/conservatives, red/blue states, minority/white, Obama asked, 'Do we participate in the politics of hope? Hope in the face of difficulty, hope in the face of uncertainty, the audacity of hope?' He affirmed their belief in American exceptionalism. 'I stand here tonight knowing that my story is part of the larger American story ... and that in no country on Earth is my story even possible' (*Washington Post*, 27 July 2004).

But neither Clinton nor most Americans thought that Obama, only a state senator when he gave that speech, would seek the presidential nomination in 2008 (Todd and Gawiser, 2009). And it was not only the speech that made Obama a celebrity. He was the son of a white woman from Kansas and an African father, with an Indonesian stepfather. Born in Hawaii, he had lived in Indonesia, and then with his white grandparents in Hawaii. Educated in Roman Catholic and Muslim schools, he became the first black editor of the *Harvard Law Review*, authored an autobiography, *Dreams From My Father* (1995) and *The Audacity of Hope* (2007); worked as a lawyer and community worker on Chicago's South Side; lectured at the University of Chicago and abandoned agnosticism and joined the Trinity United Church of Christ led by the Reverend Jeremiah Wright (Obama, 2007; Mendell, 2008). His name Hussein, fused with his race, seemed to present insurmountable obstacles.

For many he was not black enough, someone who was not a descendant of slaves; who had never known segregation and who did not appreciate the struggles of the civil rights generation. In 1999, he challenged Bobby Rush, a former Black Panther leader, and four-term incumbent of the House of Representatives (Mendell, 2008). Rush told the press, 'Barack is a person who read about the civil rights protests and thinks he knows all about them.' (*New Yorker*, 17 November 2008). Obama was decisively defeated.

Many commentators divided Democratic voters into two camps – those who had known or participated in the movement supported Clinton and young, middle class campaigners who backed Obama. Although there is some merit in this, it ignores people like the Reverend Joseph Lowery, King's friend and co-founder of the SCLC, who supported Obama from the beginning. And Obama addressed the criticism that he and the new African American politicians did not acknowledge the sacrifices of the older generation. At Brown Chapel AME Church in Selma, Alabama, on 4 March 2007 he honoured 'the Moses generation' and described his as 'the Joshua generation.' 'I'm here because somebody marched. I'm here because you all sacrificed for me. I stand on the shoulders of giants' (*New Yorker*, 17 November 2008; Ifill, 2009). His use of biblical prophets resonated with the audience. Many became less sceptical but most backed Hillary because they admired Bill Clinton and they wanted the Democrats to win. They were sure a black man could not. It was one of the strangest features of the primaries that her husband lost her many black supporters.

Post-Racial Politics?

Those who see this campaign as post-racial politics have a serious problem reflected in the newspaper headline: 'How black can he be before he alienates white voters?' A headline posing the question, 'How white can he be before he alienates black voters?' is unimaginable. The report acknowledged race was the most contentious issue and Americans preferred 'the middle path between perceived extremes.' According to one academic: '... Obama is the ideal middle way person – he is just as white as he is black.' Another claimed white people were weary of black people who denounced them as racists (*Global Edition of the New York Times*, 9 June 2008; Mendell, 2007). Obama commented on how some saw his convention speech 'to mean that we have arrived at a "postracial politics" or that we already live in a color-blind society.' Proclaiming Americans were one people did not mean 'that the fight for equality had been won' or that the problems were 'self-inflicted' (Obama, 2007).

But critics ignored this. Ralph Nader, an independent candidate, claimed it was only Obama's race that made him a candidate and that Obama ignored social and environmental problems. 'He wants to appeal to white guilt. ... Basically he's coming on as someone who is not going to threaten the white power structure, whether it is corporate or whether it is oligarchic. And they love it. Whites just eat it up' (*Boston Globe*, 26 June 2008).

However, many white Americans believed that Obama represented an era of post-racial politics. Black journalist, Gwen Ifell noted, '[T]he race test seemed peculiar to many of Obama's supporters who wanted to believe they did not see race when they looked at their candidate' (Ifill, 2009). The *New Yorker* editorialised (30 June 2008): 'Over the years, Obama has carefully calibrated his political message, and he has won a grudging respect among some conservatives.' Republican Ken Mehlman believed Obama was the black man the Republican Party needed because he was 'African American with no US roots and white voters viewed him through a different prism than

they had other [black] presidential candidates, most notably, Jesse Jackson'
(Todd and Gewiser, 2009). But for another black journalist, post-racial was
'not a new chapter in America's racial history; it shreds the entire book
and then burns the rest.' Post-racial African Americans will neglect the disadvantaged blacks 'or blame them for their own situation' (*The Nation*, 9
August 2008). African American doubts persisted. Obama's criticisms of single black parents and young men made him, in Jackson's view, 'too white'
and for Sharpton, Obama was a 'race-neutral candidate' (*New York Times*,
18 January 2008). Later Jackson, unaware that a TV microphone was live,
muttered, 'Barack's been talking down to black people. I wanna cut his nuts
off (*The Guardian*, 16 July 2008).'

But Obama did not want to be pigeon-holed as the black candidate. At a
November 2006 meeting to discuss his candidacy, he and his advisors spent
five minutes on race and decided 'the tone of the campaign would not be
defined by the colour of his skin' (*International Herald Tribune*, 12 February
2008). He was ambivalent about 1960s liberalism. The Movement made his
career possible but too many, like his mother, were trapped into a romantic
version of those years. In *Audacity of Hope*, he claims the attacks on American imperialism, monogamy and religion were 'proclaimed without fully
understanding the value of such constraints, and the role of victim was too
readily embraced as a means of shedding responsibility, or asserting enti-
tlement, or claiming moral superiority over those not victimized' (Obama,
2007). He admires Ronald Reagan who '. . . spoke to America's longing for
order, our need to believe that we are not subject to blind, impersonal forces
but we can shape our individual and collective destinies, so long as we redis-
cover the traditional values of hard work, patriotism, personal responsibility,
optimism, and faith.' Reagan's critics were seen as he wanted them to be,
as 'a band of out-of-touch, tax-and-spend, blame-America-first, politically
correct elite' (Obama, 2007). Obama was labelled an elitist but for very
different reasons.

Iowa and New Hampshire

Clinton underestimated the young senator's organisation. Within months of
explaining to a small crowd on a freezing November day why he wanted to
be president, he raised over $30 million mainly from small donors via the
Internet. And although his chief advisor David Axelrod and his campaign
manager David Plouffe wanted no open discussion of race, Obama had
to prove he could win white votes and fulfil his and Axelrod's dream to

be a history-making agent for change (*The Observer*, 7 July 08). This had to be established early because of Clinton's lead of 30 to 40 points (Thomas, 2009). Iowa was white, it selected delegates by caucus, and a win would make him a serious contender.

Iowa revealed the formidable grassroots machine that revolutionised American electoral politics. The successes of the civil rights movement (Obama, 2007) showed him how to combine old-style politics, launch with a 'why-I-want-to-be-president' speech (Todd and Gawiser, 2009), endorsements from prominent people like Edward Kennedy, and trade unionists, along with exploiting the communications revolution to recruit new, especially younger voters and register more minority voters. The 2000 and 2004 elections proved registration was meaningless unless masses of volunteers got people to the polls and lawyers were organised to challenge fraud. Obama had 35 field offices in Iowa and on a snowy night over 250,000 turned out for the caucus. Clinton organisers expected 90,000. Twenty-two per cent of them were 25 or younger and only 5 per cent of them supported Clinton. She was a distant third behind Obama and Edwards. An African American carried one of the whitest states, transforming him from rank outsider into serious challenger. In New Hampshire he had a 23 point lead but his arrogance and her tears ensured Clinton's big victory. Many saw him as an elitist who did not respect his opponent and women voters and older voters were angry with him. Her landslide cast doubt on his ability to win white voters, especially blue-collar men, and made her determined to fight on. It became the longest and toughest primary campaign in American history (Thomas, 2009).

Race and the Democratic Primary Campaign

After her comeback in New Hampshire, Clinton needed a knock-out blow in South Carolina. She polled better than Obama, especially with crucial black voters. She supported Bill Clinton's demand to campaign there. He was proud of his title as "America's first black president" and he was confident that his popularity would trump the northern, black candidate. It was logical. But it was a disaster for him and for her (Thomas, 2009).

In this first southern contest, Hillary lead by 13 points (40 to 27) and needed only 25 per cent of the black vote. But Bill Clinton alienated the press with intemperate outbursts and his attacks on Obama became increasingly personal. To make Obama a race candidate, Clinton compared him to Jesse Jackson who had won South Carolina in 1998 with strong appeals to the African American community. The harder he tried to marginalise Obama the more black voters deserted Hillary. Obama won 84 per cent of the black vote and trounced Clinton 48 to 28. Edwards won 23 per cent, mainly white, blue-collar voters.

Some suggest the Clinton campaign did not play the race card after this crushing defeat (Thomas, 2009). And Bill Clinton even complained that Obama exploited the Jackson remark and it was Obama who 'played the race card on me' (Ifill, 2009). Bill Clinton's performance persuaded veteran civil rights worker and Congressman, John Lewis, to switch support from Hillary to Obama. She denied her campaign played on racial fears. But some saw her TV ad during the Texas primary as doing exactly that. A blond white child and two others who 'seem vaguely Latino' sleep, watched over by their mother. A hand reaches for a telephone. Hillary Clinton in a smart suit picks it up. The voice-over asks who would they want to pick up the phone at 3 a.m. during a crisis. Orland Patterson saw in it 'symbols of racism and slavery' and the 'racist epic "Birth of a Nation" ... with its portrayal of black men lurking in the bushes around white society.' The message was Mrs Clinton would save them but Obama would not because an Obama presidency 'would be dangerous'; he is 'the danger, the outsider within.' It might not have been her intention but he saw it 'as trading on the darkest messages of a twisted past ...' (*New York Times*, 11 March 2008). Whatever one's view of this interpretation, it demonstrated the racial minefield Clinton had to negotiate.

Clinton's campaign, short of money and riven by feuds, focused on and won the large states but Obama ran in all, including small caucus states. Gradually he built an insurmountable lead in committed delegates. But she fought on. And she was helped by the Reverend Jeremiah Wright, who had converted Obama from sceptic to Christianity, officiated at his wedding and baptised his children (Ifill, 2009). Obama wrote in 2007 about his pastor telling him, 'Some of my fellow clergy don't appreciate what we're about. They feel like we're too radical. Others we ain't radical enough.' Too radical explains his 'disinvitation' to Obama's campaign launch. Axelrod and Plouffe were worried and decided to check old sermons. In the heat of the campaign, they had failed to do it. Their mistake meant that Wright's anti-American sermons were discovered by ABC news, appeared on YouTube and were repeated constantly on TV until election day. In one, Wright asks what blacks have and shouts his answer, 'The government gives them drugs, builds bigger prisons ... and then wants us to sing "God Bless America." No, no, no. God damn America ....' Like Malcolm X after JFK's assassination, Wright explained 9/11 as, 'The chickens have come home to roost'

(ABC News, 13 March 2008). His sermon fed white racism and made African Americans appear to be unpatriotic supporters of terrorism – all later exploited by the McCain campaign.

Race could not be avoided. Obama went to Philadelphia and at the Constitutional Museum, on a stage draped with American flags, he said that he was aware that the news media saw his campaign through a racial prism. He admitted Wright's comments 'were . . . divisive at a time when we need unity; racially charged at a time when we need to come together to solve monumental problems . . . problems that are neither black or white or Latino or Asian, but rather problems that confront us all.' But he stressed, 'I can no more disown him that I can disown the black community. I can no more disown him than I can my white grandmother. . . .' He reminded his audience of the anger and discrimination that Wright and his generation had had to face. It was their courage that had made his candidacy possible. Obama said he sympathised with whites in an uncertain world where they saw their dreams 'drop away'; were told to bus their children to school; heard about blacks benefiting from affirmative action for jobs and college places, and that resentment could result in prejudice. But those who viewed America through race, like Wright, saw the nation as static and that was untrue. 'America can change. That is the true genius of this nation. What we have achieved gives us hope – the audacity to hope – for what we can and must achieve tomorrow' (WorldNetDaily, 18 March 2008). An intelligent address on the most sensitive issue in America turned potential disaster into triumph. Wright replied with incendiary interviews and Obama resigned from the church and disowned his former mentor. And the preacher's rage highlighted Obama's moderation. Wright's ranting lingered on but the focus shifted more to making Obama the foreigner, the unpatriotic outsider. The race question did not die. In the Democratic melodrama, Hillary Clinton, after a drubbing in North Carolina and a narrow win in Indiana, spoke to *USA Today*. She said she was the only candidate who could win and mentioned a report 'that found out how Senator Obama's support among working, hardworking Americans, white Americans, is weakening again, and how whites in both states who had not completed college were supporting me. There's pattern emerging here.' An editorial in the *New Yorker* warned she would 'be wise to avoid this sort of demographic analysis – and, more important, to abandon the dishonorable political strategy that underlies it' (19 May 2008). The same appeal to the white working class with its racist overtones was also persistently exploited by the Republicans.

But Hillary Clinton is not a racist and her words reflected desperation. She increasingly viewed Hispanic voters as a *contrafuegos* – her firewall.

Sergio Bendixen, a Clinton pollster was reported as saying, 'The Hispanic voter – and I want to say this very carefully – has not shown a willingness or affinity to support black candidates' (*The Times*, 4 February 2008). The Clintons denounced this but campaign spokespersons continued to appeal to Hispanic voters' perceived prejudice. An organiser in Texas complained that blacks only looked after their own 'and never supported us and there is a lot of bad feeling about that' (Candidato USA.org, 3 August 2008). But the firewall failed and on 7 June Hillary Clinton bowed out and, somewhat half-heartedly, endorsed Obama. But the doubts she had expressed remained after Obama had clinched the nomination. He was warned that his 'Appalachian problem,' racism and evangelical religion, could cost him the key states of Ohio, Pennsylvania and Virginia (*New Yorker*, October 2008). His southern supporters were worried he would not appeal to the region's populists. In June, Gerald McEntee of the AFL-CIO, stated, 'I would say he should have an Appalachian strategy' (*New York Times*, 20 June 2008).

The End of Culture Wars? The Democratic Convention

Heated debates, even violence, over the persistence of racism, poverty, abortion and gay rights had been central in politics since 1968 but at the Democratic National Convention it seemed that the culture wars were buried. Senator Ted Kennedy, shortly after treatment for brain cancer, told cheering delegates in Denver, 'Barack Obama will close the book on the old politics of race, gender and group against group and straight against gay. . . . The hope rises anew.' And Hillary Clinton urged the women who had voted for her to support Obama because they believed in 'deep and meaningful equality – from civil rights to labor rights, from women's rights to gay rights, for ending all discrimination . . . .' (ABC News, 26 August 2008). And on the last night, Obama addressed 80,000 people in Denver's football stadium. 'I know there are differences on same-sex marriage, but surely we can agree that our gay and lesbian brothers and sisters deserve the right to visit the person they love in hospital and live lives free of discrimination.' He acknowledged differences over abortion but emphasised all Americans agreed on the need for fewer unwanted pregnancies. The speech was given on the 45th anniversary of King's speech in 1963 but he did not mention Dr King directly and instead referred to 'a young preacher from Georgia [who spoke] of his dream' (*New York Times*, 28 August 2008).

Obama throughout the primaries and election campaign spoke to massive audiences: an estimated 75,000 in Portland, 21,000 in Seattle and

100,000 in St Louis. When Obama stood in front of the St Louis throng, John McCain spoke to 7000 in Concord North Carolina and accused Obama of 'socialism' (*Miami Herald*, 19 October 2008). These unprecedented rallies almost matched the 200,000 crowd he addressed in Berlin, Germany. And after his success in Europe, Obama expected a huge boost in the polls but the McCain team ran a TV advertisement depicting Obama as a celebrity similar to Britney Spears and Paris Hilton. It was very effective (Todd and Gawiser, 2009). It was a legitimate attack advertisement and set the continued themes that Obama was a celebrity incapable of making the right decisions as president. He was not an ordinary Joe. Like Clinton, McCain used white working-class men as examples of Republican voters. In the third debate he constantly referred to Joe 'the plumber' Wurzelbacher as the man who would suffer under Obama. Unfortunately for McCain, Joe was no plumber, owed back taxes and would benefit from Obama's tax plans (*Business Week*, 16 October 2008). This appeal to 'ordinary Joes' and repeated references to Obama's arrogance was one way to use the issue of race. Attacking Obama as an elitist is part of the politics of euphemism. One of the key stereotypes of, especially men, who seek to improve themselves, is that they do not 'know their place.' Ambitious blacks were 'uppity niggers' and this was a major theme that McCain and his running mate took to the road.

Pressing the Self-destruct Button

John McCain's hero is Robert Jordan, the republican fighter in Hemingway's *For Whom the Bell Tolls*. It is appropriate. Jordan carries out a mission that he knows is 'doomed to failure. But he still went to blow the bridge . . . in an attack that he knew could not succeed. It's a – it's a beautiful story.' It was McCain's story in 2000 and 2008. The self-styled 'maverick' of American politics seemed to thrive on defeat, whether in the military, his personal and financial scandals or attacks on important elements of Republican support. The press rarely questioned his maverick qualifications (Welch, 2008). However, Obama was quick to point out that McCain's voting record was 90 per cent in support of Bush and it was time for a change.

Then McCain pushed the button and the going was easy. One week after the Democratic Party Convention, McCain announced the unknown governor of Alaska, Sarah Palin, would be his vice presidential candidate. Governor Palin was 'an extraordinary selection' (*The Observer*, 2 November 2008). Perhaps, his friend, renegade Democrat Joe Lieberman, would have been his personal choice, but Lieberman was impossible because he was Jewish and pro-choice on abortion. Palin was not. Initially, she appealed to McCain campaign managers because they thought she would weaken Obama's call for change and attract angry Clinton women (Thomas, 2009). But McCain had derided Obama's inexperience; and claimed he was unfit to be commander-in-chief, and he came from a distant state (almost writing-off Hawaii as a foreign land). Obama was a community worker and political novice. Palin? She had been mayor of a small Alaska town of 9000 and two years as governor of a state with less than 700,000 inhabitants. Her foreign policy knowledge was non-existent although she said she could see Russia from her house and Canada bordered her state. Chosen to attract disaffected Clinton supporters, her view that victims of incest or rape be refused abortions and only receive counselling alienated independents and moderate pro-life supporters. Her youth only underlined McCain's age and that made many worried she might become president. But her fundamentalist conservatism reassured the party base that they should vote for McCain.

Both seemed to thrive as underdogs. But the campaign became nasty as they strove to win over older women and blue-collar workers. Increasingly Obama was portrayed as un-American, a theme that had started with an ABC news interview when he was criticised for not wearing an American flag lapel badge. McCain and Palin continually asked, 'Who is the real Barack Obama?' (Ellis, 2008). Apparently they had not read his two bestselling books. And Palin took things to an extreme. In Clearwater, Florida, she told an almost totally white crowd, 'I am just so fearful that this is not a man who sees America the way I see America.' She said that Obama, who was acquainted with William Ayers a former Weatherman bomber, was 'someone who sees America as imperfect enough to work with a former domestic terrorist who targeted his own people.' Within a week clips from her rallies showed people shouting 'Kill him,' 'Treason,' 'Off with his head' and 'He is a bomb.' In Ohio a man described Obama as a 'one-man terror cell' (Thomas, 2009). Amazon sold a 'Terrorist' facemask of Obama. Fox News reporters frequently called him Osama to link him with the Al-Qaeda leader Bin Laden. Polls showed that his middle name, Hussein, proved to many Americans he was a Muslim who had attended a 'civilian maddrassa', and, if elected, would take the oath on the Koran. McCain came to realise the danger of this rhetoric and when a woman declared Obama was an Arab, McCain quickly denied it (Thomas, 2009).

In the end it was not only the dismal performances of McCain in the debates, it was Palin's divisive denunciations that helped in their defeat. Portraying Obama as an un-American, socialist delighted true believers but for the majority of voters it proved Palin was unfit to hold office. Sixty per cent considered Palin unfit and only 36 per cent of crucial independents believed she was an appropriate choice. The Republicans' hope she would win Clinton supporters proved wrong. Only 12 per cent thought she had the necessary qualifications (Todd and Gawiser, 2009). Joe Biden the long-term Senator for Delaware with a formidable knowledge of foreign affairs and Democratic nominee for vice president (*Wall Street Journal*, 27 August 2008) was seen by two-thirds of national voters as a president if required (Todd and Gawiser, 2009).

In fairness to Palin, McCain's response to the economic meltdown did the most damage. From his assertion that 'the fundamentals of the economy are sound' to the theatrical attempt to stop the first debate, rushing back to Washington supposedly to win Republican support to bail out the banks, showed him unfit to handle the greatest crisis since the Great Depression (Thomas, 2009). McCain, the man who loved to lose, was at his most gracious when he conceded defeat (*The Guardian*, 6 November 2008). But the Republicans faced long-term stark choices. The numbers of white, blue-collar, male voters, who largely support Republicans, are in decline as a group. Obama won the majority of white voters in 17 states. The Republicans lost every state on the eastern seaboard (apart from Georgia and South Carolina), the suburbs and young voters and are in danger of becoming a party of the Deep South and some rural states. And even there, if more African Americans had voted in Mississippi, Obama might have carried the state (Todd and Gawiser, 2009). The low turnout might be explained by the state's persisting plantation culture (Asch, 2008).

The First African American President

After centuries of slavery, segregation and lynching and 44 years after the Voting Rights Act a black man was the 44th president. This was a revolution. For people who had fought for civil rights, King's dream had come true as they watched the president-elect, his wife and two daughters walk onto the stage to be greeted by thousands of all races in Grant Park, Chicago on election night. Jesse Jackson and millions of Americans wept with joy and disbelief. Obama cried. He wept for his grandmother who had died on election day. He fulfilled the vision spelt out in his 2004 speech, and repeated that night, that Americans would not be divided into red and blue states, young against old, poor opposed to rich, white versus black, city versus rural, female against male, straight versus gay. And George W. Bush congratulated him: 'This moment is especially uplifting for a generation of Americans who witnessed the struggle for civil rights with their own eyes – and four decades later see their dream fulfilled' (*The Guardian*, 6 November 2008).

The day before the inauguration 90-year-old Pete Seeger, labour and civil rights minstrel, performed with Stevie Wonder and Bruce Springstein, and Gene Robinson, the gay Episcopalian bishop, gave thanks. On 20 January 2009 two million people gathered in Washington to cheer Obama and boo Bush. Some liberals were upset that the anti-gay marriage evangelist Rick Warren gave the invocation but delighted that the Reverend Joseph Lowery, SCLC founder, offered the closing blessing. It was all part of Obama's inclusiveness.

The day was bright and bitterly cold but Obama did not try to lift the crowd with great oratory. He referred to JFK, LBJ and his hero Abraham Lincoln. The British editor of *The Guardian*, described the Emancipation Proclamation and Obama's inauguration as 'bookends to the darkest stain on America's history.... Obama put it simply: "A man whose father less that 60 years ago might not have been served at a local restaurant can now stand before you to take a most sacred oath" ' (21 January 2009). The overwhelming response was one of optimism and a reborn faith in the American Dream; for those who preferred the dark side of politics, the heavily armoured presidential limousine was 'The Beast' and Obama was the fruit of miscegenation and he 'Must Die' (Blog, Barack Hussein Obama is Antichrist', 12 February 2009). The reaction of ultra-conservative broadcaster Rush Limbaugh was less apocalyptic; he only prayed that the 44th president would fail. While the disturbed and desperate wept and cursed, Obama quickly issued numerous executive orders and signed legislation that cheered his supporters.

Executive Orders

The fastest way for a president to act to reverse a predecessor's policies in his first days in office is by executive orders. Obama issued many on the first day. All interrogations had to follow the US Army Field Manual; all CIA-run secret prisons would be closed; Red Cross must be given access to all detainees. America would comply with the Geneva Conventions and no prisoners would be "rendered". Guantanamo detainees cases would be reviewed and the camp closed in one year. Military commissions were suspended and a Special Task Force, with leading Administration officers, would undertake a comprehensive review of detainee policy (*New York Times*, 23 January 2009). He later reversed his opposition to military tribunals but ensured civil rights for prisoners (*The Guardian*, 15 May 2009). On the same day he lifted the ban on funding family planning groups which advised on abortion when working overseas (ABC News, 8 March 2009). He said he knew people were unhappy about stem cell research but argued the consensus favoured it, removing federal funding restrictions imposed by Bush. Republican, Christopher Smith of New Jersey called him 'the abortion president' (*New York Times*, 9 March 2009). The Catholic bishops had already warned him not to relax restrictions on abortion because they would be an 'attack' on the church (*Chicago Tribune*, 17 November 2008).

On 26 January 2009, the Administration established environmental priorities. President Obama signed two executive orders on new rules for the auto industry, and Secretary of State Hillary Clinton appointed a special envoy for climate change. Obama said the planet faced global warming and dwindling resources. He wanted 'energy independence.' The EPA would permit California's tougher auto emission standards that had been overturned by the courts. Federal transportation officials would draw up new rules to direct automakers to make more fuel-efficient cars by 2011. These were part of the proposals to boost the economy and have 460,000 Americans working on clean energy and to double alternative energy capacity by 2012. The Administration claimed it would save $2 billion annually, make 75 per cent of federal buildings more efficient and energy bills would be cut by insulating 2 million homes (White House.gov, 26 January 2009).

Eight days after he was sworn in, he signed acts passed by Congress in the dying days of the Bush Administration. Bush twice vetoed Medicaid health insurance acts to benefit an additional four million children in low-income families. In February, Obama signed a similar law (*New York Times*, 4 February 2009). And the Lilly Ledbetter case against Goodyear tire would not be repeated. Ledbetter had suffered pay discrimination for 19 years (see Chapter 9). The new law, The Lilly Ledbetter Fair Pay Act, protected workers regardless of gender, race or disability. She had spoken at the Democratic Convention, campaigned for a black man, travelled on the presidential train to the inauguration and danced with the President at the inaugural ball – a working-class white woman from Alabama dancing with a Yale-educated African American President from Chicago (*Time*, 29 January 2009). It captured the extraordinary events of 2009.

Appointments

But Obama was no revolutionary socialist as Republicans had portrayed him and this search for consensus was seen in his appointments. They, like the executive orders, showed he was determined to close the book on George Bush and neo-conservatism. But his first appointment had more to do with internal Democratic Party politics. Despite speculation, there was only one person for the top Cabinet post, Secretary of State, and that was his long-time rival Hillary Clinton. She was nominated and rapidly confirmed. Her appointment pleased many feminists and African American women. But presidents always displease lobbies in their party. Demands were early and complaints became louder; too few black members; not enough Hispanics and too many white males. Brent Walker of the League of United Latin Americans was worried that 'there are few Latinos in the Cabinet so far.' Kim Gandy, the president of NOW, was disappointed that there were so many white men nominated (*San Francisco Chronicle*, 15 December 2008).

There is some merit to the complaints. Timothy Geithner, former head of the New York Federal Reserve, was appointed Secretary of the Treasury. Robert Gates, a Republican and Bush appointee, was Secretary of Defense. African Americans who hoped to have one of theirs as head of HUD were disappointed when Shaun Donovan was nominated and confirmed. The new Attorney General Eric Holder Jr is African American. Although he had had a dispute with Jesse Jackson when he denied that Raynard Johnson was lynched in Mississippi in 2000 (*LA Times*, 9 January 2009), Holder had a distinguished career in civil rights. After his confirmation, he spoke at a celebration of Black History Month and outraged the popular media by calling the United States a 'nation of cowards' because people would not talk frankly about race. Although much progress had been made, every Saturday and Sunday America was as segregated as it had been 50 years ago (*New York Times*, 11 February 2009).

The Cabinet reflected a desire for consensus in some respects such as keeping the Republican Robert Gates. But with others, such as Melanne Verveer the first Ambassador-at-Large for Global Women's Issues, Hispanics such as Ken Salazar at Interior, Obama made a clear break with the old administration. Lisa Jackson was the first African American to head the EPA – reflecting the successful alliance between environmentalists and the civil rights movement. Susan Rice was made UN ambassador. Nobel Prize winner Steven Chu, Energy Secretary and General K. Shinseki at Veteran Affairs were leading posts for Asian Americans. LGBT blog sites were full of complaints that no one represented them but the first openly gay people – lesbians Nancy Sutley and Elaine Kaplan – were appointed (*New York Times*, 22 March 2009) – although later he angered many for allowing the military to dismiss gays (*Huffington Post*, 7 May 2009). But it was not only ethnicity, gender or sexual orientation that shaped his appointments.

Obama had run a fifty state campaign and did well in the West, and western politicians were included with an eye on the 2012 election.

It's the Economy

Obama's re-election depends on his handling of the greatest economic crisis since 1929. He sent the American Recovery and Reinvestment Plan to Congress asking for $787 billion including $260 billion to help middle and working class families. It included a $2500 tax credit on college tuition and at least $7500 credit for first-time home buyers. Despite consulting Republican leaders in Congress, not a single Republican in the House supported it and only three in the Senate. Obama signed it on 13 February (*The Guardian*, 14 February 2009). It was not a good start for 'reaching-across-the-aisle.' Many Republican governors had lined up to say they would refuse the money and then admitted they would not. Rupert Murdoch's *New York Post* published a cartoon which showed two policeman after they had killed a chimpanzee with the caption "They'll have to find some one else to write the next stimulus bill.' Murdoch said it was not racist but apologised to his readers five days later. Republicans failed to provide an alternative policy and seemed to bank on it failing.

Obama's popularity according to the polls rose to the mid-60 or 70 per cent. He went before a joint session of Congress on February 25 and thanked members for the stimulus act which he claimed would create or save 3.5 million jobs and appealed to them, but primarily the nation, to support a huge budget proposal to increase taxes on the wealthy, curb bonuses for CEOs, and fund massive programmes for environmental, educational and internal improvement schemes among many others (*New York Times*, 19 January 2009). The Democrats cheered but the Republican leadership, including Senator John McCain, attacked the proposals for plunging the country into a huge deficit and they called for tax cuts (BBC News, 25 February 2009). Obama was accused by Republicans of perpetually campaigning when he visited many states whipping up support for the budget. In contrast, Obama's policies were endorsed unanimously at a G20 summit in London where he arranged to negotiate with the Russians on missile limitation. He continued his tour, and NATO members decided to provide greater support in Afghanistan. He moved on to Istanbul and assured the Turkish parliament that America was not fighting a war against Islam and finally went to Baghdad to tell the troops that most of them would be leaving within a year. He was not only popular in Europe but also in the United

States where 75 per cent were certain they would be better off economically in four years and 58 per cent of those who had voted for McCain agreed.

Courting Problems

Despite this popularity, the Supreme Court posed serious problems. On 9 March 2009, by 5-4, *Bartlett v Strickland* restricted the Voting Rights Act (1965), when it ruled no state was required to draw voting districts where African Americans were less than a majority of the voting-age population. North Carolina had protected areas where minorities were only 39 per cent. The Act had not stipulated any percentage and this decision drew the first clear line. Dissenting justices argued that voters would be packed into districts of 50 per cent and would mean 'contracting the number of districts where racial minorities are having success in transcending racial divisions.' However, Justice Anthony M. Kennedy, while voting with the majority, warned about the legacy of racial discrimination and he wanted only incremental steps in cutting back voting rights protections. 'Racial discrimination and racially polarized voting are not ancient history.' But the Voting Rights Act was intended to hasten the 'waning of racism in American politics' not 'entrench racial differences' (*New York Times*, 9 March 2009). Although Roberts challenged the reasoning of Congressmen for extending the Act, he backed away from a direct confrontation preferring to make an incremental step. In *Northwest Austin Municipal Utility District Number One v Holder* challenged Section 5 of the act requiring preclearance by the Justice Department before changes were made in jurisdictions where there had been abuses in practices and procedures. This section was designed to prevent discrimination in voting and districting and Congress overwhelmingly voted to renew the act for another 25 years. By a vote of eight to one the Court refused to rule on its constitutionality and Roberts agreed that the Court was a co-equal part of government which allowed for future cases and the Court also ruled that districts which had complied for ten years could 'bail out' of the requirements (FindLaw.com, 22 June 2009). This drastically reduced the time voted by Congress which had been 25 years. Not surprisingly, the only dissenter was Clarence Thomas who argued that Section 5 was unconstitutional.

Obama's first nominee, Judge Sonia Sotomayor, a Puerto Rican woman brought up in public housing in the Bronx, was to replace retiring liberal John Souter. Her nomination presented problems for Republicans because they needed Hispanic voters. Eight Republicans, such as Senator Lindsey

Graham (SC), gave reluctant support whereas Alabama Senator, Jeff Sessions, led 31 Republicans to vote against her because of a speech she made years earlier when she said the Court a 'wise Latina woman.' He said she was not impartial because of a speech she made years earlier when she said the Court needed a 'wise Latina woman.' He argued she was not impartial. Sessions had been unanimously rejected for a federal justice post by the Senate in 1982 because of his racism. He said the KKK was 'OK' until he discovered they were 'pot-smokers.' A white lawyer was a 'disgrace to his race' for supporting African Americans' right to vote. Al Franken's election for Minnesota, following eight months of legal challenges, gave Democrats 60 Senate seats – a filibuster-proof majority. And if Obama wins a second term the balance of the Court will shift. Neo-conservatives will then lose their important power base.

And other courts gave Obama difficulties. The 10th Federal Appeals Court ruled that same-sex couples were entitled to employee health benefits under a federal insurance programme. The federal government claimed it would violate the Defense of Marriage Act of 1996. Obama had either to defend LGBT rights as promised or to refuse in the hope of winning some Republican support for the budget (*New York Times*, 12 March 2009).

But Republicans divisions help him. In the elections for a new chairman for the Republican Committee, one candidate distributed a Christmas DVD that was widely interpreted as racist. The two African American candidates, Kenneth Blackwell and Michael Steele defended him but he was forced to drop out (*New York Times*, 27 December 2008). South Carolinian, Mike Dawson did when it was revealed he was a member of an all-white country club (ABC News, 7 January 2009). In an attempt to widen the party's appeal, African American Michael Steele was elected. He promised the GOP would be the 'hip-hop' party. But as attacks on him mounted, he complained that he was tired of the excuses for Republican defeats (*Boston Herald*, 23 March 2009). Two leading Republican contenders confessed to adultery and Sarah Palin unexpectedly resigned as Governor of Alaska on 3 July 2009. Her critics, in both parties, speculated about her future plans, but for many she personified 'the politics of resentment.' '[S]he stands for a genuine movement: a dwindling white nonurban America that is aflame with grievances and awash with self-pity' (Frank Rich, Op-Ed., *New York Times*, 11 July 2009).

Instead of seeking consensus Republicans chose to oppose all of Obama's efforts and assiduously played the race card while Glenn Beck of Fox News on TV declared Obama was a racist – 'he has a deep-seated hatred of white people and white culture' (Fox News, 28 July 2009). Other white folks refused to believe they had a black president claiming he was not a US citizen, Beck and others in the 'birther' movement also led the battle against health care. Republican Cairg Shirley, of Shirley Bannister Associates responsible for the Willie Horton campaign, distributed videos portraying Obama as Hitler and, ironically, a tyrannical advocate of eugenics, taking up Newt Gingrich and Sarah Palin's claims that health care reform would see 'death panels' that would refuse expensive care to the elderly and the disabled (Rachel Maddox, MSNBC, 13 August 2009). For others, Obama's intention was to win reparations for slavery. The all-white mobs shouted down pro-reformers, yelled 'Kill Obama' and held mock lynching parties (*Washington Post*, 16 August 2009).

Republican resistance to the struggle for reform, exploiting racism, is reminiscent of the George Wallace campaigns. As Fanny Lou Hamer cautioned in 1977, 'Mac, we ain't free yet' (Dittmer, 1995). The young man who held the sign on inauguration day in 2009, 'WE **HAVE** OVERCOME', may not have realised that many who participated in the 1960s struggle thought the same. Almost as significant as Obama's triumph were the record number of death threats he received and the mounting number of attacks on minorities between 2008 and 2009 and the Department of Homeland Security warned that right-wing extremists posed a serious threat (*New York Times*, 11 June 2009). Liberals who thought they had buried conservatism in the 1960s soon discovered that they had to live under it for most of their lives.

BIBLIOGRAPHY

Abernathy, Ralph David. *And the Walls Came Tumbling Down*. Harper and Row, New York, 1989.

Adams, Frank T. *James A. Dombrowski: An American Heretic, 1897–1983*. The University of Tennessee Press, Knoxville, 1992.

Allen, James, *et al*. *Without Sanctuary: Lynching Photography in America*. Twin Palm Publishers, Santa Fe, New Mexico, 2000.

Alexander, Paul. *Man of the People: The Life of John McCain*. John Wiley & Sons, Hoboken, New Jersey, 2003.

Ambrose, S. *Eisenhower: The President*. Simon and Schuster, New York, 1984.

Ambrose, S. *Nixon*. 3 vols. Simon and Schuster, New York, 1989.

Anderson, Terry. *The Movement and the Sixties: Protest in America from Greensboro to Wounded Knee*. Oxford University Press, New York, 1995.

Arsenault, Raymond. *Freedom Riders: 1961 and the Struggle for Racial Justice*. Oxford University Press, New York, 2006.

Asch, Chris Myers. *The Senator and the Sharecropper: The Freedom Struggle of James O. Eastland & Fanny Lou Hamer*. The New Press, New York, 2008.

Aughey, Arthur, A.G. Jones and W. T. M. Riches. *The Conservative Political Tradition in Britain and the United States*. Pinter Press, London, 1992.

Bass, Jack. *Taming the Storm: The Life and Times of Judge Frank M. Johnson, Jr and the South's Fight Over Civil Rights*. Doubleday, New York, 1993.

Beals, Melba Pattillo. *Warriors Don't Cry*. Pocket Books, New York, 1994.

Berkowitz, Edward D. 'A Historical Preface to the Americans with Disabilities Act,' in Bernstein, B. J. ed. *Politics and Policies of the Truman Administration*. Quadrangle Books, Chicago, 1970.

Bernstein, I. *Promises Kept: John F Kennedy's New Frontier*. Oxford, New York, 1991.

Beschloss, Michael R., ed. *Taking Charge: The Johnson White House Tapes, 1963–1964*. Simon & Schuster, New York, 1997.

Blackmon, Douglas A. *Slavery By Another Name: The Re-Enslavement of Black Americans from the Civil War to World War II*. Anchor Books, New York, 2008.

Blight, David. W. *Race and Reunion: The Civil War in American Memory*. Harvard University Press, Cambridge, 2001.

Blum, J. M. *Years of Discord: American Politics and Society, 1961–1974*. W. W. Norton, New York, 1991.

Bovard, James. *Attention Deficit Democracy*. Palgrave Macmillan, New York, 2005.

Boyarsky, Bill. *Ronald Reagan: His Life and Rise to the Presidency*. Random House, New York, 1981.

Boyer, Paul. *When Time Shall Be No More: Prophecy Belief in Modern American Culture*. Harvard University Press, Cambridge, 1992.

Boyer, Peter J. 'Man of Faith: Can Jesse Jackson Save Himself?' *The New Yorker*, 22 October 2001, pp. 50–65.

Boyer, Peter J. 'The Worrier: Newt Gingrich Returns.' *The New Yorker*, 26 November 2001, pp. 48–53.

Bracey Jr, J. H., August Meier, and Elliott Rudwick. *The Afro-Americans: Selected Documents*. Allyn and Bacon, Boston, 1972.

Branch, Taylor. *Parting the Waters: Martin Luther King and the Civil Rights Movement, 1954–63*. Macmillan, London, 1989.

Branch, Taylor. *Pillar of Fire: America in the King Years, 1963–65*. Simon and Schuster, New York, 1998.

Brandt, Eric, ed. *Dangerous Liaisons: Black Gays and the Struggle for Equality*. The New Press, New York, 1999.

Buell, Frederick. *From Apocalypse to Way of Life: Environmental Crisis in the American Century*. Routledge, New York, 2004.

Burner, Eric R. *and gently shall lead them: Robert Moses and Civil Rights*. New York University Press, New York,1994.

Burns, James McGregor. *Roosevelt: The Soldier of Freedom*. Harcourt Brace Javanovich, New York, 1970.

Cannon, Lou. *President Reagan: The Role of a Lifetime*. Touchstone, New York, 1991.

Caro, Robert A. *The Years of Lyndon Johnson:* Vol.3. *Master of the Senate*. Jonathan Cape, New York, 2002.

Carson, Clayborne. *In Struggle: SNCC and the Black Awakening of the 1960s*. Harvard University Press, Cambridge, Mass., 1981.

Carson, Clayborne, ed. *The Student Voice, 1960–1963*. Meckler, Westport, Conn, 1990.

Carter, Dan T. *The Politics of Rage: George Wallace, the Origins of the New Conservatism, and the Transformation of American Politics*. Louisiana State University Press, Baton Rouge, 1995.

Carter, Jimmy. *Keeping Faith: Memoirs of a President*. Collins, London, 1992.

Carville, James. *We're Right, They're Wrong: A Handbook for Spirited Progressives*. Random House, New York, 1996.

Chalmers, David M. *Hooded Americanism: The History of the Ku Klux Klan*. Quadrangle, Chicago, 1965.

Cleaver, Eldridge. *Soul on Ice*. Dell Publishing Company, New York, 1968.

Clinton, Bill. *My Life*. Hutchison, London, 2004.

Cockburn, Alexander and Jeffrey St Clair. *Whiteout: The CIA, Drugs and the Press*. Verso, London, 2001.

Cone, James H. *Martin & Malcolm & America: A Dream or a Nightmare*. Fount Paperbacks, London, 1993.

Cone, James H. *Martin & Malcolm & America: A Dream or a Nightmare*. HarperCollins, Glasgow, 1995.

Cooper, W. J. and Thomas Terrill. *The American South: A History*. Alfred Knopf, London, 1991.

Cose, Ellis. *Color-Blind: Seeing Beyond Race in a Race-Obsessed World*. Harper-Collins, New York, 1998.

Crawford, Vicki, Jacqueline Rouse and Barbara Woods. *Women in the Civil Rights Movement: Torchbearers and Trailblazers*. Indiana University Press, Bloomington, Indiana, 1993.

Dallek, Robert. *Lone Star Rising: Lyndon Johnson and His Times, 1908–1960*. Oxford, New York, 1991.

Dalleck.Robert. *John F. Kennedy: An Unfinished Life, 1917–1963*. Allen Lane, London, 2003.

Dallek, Robert. *Ronald Reagan: The Politics of Symbolism*. Harvard University Press, Cambridge, Mass., 1984.

Daniel, Pete. *The Shadow of Slavery: Peonage in the South, 1901–1969*. The University of Illinois Press, Urbana, 1972.

Daniel, Pete. *Standing at the Crossroads: Southern Life in the Twentieth Century*. Hill & Wang, New York, 1986.

Daniel, Pete. *Lost Revolutions: The South in the 1950s*. The University of North Carolina Press, Chapel Hill, 2000.

Davis, Angela. *An Autobiography*. Random House, New York, 1988.

Davis, Angela. *Women, Race & Class*. Vintage, New York, 1983.

Davis, Angela. 'Civil Liberties and Women's Rights: Twenty Years On,' *Irish Journal of American Studies*, 1994, vol. 3, 17–30.

Davis, David Brion. *The Problem of Slavery in the Age of Revolution, 1770–83*. Cornell University Press, Ithaca, 1975.

Davis, David Brion. *In Human Bondage: The Rise and Fall of Slavery in the New World*. Oxford University Press, New York, 2006.

Dawley, Alan. *Struggles for Justice: Social Responsibility and the Liberal State*. The Belknap Press of the Harvard University Press, Cambridge, Mass., 1991.

D'Emilio, John. *Lost Prophet: The Life and Times of Bayard Rustin*. Free Press, New York, 2003.

Divine, Robert, ed. *The Johnson Years*. University Press of Kansas, Lawrence, 1994.

Diggins, John P. *The Proud Decades: America in War and Peace, 1941–1960*. W. W. Norton, New York, 1989.

Dittmer, John. *Local People: The Struggle for Civil Rights in Mississippi*. Urbana, Illinois, 1995.

Douglass, Frederick. *Life and Times of Frederick Douglass*. Collier Macmillan, London, 1962.

Dray, Philip. *Capitol Men: The Epic Story of Reconstruction Told Through the Lives of the First Black Congressmen*. Houghton and Miflin, New York, 2008.

Draper, Robert. *Dead Certain: The Presidency of George W. Bush*. Free Press, New York, 2007.

D'Souza, Dinesh. *The End of Racism*. Free Press, New York, 1995.

Duberman, Martin. *Paul Robeson*. Pan Books, New York, 1989.

Dye, Thomas R. and Harmon Zeigler. *The Irony of Democracy: An Uncommon Introduction to American Politics*. Harcourt Brace, Fort Worth, 2000.

Dyson, Michael E. *Making Malcolm: The Myth and Meaning of Malcolm X*. Oxford University Press, New York, 1995.

Ehrenreich, Barbara. *Nickel and Dimed: Undercover in Low-wage USA*. Granta Books, London, 2001.

Ellis, Ian. *To Be President: Quest For the White House*. Politico's, London, 2009.

Ely, James C. *The Crisis of Conservative Virginia: The Byrd Organization and the Politics of Massive Resistance*. University of Tennessee Press, Knoxville, 1976.

Emery, Fred. *Watergate: The Corruption and Fall of Richard Nixon*. Jonathan Cape, London, 1994.

Essien-Udom, E. U. *Black Nationalism: A Search for Identity in America*. Dell, New York, 1964.

Faderman, Lillian. *Old Girls and Twilight Lovers: A History of Lesbian Life in Twentieth Century America*. Penguin, London, 1992.

Fairclough, A. *To Redeem the Soul of America: The Southern Christian Leadership Conference and Martin Luther King, Jr*. University of Georgia Press, Athens, GA, 1987.

Faludi, Susan. *Backlash: The Undeclared War Against Women*. Chatto & Windus, London, 1992.

Fannin, Mark. *Labor's Promised Land: Radical Visions of Gender, Race and Religion in the South*. University of Tennessee Press, Knoxville, 2003.

Fleming, Cynthia Griggs. 'Black Women Activists and the Student Nonviolent Coordinating Committee: The Case of Ruby Doris Smith Robinson,' *Irish Journal of American Studies*, 1994, vol. 3, 31–54.

Foner, Eric. *Free Soil, Free Labor, Free Men: The Ideology of the Republican Party Before the Civil War*. Oxford, New York, 1970.

Foner, Eric. *Reconstruction: America's Unfinished Revolution, 1863–1877*. Harper and Row, New York, 1988.

Fosl, Catherine. *Subversive Southerner: Anne Braden and the Struggle for Racial Justice in the Cold War South*. Palgrave Macmillan, New York, 2002.

Fraser, Tom. 'Two American Presidents and Israel: Studies in Ambiguity,' *Irish Journal of American Studies*, 1994, vol. 3, 193–114.

Freidenberg, Daniel M. *Sold to the Highest Bidder: The Presidency from Dwight D. Eisenhower to George W. Bush*. Prometheus Books, Amherst, New York, 2002.

Furgurson, Ernest. *Hard Right: The Rise of Jesse Helms*. W. W. Norton, New York, 1986.

Garrow, David. *Bearing the Cross: Martin Luther King Jr and the Southern Christian Leadership Conference*. Jonathan Cape, London, 1988.

Garrow, David. *Liberty and Sexuality: The Right to Privacy and the Making of Roe v Wade*. Macmillan Publishing Company, New York, 1994.

Garson, Robert A. *The Democratic Party and the Politics of Sectionalism, 1941–1948*. Louisiana State University Press, Baton Rouge, 1974.

Gates Jr, Henry L. *Colored People*. Viking, London, 1995.

Giddings, Paula. *When and Where I Enter: The Impact of Black Women on Race and Sex in America*. Bantam, New York, 1984.

Gilmore, Glenda Elizabeth. *Defying Dixie: The Radical Roots of Civil Rights, 1919–1950*. W. W. Norton, New York, 2008.

Glad, Betty. *Jimmy Carter: In Search of the Great White House*. W. W. Norton, New York, 1980.

Gore, Albert. *The Eye of the Storm: A People's Politics for the Seventies*. Herder & Herder, New York, 1970.

Gore, Albert. *Let the Glory Out: My South and its Politics*. Viking Press, New York, 1972.

Graham, Hugh Davis. *The Civil Rights Era: Origins and Development of a National Policy, 1960–1972*. Oxford, New York, 1990.

Graham, Hugh Davis, ed. *Civil Rights in the United States*. Pennsylvania State University Press, University Park, PA, 1994.

Green, James R. *Grass Roots Socialism: Radical Movements in the Southwest, 1895–1943*. Louisiana State University Press, Baton Rouge, 1978.

Green, Mark. *Losing Our Democracy: How Bush, the Far Right, and Big Business Are Betraying America – And How to Stop It*. Source Books, Naperville, Illinois, 2007.

Greenburg, Jan Crawford. *Supreme Conflict: The Inside Story of the Struggle for Control of the United States Supreme Court*. Penguin Books, London, 2008.

Greene, John R. *The Limits of Power: The Nixon and Ford Administrations*. Indiana University Press, Bloomington, 1992.

Greene, Lee S. *Lead Me On: Frank Goad Clement and Tennessee Politics*. University of Tennessee Press, Knoxville, 1982.

Greene, Melissa Fay. *Praying for Sheetrock*. Secker and Warburg, London, 1992.

Grubbs, Donald H. *Cry From the Cotton: The Southern Tenant Farmers Union and the New Deal*. University of North Carolina Press, Chapel Hill, 1971.

Guinier, Lani. *The Tyranny of the Majority: Fundamental Fairness in Representative Democracy*. Free Press, New York, 1994.

Hahn, Steven. *A Nation Under our Feet: Black Political Struggles in the Rural South From Slavery to the Great Migration*. Harvard University Press, Cambridge, 2003.

Halberstam, David. *The Fifties*. Fawcett Columbine, New York, 1993.

Hamby, A. L. *Beyond the New Deal: Harry S Truman and American Liberalism*. Columbia University Press, New York, 1973.

Hill, Patricia, et al. *Call and Response: The Riverside Anthology of the African American Literary Tradition*. Houghton Miflin, London, 1998.

Hodes, Martha. *White Women, Black Men: Illicit Sex in the 19th-Century South*. Yale University Press, New Haven, 1997.

Honey, Michael J. *Going Down Jericho Road: The Memphis Strike, Martin Luther King's Last Campaign*. W. W. Norton, New York, 2007.

Howard, Gerald. *The Sixties*. Washington Square Press, New York, 1982.

Hudson, Cheryl and Gareth Davies. *Ronald Reagan and the 1980s: Perceptions, Policies, Legacies*. Palgrave Macmillan, Basingstoke, 2008.

Ifill, Gwen. *The Breakthrough: Politics and Race in the Age of Obama*. Doubleday, New York, 2009.

Issel, William. *Social Change in the United States, 1945–1983*. Macmillan, Basingstoke, 1985.

Jackson, K. T. *The Ku Klux Klan in the City, 1915–1930*. Ivan R. Dee, Chicago, 1992.

Jackson, Thomas F. *From Civil Rights to Human Rights: Martin Luther King, Jr: And the Struggle for Economic Justice*. University of Pennsylvania Press, Philadelphia, 2007.

Jamison, Ross. *Too Little Too Late: President Clinton's Prison Legacy*. The Center on Juvenile Crime and Criminal Justice, San Francisco, 2002.

Johnson, Haynes. *Sleepwalking Through History: America in the Reagan Years*. W. W. Norton, New York, 1991.

Johnson, Lyndon B. *The Vantage Point: Perspectives of the Presidency, 1963–1969*. Popular Library, New York, 1971.

Jones, James H. *Bad Blood: The Tuskegee Syphilis Experiment*. The Free Press, New York, 1993.

Kaufman, Burton I. *The Presidency of James Earl Carter, Jr*. University of Kansas Press, Lawrence, 1993.

Kessler, Glenn. *The Confidante: Condoleezza Rice and the Creation of the Bush Legacy*. St Martin's Press, New York, 2007.

Kearns, Doris. *Lyndon Johnson and the American Dream*. Signet, New York, 1976.

Kerber, Linda and Jane Sherron De Hart. *Women's America: Refocusing the Past*. Oxford University Press, New York, 1991.

King, Coretta Scott, 'Keynote Address – AIDS Memorial Quilt,' www.Gifts of Speech.com. 1999.

King Jr, Martin Luther. *Chaos or Community*. Hodder and Stoughton, London, 1967.

Klein, Joe. *The Natural: The Misunderstood Presidency of Bill Clinton*. Hodder & Stoughton, 2002.

Klibaner, Irwin. *Conscience of a Troubled South: The Southern Conference Educational Fund, 1941–1966*. Carlson Publishing, New York, 1989.

Klinkner, Philip A. with Rogers W. Smith. *The Unsteady March: The Rise and Decline of Racial Equality in America*. University of Chicago Press, Chicago, 1999.

Knight, Douglas M. *Street of Dreams: The Nature and Legacy of the 1960s*. Duke University Press, Durham, NC, 1989.

Kolbert, Elizabeth. 'The Calculator: Putting a Value on Three Thousand Lives.' *The New Yorker*, 25 November 2002, pp. 42–9.

Kolbert, Elizabeth. 'The People's Preacher: Al Sharpton Would Walk Naked Rather than Wear Your Wretched Dress,' *The New Yorker*, 18 and 25 February 2002, pp. 156–67.

Kutler, Stanley I., ed. *Abuse of Power: The New Nixon Tapes*. Simon & Schuster, New York. 1998.

Lamis, Alexander P. *The Two Party South*. 2nd ed. Oxford, New York, 1990.

Lasky, M. J. *The Hungarian Revolution*. Martin Secker & Warburg, London, 1957.

Laue, James H. *Direct Action and Desegregation, 1960–1962: Toward A Theory of the Rationalization of Protest*. Carlson Publishing, New York, 1989.

Lee, Chana Kei, *For Freedom's Sake: The Life of Fanny Lou Hamer*. University of Illinois Press, Urbana, 2000.

Leslie, Ian. *To Be President: Quest for the White House 2008*. Politico's, London, 2008.

Lewis, John. *Walking with the Wind: A Memoir of the Movement*. Simon & Schuster, New York, 1998.

Lewis, "Brief History of Prince Edward County's Desegregation Fight," htpp/www.civil rights memorial.org (accessed 9 January 2009).

Lewis, George. *Massive Resistance: The White Response to the Civil Rights Movement*. Hodder Arnold, London, 2006.

Litwack, Leon F. *Trouble in Mind: Black Southerners in the Age of Jim Crow*. Alfred Knopf, New York, 1998.

Lowi, Theodore J. and Benjamin Ginsberg. *American Government*. W. W. Norton & Company, New York, 1998.

Loevy, Robert D. ' "To Write it in the Books of Law:" President Lyndon B. Johnson and the Civil Rights Act of 1964,' in Bernard Firestone and Robert Vogt, eds. *Lyndon Baines Johnson and the Uses of Power*. Greenwood, New York, 1980.

McAdam, Doug. *Freedom Summer*. Oxford, New York, 1988.

McCullough, David. *Truman*. Simon & Schuster, New York, 1992.

McCoy, D. R. and Richard Donald. *Quest and Response. Minority Rights and the Truman Administration*. University Press of Kansas, Lawrence, 1973.

McCoy, D. R. *The Presidency of Harry S. Truman*. University Press of Kansas, Lawrence, 1984.

Males, Mike. *The Scapegoat Generation: America's War on Adolescents*. Common Courage Press, Monroe, ME, 1996.

Marable, Manning. *Race, Reform and Rebellion: The Second Reconstruction in Black America, 1945–1982*. University Press of Mississippi, Jackson, 1997.

Mark, David. *Going Dirty: The Art of Negative Campaigning*. Rowman &Littlefield, New York, 2007.

Matusow, A. J. *The Unravelling of America. A History of Liberalism in the 1960s*. Harper & Row, New York, 1986.

Mayer, Jane and Jill Abramson. *Strange Justice: The Selling of Clarence Thomas*. Houghton and Miflin, New York, 1994.

Meier, August and Elliott Rudwick, 'The Bus Boycott Movement Against Jim Crow Streetcars in the South,' in David Garrow, ed. *We Shall Overcome: The Civil Rights Movement in the United States in the 1950s and 1960s*. Carlson Publishing, New York, 1989.

Meier A. and R. Rudwick. *From Plantation to Ghetto*. Hill & Wang, New York, 1970.

Mendell, David. *Obama: From Promise to Power*. Amistad, Harper-Collins, New York, 2008.

Merl, E. *Seedtime of the Modern Civil Rights Movement: The President's Committee on Fair Employment Practice, 1941–1946*. Louisiana State University Press, Baton Rouge, 1991.

Miller, Loren. *The Petitioners: The Story of the Supreme Court and the Negro*. Meridian, New York, 1967.

Miller, Merle. *Plain Speaking: Conversations with Harry S. Truman*. Victor Gollancz Ltd., London, 1974.

Miller, Neil. *Out of Our Past: Gay and Lesbian History from 1869 to the Present*. Vintage, London, 1995.

Miller, Timothy. *The Hippies and American Values*. University of Tennessee Press, Knoxville, 1991.

Milligen, Stephen. 'Silencing the Critics: Rebuilding the FBI Myth,' *The Irish Journal of American Studies*, vol. 10, 2001, pp. 113–31.

Mills, Kay. *This Little Light of Mine: The Life of Fanny Lou Hamer*. The University Press of Kentucky. Lexington, 2007.

Moore, Michael. *Stupid White Men . . . and Other Sorry Excuses for the State of the Nation*. Regan Books, New York, 2001.

Moraga, C and Gloria Anzaluda. *This Bridge Called My Back: Writing of Radical Women of Color*. Kitchen Table, Women of Color Press, New York, 1983.

Morris, Aldon. *The Origins of the Civil Rights Movement: Black Communities Organizing for Change*. Free Press, New York, 1984.

Morrison J and R. K. Morrison. *From Camelot to Kent State: The Sixties Experience in the Words of Those Who Lived It*. Times Books, New York, 1987.

Myrdal, Gunnar. *An American Dilemma*. McGraw Hill, Toronto, 1964.

Murray, Pauli. *Pauli Murray: The Autobiography of a Black Activist, Feminist, Lawyer, Priest, and Poet*. University of Tennessee Press, Knoxville, 1989.

Navasky, Victor. *Kennedy Justice*. Atheneum, New York, 1971.

Neubeck, Kenneth J. and Noel A. Cazenave. *Welfare Racism: Playing the Race Card Against America's Poor*. Routledge, New York, 2001.

Nightingale, C. H. *On the Edge: A History of Poor Black Children and Their American Dreams*. Basic Books, New York, 1993.

Nixon, Richard. *The Memoirs of Richard Nixon*. Sidgewick and Jackson, London, 1978.

Oates, Stephen B. *Let the Trumpet Sound: A Life of Martin Luther King, Jr*. HarperPerennial, New York, 1994.

Obama, Barack. *Dreams From My Father*. Cannongate, Edinburgh, 2007.

Obama, Barack. *The Audacity of Hope: Thoughts on Reclaiming the American Dream*. Cannongate, Edinburgh, 2007.

O'Reilly, Kenneth. *Black Americans: The FBI Files*. Carroll & Graf Inc., New York, 1994.

Pascoe, Peggy. *What Comes Naturally: Miscegenation Law and the Making of Race in America*. Oxford University Press, New York, 2009.

Parish, Peter. *The American Civil War*. Eyre Metheun, London, 1975.

Patini, Michael. 'Last Will and Testament of William Jefferson Clinton.' *Esquire*, December, 2000.

Patterson, James I. *Great Expectations: The United States, 1945–1974*. Oxford University Press, New York, 1996.

Payne, Charles M. *I've Got the Light of Freedom: The Organizing Tradition and the Mississippi Freedom Struggle*. University of California Press, Berkeley, 1996.

Perlstein, Rick. *Nixonland: The Rise of a President and the Fracturing of America*. Scribner, New York, 2008.

Pinkney, Alphonso. *Red Black and Green: Black Nationalism in the United States*. Cambridge, London, 1976.

Portis, Larry, ed. *Terror and Its Representations: Studies in Social History and Cultural Expression in the United States and Beyond*. Presses Universitaires de la Mediteterranee, Montpellier, 2008.

Powell, Colin (with Joseph E. Perisco). *My American Journey*. Ballantine Books, New York, 1996.

Proudfoot, Merrill. *Diary of a Sit-In*. University of Illinois Press, Urbana, Illinois, 1990.

Quarles, Benjamin. *The Negro in the American Revolution*. University of North Carolina, Chapel Hill, 1961.

Raines, Howell. *My Soul is Rested: Movement Days in the Deep South Remembered*. Penguin, New York, 1977.

Ralph, James R. *Northern Protest: Martin Luther King Jr, Chicago, and the Civil Rights Movement*. Harvard, London, 1993.

Rankin, Mrs Annie James. "Autobiography," handwritten 13 page document, Mississippi Digital Archive, Tougaloo College.

Redkey, Edwin S. *Black Exodus: Black Nationalism and Back to Africa Movement, 1890–1910*. Yale University, New Haven, 1969.

Reed, Merl E. *Seedtime of the Modern Civil Rights Movement: The President's Committee on Fair Employment Practice, 1941–1946*. Louisiana State University Press, Baton Rouge, 1991.

Renshon, Stanley A. *High Hopes: The Clinton Presidency and the Politics of Ambition*. Routledge, New York, 1998.

Republic of New Africa archive, Mississippi Digital Library, Tougaloo, College.

Rhea, Joseph Tilden. *Race Pride and the American Identity*. Harvard University Press. Cambridge, 1997.

Riches, Juila K. 'Fetal Attraction: The Politics of Foetal Protection in the Law.' Unpublished doctoral dissertation, Georgetown University, 2002.

Riches, W. T. M. 'White Slaves, Black Servants and the Question of Providence: Servitude and Slavery in Colonial Virginia,' *The Irish Journal of American Studies*, vol. 8, 1999, 1–33.

Riches, W. T. M., ed. *The Turbulent Decade: The United States in the 1960s*. Irish Association for American Studies, 1987.

Rowbotham, Sheila. *A Century of Women: The History of Women in Britain and the United States*. Penguin Books, London, 1997.

Rudwick, Elliott M. *Race Riot in East St Louis, July 2, 1917*. Southern Illinois University Press, Carbondale, Illinois, 1964.

Rudwick, Elliott M. *W. E. B. Du Bois. Propagandist of Negro Protest*. Atheneum, New York, 1968.

Ruiz, Vicki and Ellen Carol DuBois. eds. *Unequal Sisters: A Multi-Cultural Reader in US Women's History*. New York, Routledge, 1994.

Safford, Joel L. 'John C. Calhoun, Lani Guinier and Minority Rights,' *Political Science and Politics*, June 1995, 211–216.

Sandweiss, Martha A. *Passing Strange: A Gilded Age Tale of Love and Deception Across the Color Line*. Penguin Press, New York, 2009.

Schlesinger, Jr., Arthur. *Robert Kennedy and His Times*. Futura, London, 1979.

Seeger, Pete and Rob Reiser. *Everybody Says Freedom: A History of the Civil Rights Movement in Songs and Pictures*. W. W. Norton, New York, 1989.

Shaffer, Stephen and Charles W. Menifield. 'Representation of African American Interests in the Contemporary Mississippi State Legislature.' Paper present to the Southwestern Social Science Association, New Orleans, 2002.

Shull, Steven A. *A Kinder, Gentler Racism? The Reagan-Bush Civil Rights Legacy*. M. E. Sharpe, New York, 1993.

Signorile, Michelangelo. *Queer Nation: Sex, the Media and the Closets of Power*. Abacus, London, 1993.

Sitkoff, Harvard. *The Struggle for Black Equality, 1954–1992*. Hill and Wang, New York, 1993.

Smith, Rogers. *Civic Ideals: Conflicting Visions of Citizenship in US. History*. Yale University Press, New Haven, 1997.

Smith, Therese. *"Let the Church Sing!": Music and Worship in a Black Mississippi Community*. University of Rochester Press, Rochester, 2004.

Stein, Judith. *The World of Marcus Garvey: Race and Class in Modern Society*. Louisiana State University Press, Baton Rouge, 1986.

Stockman, David. *The Triumph of Politics: The Inside Story of the Reagan Administration*. Avon, New York, 1987.

Stokes, Melvyn and Rick Halpern, eds. *Race & Class in the American South Since 1890*. Berg, Oxford, 1994.

Stoper, Emily. *The Student Nonviolent Coordinating Committee: The Growth of Radicalism in a Civil Rights Organization*. Carlson Publishing, New York, 1989.

Summers, Anthony. *The Arrogance of Power: The Secret World of Richard Nixon*. Victor Gollanz, London, 2000.

Tate, Gayle T. and Lewis Randolph, eds. *Dimensions of Black Conservatism in the United States*. Palgrave, New York, 2002.

Thernstrom, Stephan and Abigail Thernstrom. *America in Black and White: One Nation Indivisible*. Simon and Schuster, New York, 1997.

Thomas, Clarence. *My Grandfather's Son: A Memoir*. Harper Collins, New York, 2007.

Thomas, Evan. *"A Long Time Coming": The Inspiring, Combative 2008 Campaign and the Historic Election of Barack Obama*. Public Affairs, London, 2009.

Thornton, J. Mills. 'Challenge and Response in the Montgomery Bus Boycott of 1955–1956,' in David Garrow, ed. *The Walking City: The Montgomery Bus Boycott, 1955–1956*. Carlson Publishing, New York, 1989.

Thrasher, Sue. Unpublished 'Interview with Anne Braden,' 18 April 1981.

Todd, Chuck and Sheldon Gawiser. *How Barack Obama Won: A State-By-State Guide to the Historic 2008 Presidential Election*. Vintage Books, New York, 2009.

Topping, Simon. *Lincoln's Lost Legacy: The Republican Party and the African American Vote, 1928–1952*. University Press of Florida, Gainesville, 2008.

Truman, Harry S. *Memoirs: Years of Trial and Hope*. Doubleday & Company, Inc., New York, 1956.

Tuck, Stephen. "African American Protest," in Cherl Hudson and Gareth Davies, eds. *Ronald Reagan and the 1980s: Perceptions, Policies, Legacies*. Palgrave Macillan, Basingstoke, 2008.

Tuttle, William. *Race Riot: Chicago in the Red Summer of 1919*. Oxford University Press, New York, 1980.

Wadden, Alex. *Clinton's Legacy? A New Democrat in Governance*. Palgrave, Basingstoke, 2002.

Washington, James M. *A Testament of Hope: The Essential Writings and Speeches of Martin Luther King Jr*. HarperCollins, New York, 1991.

Watters, Pat. *Down To Now: Reflections on the Southern Civil Rights Movement*. Pantheon, New York, 1971.

Weisbrot, Robert. *Freedom Bound: A History of America's Civil Rights Movement*. W. W. Norton, New York, 1990.

Welch, Matt. *McCain: The Myth of the Maverick*. Palgrave Macmillan, New York, 2008.

Werner, Craig. *A Change is Gonna Come: Music, Race and the Soul of America*. Cannongate Books, London, 2002.

West, Cornell. *Keeping Faith: Philosophy and Race in America*. Routledge, New York, 1993.

White, John. *Black Leadership in America, 1895–1968*. Longman, London, 1985.

Whitfield, Stephen A. *A Death in the Delta: The Story of Emmett Till*. Collier Macmillan, London, 1988.

Wickham, DeWayne. *Bill Clinton and Black America*. Ballantine Publishing Group, New York, 2002.

Weidner, Donald. *A History of Africa South of the Sahara*. Vintage Books, New York, 1962.

Wirt, Frederick M. *'We Ain't What We Was:' Civil Rights in the New South*. Duke University Press, Durham, NC, 1997.

Wolters, D. *The New Negro on Campus: Black College Rebellions of the 1920s*. Princeton University Press, Princeton, 1975.

Woods, Randall B. *LBJ: Architect of American Ambition*. Harvard University Press, Cambridge, 2006.

Wynn, Neil A. *The Afro-American and the Second World War*. Paul Eleck, London, 1976.

Yarborough, Tinsley. *Judge Frank Johnson and Human Rights in Alabama*. University of Alabama Press, Tuscaloosa, 1981.

Young, Andrew. *An Easy Burden: The Civil Rights Movement and the Transformation of America*. Harper Collins, New York, 1996.

Zilversmitt, H. *The First Emancipation: The Abolition of Slavery in the North*. University of Chicago Press, Chicago, 1967.

Zinn, Howard. *A People's History of the United States*. Harper & Row, New York, 1980.

INDEX

253

Index 255

Bush v Gore (2000), 197
bussing, 102, 103, 106, 110, 113, 116, 117, 141, 144, 213, 220, 231
Byrd, Harry, 20, 125
Byrd, Jr., James, 201

Calhoun, John C., 2, 60, 167
Camp Sister Spirit, 204
Cancer Alley, 219
Capitol Transport Company, 12
Carmichael, Stokeley, 78
Carney, James, 17
Carson, Julia, 153
Carswell, G. Harold, 101–4
Carter, Jimmy, 110, 111, 113, 117, 142
Carter, Lillian, 127
Carville, James, 202
Chambliss, Robert, 66
Chaney, James, 73, 111
Chao, Elaine, 210
Charleston Hospital Strike, 97–8
Cheney, Richard, 197–8, 211
Cherry, Bobby Frank, 67
Chicago, 5, 10, 12, 13, 82–3, 93–4, 96, 105, 112, 128, 164, 169, 178, 183, 188, 196, 211, 213, 218, 226, 235, 237
Chicago Freedom Movement, 83
Chisholm, Shirley, 105–6
Christian Coalition, 186
Church Arson Prevention Act, 186
Chu, Steven, 235
Citizens Councils (white), 20, 21, 41, 124–7
Civil Rights Act (1957), 25–7, 49, 100, 103, 132
(1960), 49–56
(1964), 56, 69–71, 78–79, 80, 83, 111, 113, 126, 147
Civil Rights Commission, 56, 57, 116, 117, 132, 148–9, 149, 151, 187, 200, 204
Civil Rights Restoration Act, 118, 147
Civil Rights and Women's Equity Act (1991), 147–8

Civil War, American, 1–2, 67, 80, 108, 111, 121–3, 145, 178, 192, 217
Clarke, Kenneth, 65
Clark, Jim, 76–8, 122, 132
Clark, Ramsey, 79
Clark, Septima, 97–8
Clay, William, 180
Cleaver, Eldridge, 144
Clement, Frank, 124
Clinton, Bill, 122, 144, 152
  black appointments by, 164–8
  election of 2008, 224, 225, 227, 229, 230
  as Governor, 122, 158, 159
  health reform, 176–8
  popularity of, 168, 186–7, 201
  welfare reform, 160–1, 178–81
Clinton, Hillary Rodham, 155, 163, 184, 185–6
  election of 2008 and, 224–32
  Secretary of State, 238
Cobb, Charles, 73
Cobb-Hooper, Gilda, 216
cocaine, 112, 152, 173–6, 212, 230
Cochrane, Johnny, 168
Coffin, Rev. William Sloane, 138
Cohambee River Collective, 185
Color and Democracy, 28
Colvin, Claudette, 36
Commission for Eqaul Economic Opportunity (CEEO), 13, 56, 119
Commonwealth College, 22
Communists/communism, 17, 22–4, 25, 28, 30, 61, 70, 84
Congress for Culture Freedom, 28
Congressional Black Caucus, 128, 165, 169, 196, 211, 215–16
Congress of Racial Equality (CORE), 13, 53, 57–8, 63, 65, 71–3, 76, 77, 84, 136, 187
Connally, John, 75
Connor, Eugene 'Bull', 59, 63, 122
Conyers, John, 149, 196, 216
Cooper, Annie Lee, 77
Cooper, Thomas Alvin, 193